INSPIRATIONAL TRAINING

'Have I ever told you you're my hero?
You're everything I would like to be.
I can climb higher than an eagle,
You are the wind beneath my wings.'

Larry Henley and Jeff Silbar

This book is dedicated to all those people
who were, and still are, the wind beneath
my wings. They have given me the courage,
support, inspiration and confidence to be the
best that I can be.
In return, I now share their strengths with
others – too many to mention. The special
ones will know exactly who they are when
I say 'thank you from the bottom of my heart'.
Finally, love to my family and children, Gavin and
Gemma, without whom everything would be
meaningless.

Inspirational training

Ronald Cartey

Consultant editor
George Webster

Gower

Published by
Gower Publishing Limited
Gower House
Croft Road
Aldershot
Hampshire GU11 3HR
England

Gower
Old Post Road
Brookfield
Vermont 05036
USA

British Library Cataloguing in Publication Data
Cartey, Ronald
    Inspirational training
    1. Effective teaching 2. Teaching
    I.Title
    371.3

ISBN 0 566 07708 6

Library of Congress Cataloguing-in-Publication Data
Cartey, Ronald, 1946–
    Inspirational training
Ronald Cartey.
        p.   cm.
    Includes index.
    ISBN 0-566-07708-6 (cloth)
    1. Employees—Training of—Methodology. I. Title.
HF5549.5.T7C298527 1996
658.3′ 124—dc20   95–43334
                                                                    CIP

Typeset in Palatino by Raven Typesetters, Chester and
printed in Great Britain by the University Press, Cambridge

Contents

List of figures

Preface

Learning is the responsibility of the trainer – not the trainee.

The purpose of this book is to share, with anyone whose function is, like mine, to train, teach or coach others in any subject matter, a training technique that has been developed, tried, tested and successfully practised over a number of years. It is a comprehensive version of the Trainer Development Programme which is exclusively offered by The Advanced Training Group, and has been designed to provide you with as much practical knowledge as is possible in a few short pages.

This training technique has been researched and developed by myself and is the product of studying and working with some of the most renowned trainers and speakers in the world. It is a culmination of the most effective training methods put into a simplified, yet powerful, programme – a proven method of imparting and communicating information that uses an understanding of behavioural patterns, coupled with a knowledge of the human psyche. It involves using the trainee's conscious and subconscious mind to generate accelerated learning, not just to accept information and ideas in a more positive way but also to awaken the hidden potential everybody has within themselves to develop, from what they have learned, the motivation for their own future success. It is, indeed, a training technique for trainers that, with practice, takes the art and skill of imparting knowledge into new realms, not only giving trainers the ability to train but also inspiring trainees to accept your message, retain it and, most important of all, *make positive use of it* to achieve the results they desire.

Don't just read this book – *use it*. Read each section carefully and then re-read, analysing how and when each point can be applied, highlighting each relevant suggestion. Then constantly refer back and use them as a refresher, as a reinforcer of confidence or as a reference to ensure that you consistently strive to improve your own performance.

Many trainers have written to say how invaluable they have found my techniques, as set out in this book, and to enquire about the worldwide Trainer Development Programme that uses these techniques as a foundation to develop outstanding communication skills. Do feel free to write personally to me at the address below: I shall be delighted to give you all the available information on the supporting materials and programmes.

In the meantime, I repeat, *use* this book. Take the ideas and techniques you will find in its pages, work on them, perfect them and, more importantly, *apply* them, and I guarantee that whatever success you are seeking will be yours.

Ronald Cartey
Chairman and Chief Executive
The Advanced Training Group Limited
Westminster House
Ermine Business Park
Huntingdon PE18 6XY
England

General introduction

As co-founder of the Advanced Training concept and chairman of an international training and business consultancy, the author perfected and developed the technique described in this book.

This training concept was based on the knowledge that the key to successful training is self-confidence and self-belief. It is not intelligence but, rather, the ability to release an individual's full potential that is the principal criterion for successful training. While most training is designed to impart greater knowledge or skill in specific areas, such as management, planning or communication, such training is ineffective if it fails to *motivate* the trainee to make it work and, more importantly, *encourage* them to make use of the knowledge they have gained. The skill of effective training is the ability to represent a clear, concise and easily assimilated message with such conviction the receiver will be motivated to take *positive action*.

Most people define motivation as:

- having a motive for doing something
- having an inducement to do something
- anticipating a reward for doing something
- increased enthusiasm (or hype).

but, in reality, personal motivation derives from three key elements:

- Drive

- **Attitude**
- **Confidence**.

Together these make up what the author terms 'the DAC factor'. Without it, skills and knowledge are meaningless and, for this reason, the DAC factor is fundamental to the training technique we shall be exploring in this book.

Having first looked at a number of large training establishments and the techniques employed, the author discovered that, in general, after training, trainees

- seldom changed their ways
- were often slow to take in new ideas
- experienced either no, or only a slow, improvement in results
- did not always use what they had learned to exploit personal opportunities.

In effect, the training was regarded as interesting but rarely entirely effective! Further research revealed that the reasons for this were that most trainers concentrated only on two aspects of training, these being material or course content and presentation of material.

To develop a programme that was designed to increase trainees' skill base, the average trainer

- researched their subject thoroughly
- developed the relevant points
- compiled information
- incorporated current ideas and trends
- designed a training module for delivery.

Once the trainer had designed the core programme, he or she would usually endeavour to present the new topic in a professional manner. Ideas generally considered would be:

- visuals
- programme notes
- handouts
- exercises
- method of delivery.

Then, having presented the prepared programme, adapted according to client or company requirements, the average trainer would finally assess its effectiveness through 'trainee survey forms' or even 'client feedback'. If, as frequently was the case, the programme was not a resounding success, the trainer would then change or adapt the material, reconsider and alter the presentation, and amend the handouts and the exercises until the response had been improved.

However, the one overriding aspect the research revealed was that *trainers seldom assessed their own techniques*! They reconsidered and adapted the methods but ignored the one element that was constant in every programme – themselves.

It soon became apparent that the effectiveness of any training programme – that is, effectiveness as measured by the degree of *action* that subsequently took place – depended on a number of factors:

1 the *esteem* gained by the trainer
2 the *methods* used by the trainer
3 the *communication skills* of the trainer
4 the *enthusiasm* of the trainer
5 the *passion* conveyed by the trainer
6 the *motivational skills* of the trainer.

Results therefore revolved entirely around the trainer's own expertise, and we quickly realized that *the ability to learn is the responsibility of the trainer – not the trainee*. It soon became clear that many trainers, whilst knowledgeable about their subject, had never been trained how to train. What we needed to develop was a training *technique*.

The observations from our research are still true today, the reasons being that most trainers still feel they have the responsibility, as experts in their subjects, to communicate knowledge and that it is up to the trainees to assimilate and make use of that knowledge. This makes no provision for the human element. Whilst tutors and trainers frequently change their material, they do not change their own style or presentation technique despite the fact that their trainees come with widely differing backgrounds, have vastly differing attitudes, differing levels of intelligence and differing needs. In practice, every person seeking education, special skills, business success, improved sporting techniques, personal betterment or any form of knowledge about any subject can achieve their aspirations if they want to.

No two people are exactly the same and it was with this in mind that the author decided to develop a training technique with a more humanistic, rather than mechanistic, approach to training people of all levels of ability and from all backgrounds and lifestyles – a technique that would

● be effective, regardless of the training environment
● apply to *any* discipline – for example, sports, dancing, business, academia

- have no time constraints
- retain the trainer's style or personality traits
- generate results more quickly.

To determine an effective training method which would incorporate these criteria, further research was conducted into recognized educational, teaching and coaching methods used around the world. These were monitored and measured for positive effectiveness and, from this, it clearly emerged that one of the most powerful techniques derived from the principles of holistic learning.

This system was developed primarily for educational purposes by a number of eminent psychologists and adopted by educational specialists in many parts of the world with remarkable success in the fields of medicine, science and languages. The principles of holistic learning were first discovered by a leading Bulgarian psychologist, Dr Georgi Lazanov who established, through many years of research, that people's ability to learn is virtually limitless. He described it as 'tapping the reserves of the mind', claiming that people who had experimented with his methods found that they began, for the first time, to discover who they were and what they could do. One eminent specialist in human psychology went even further, saying that Lazanov's system was allowing the human race to learn that the mind has limitless capacity and that we will soon be able to realize and use powers that we are not yet even capable of imagining. Some observers have described holistic learning as 'superlearning' since there are now many examples of students who have, for example, mastered new languages in days, or even hours, through the process. The system comprises a scientific approach through which trainers look at individuals with the aim of determining what makes them *accept* whatever it is that is imparted. It exploits an individual's *natural ability to learn*, rather than relying on their level of *intelligence*, and results in *total learning*.

Lazanov and other physiologists and psychologists worldwide undertook complex research into the way in which the human mind works and reached the common conclusion that not only do we only use a fraction of our capabilities, but we have no idea as to our potential capabilities until we unlock them from our minds. We all have barriers that create conflict between the mind and the body and, to overcome them and allow us to use the full power of our beings, the mind and the body must be brought together as a holistic entity. To achieve this, three elements must combine with the body:

1 **Logic**: The human brain is divided into two distinct halves. The left-hand side, which controls our logical instincts, is devoted to:

- logical reasoning
- thought
- data simulation
- factual learning.

2 **Emotions**: The right-hand side of the brain, which controls our creative instincts, is devoted to:

- imagination
- creativity
- visualization
- aspirations
- extrasensory perception
- intuition.

3 **Physical functions:** In the centre of the brain is a support section which contains an area determining:

- health
- physical performance
- self-awareness
- autogenics.

Holistic learning utilizes existing logical, emotional and physical abilities. The technique's success derives from removing any conflict between the left-hand and right-hand sides of the brain, thereby creating harmony between all aspects of the mind and ensuring that the body is in accord with that harmony. It can be used to learn any type of factual information, such as mathematics, languages, geography or history and it can also be used to learn how to succeed in business, at sport, in music or any other aspect of our lives.

Holistic learning ensures that every trainee, whatever their background, personal circumstances or abilities, will become much more receptive to ideas, suggestions and facts than is ever possible through conventional teaching methods that merely rely on the individual's ability to absorb information.

The system was originally developed and used within the academic and scientific sector. The technique explored in this book extends the principles of the holistic approach into commercial applications, where time, people and costs must also be taken into consideration. Accordingly, this application of the technique is designed to speed up the process without losing sight of either the total learning aspect or the concept of applied humanistic psychology.

The first step towards achieving these goals was to identify the principal criteria for enhanced learning, with the objective of matching them with various communication techniques and thereby developing a truly effective training concept which would be independent of differing situations, variables or style. For example:

1 **Situations** differ according to whether we are, for example:

- advising on how to improve selling techniques
- encouraging better results on the sportsfield
- teaching poise and deportment to dance students.

These factors are usually influenced by many other factors, such as whether we are sharing knowledge or instructing techniques to improve individual performance and also whether we are operating on a one-to-one basis, with a small group or with, perhaps, a hundred or more people at a time.

2 **Variables** include the discipline in which delegates are being trained, coached or taught, for example:

- sales management
- sports
- dance
- art

or the location of the training environment, for example:

- classroom
- lecture theatre
- conference hall
- sportsfield

or the training method being employed, for example:

- lecturing
- coaching
- role-playing.

3 **Style** encompasses each trainer's own individual approach and methods and therefore differs widely between trainers. While trainers must retain their own individual style, to achieve a change in their underlying personal views, we had to develop a disciplined, structured

technique which allowed them both to accept new ideas and helped to generate change in their individual patterns and actions.

The first step was therefore to identify, through research and experience, learning criteria that would enable us to understand how to communicate effectively to achieve the most effective learning state.

The *five key criteria for enhanced learning* were accordingly established as follows:

1 **Teacher/trainer/coach acceptance**. We noticed that if the trainee neither liked nor respected the trainer, the training was never accepted. A similar situation sometimes occurs at school where children who have previously shown little interest in a subject suddenly excel in it simply because they have a new teacher whom they like more than the previous one or, conversely, fail in their favourite subject because they dislike the new teacher. Thus, the first criterion had to generate the reaction of the trainee towards the trainer: 'I *like* them', or 'I *respect* them.'

2 **Practical and useful ideas**. People always look for practical and useful ideas to satisfy the logical aspect of the learning process. We observed that, even though much of what trainers communicated was theoretical, the trainee needed to agree with what was said on the basis that it made good sense. Whilst an individual may generally have felt that what they were told was theoretically correct, it did not always mean that they adopted the suggestion or allowed it to change their own behaviour or style. Therefore, we needed to obtain the reaction 'It makes *sense*', or 'It will *work*.'

3 **Interesting concepts**. We discovered that the trainee's mental stimulation was a key element in the learning process. When we re-examined the holistic approach, in which it had been established that total learning draws on the left-hand side of the brain for logical and practical ideas and on the right-hand side for creativity, we then understood the importance of mental stimulation. Trainees need to be able to visualize ideas working. It is one thing to gain agreement that something will work, but quite a different matter to make it appear real. By using visualization techniques we can generate ideas and images in the mind so that trainees can see it work, even though they may be in a lecture room, on a sportsfield or in any other learning situation. By appealing to the creative side of the mind, it is possible to stimulate the brain and thus make training programmes interesting. The reaction we were looking for was 'That's worth listening to.'

4 **Topic or result acceptance**. We frequently noticed that a trainee showed agreement with what had been said more to placate the trainer

than to accept the information. Training is meaningless unless trainees agree with what is communicated. What we needed to develop was the acceptance of information to produce the constant reaction: 'Yes I *agree* with the message/research/facts/results this topic generates.'

5   **Self-belief**. Self-belief was determined as the key element and by far the most important criterion of learning. We noted that despite everything they may have learned from training, at the conclusion of developing every idea and irrespective of what was accepted, unless the trainees believed they could *do it for themselves*, little or no action took place. The biggest challenge for accepting new ideas and the main criterion for accepting change is that the trainee firmly believes that 'it *will* work for *me*'. It is all very well for the trainee to say 'Yes, I like and respect the trainer', 'Yes, that makes good sense', 'Yes, I can see it will work' and 'Yes, I can see what results it will produce', but unless the trainer is able to generate self-confidence in trainees so that they can see it working for *them*, that *they themselves* do have the ability, that *they can* generate the skills they want, that *they will* be able to develop confidence in themselves, learning will never take place.

Truly effective training that will inspire others to succeed should therefore be based on satisfying these five learning criteria. The next step was to match them to *five teaching criteria*, which I identified as:

1   **Bio-rapport**
2   **Logical presentation**
3   **Mental stimulation**
4   **Subliminal influencing**
5   **Attitudinal development.**

The development of these, and the purpose of this book, is explained more fully in the following chapters.

PART I

Bio-rapport

Introduction

Bio = of the body.
Rapport = Emotional bond or connection: drawing together – the establishment or renewal of cordial relations.

Bio-rapport is another way of giving information about a trainer in order to fulfil the first criterion in the learning process – namely the rapid acceptance by trainees of the trainer's personality, knowledge, professionalism and experience.

How, then, do we develop the art, or skill, of getting people to accept us? In today's highly competitive and professional world, it is no longer enough just to smile, look happy and expect people to immediately like us, respect our authority or knowledge and accept our ideas. Trainees, in every part of the world, are much more discerning and demanding when it comes to assessing the quality of their trainers, so the first step towards becoming a highly effective trainer is to make sure that our trainees quickly bond with us. To achieve this, we must understand the two elements involved, gaining acceptance and use of body language, which together create the subconscious condition known as bio-rapport.

Acceptance of us as trainers must be won in three distinct areas. We must gain their acceptance:

1   as a professional to ensure their respect
2   as a trainer to ensure their acceptance of our ideas
3   as a person to ensure they like us as an individual.

Chapters 1, 2 and 3 deal with these three requirements separately since we deal with people within training groups and individually, both inside and outside the training venue, and also during breaks and at the end of the programme when we will be assessed as individuals as well as authoritative trainers. Chapter 4, the last chapter in Part I, deals with body language – our ability to project body movements that match the words we speak.

1 Winning acceptance as a professional

Professional = showing the skill, artistry, ability, demeanour or standard of conduct appropriate to a particular profession.

It is important to quickly establish with our trainees that we are professional, not only as trainers but also in our demeanour and conduct. To be judged as professionals we should:

- match the image
- maintain the image
- avoid 'talking-down'
- never build up self-importance
- never lie or exaggerate
- never attack the competition or competitive ideas
- avoid criticism
- be beyond reproach.

These core criteria of professionalism are explored in the remainder of the chapter.

Match the image

The key to effective training is the realization that *we* are the message and that the message itself is governed by two aspects:

- how we see ourselves
- how others see us – or their *perceived* image of us.

The first image trainees have of us is governed by the way we dress. Some trainers dress for their own comfort rather than consider the effect their appearance will have on the teaching/learning process. This can be a costly mistake, because if the trainees' first impression is that the trainer looks like a scientist when they are expecting, for example, a session on sales management, the trainer will have less chance of gaining their respect. The rule where dress is concerned is as follows:

Dress to match the trainees' **image** *of a professional who is actually engaged in the business or subject they have come to learn about.*

Dressing to match the *perceived image* is a crucial step towards gaining bio-rapport with trainees.

The business of perceived image doesn't just apply to trainers or professionals in other fields, but in all walks of life. For example, imagine that, when you collect your car from a garage after a service, you are met by a person dressed in immaculate white overalls, showing no trace of dirt. As this person hands the keys back they say they have just personally completed the service on your car themselves so you can rest assured it is absolutely perfect. What would your reaction be to this statement? Would you believe it? Of course not, because your *image* of a mechanic is that of someone who, having been working underneath a car, would be covered in oil and grease, and this particular person *does not match the image* because they are dressed in pristine whites. We can also look at this same situation in reverse. Imagine now that you have to take the car to the same garage, but this time for an electronic engine tune. On arrival, you are met by a mechanic who, wiping his oily hands on his heavily soiled blue overalls before he takes the keys, announces that he is going to take the car straight into the immaculately presented electronic tuning bay so that he can get on with the job. What would be your reaction to that? You would probably tell him to leave the car alone until an expert arrived. Why? Because we have all been conditioned to believe that a highly technically qualified electronic tuning expert is always dressed in immaculate whites. Again, *he did not match the image* because he was dressed in greasy blue overalls.

Can you now see how powerful *perceived image* is? Image applies to products, people and situations – it affects judgements and assumptions. Therefore, you must constantly ask yourself 'Do I match the image?' We are subject to a mass of conditioned images – images that bombard us daily through the media, by means of fashions, trends, advertising claims, role models, parents, colleagues, traditions and a host of other factors.

You have, of course, all heard the saying *first impressions count*. This is why you must ask yourself the following questions before you face your audience:

● Do I look the part?
● Do I give the impression of being a professional manager, speaker, negotiator or planner?

When instructing on business matters, you must look as though you have stepped straight out of a top company's boardroom. When coaching a group about the finer points of field sports, wear a smart tracksuit. When you are training people in show production, dress like a producer. When your group is expecting to learn the ins and outs of fly fishing, you should wear smart appropriate tweeds. When you look the part, you are well on the way towards gaining respect as a professional.

Maintain the image

Having accepted the importance of looking the part in terms of matching the perceived image, we must also ensure that, as we present our ideas or transfer our skills to our trainees, we do not create any form of distraction that could alter our image and divert the trainees' attention from our message. If our appearance deteriorates during the delivery of a training programme, then our image as professionals will also deteriorate. Here is a simple checklist to ensure that the correct image is maintained at all times:

● **Jackets.** For men, the rule of thumb is that if a jacket is worn (it is not compulsory), it should always be buttoned up, firstly, because men's jackets are tailored that way and, secondly, because it creates a professional image rather than a casual approach. It can also prevent potential distractions. For example, how often have you watched a speaker who, as his enthusiasm builds and his gestures become increasingly animated diverts you with the spectacle of his shirt tails gradually hanging out beneath his casually undone jacket? A sense of ridicule sets in from that point on, and the post-session conversation is then not about how useful the material was or whether the ideas will work, but centres around the question 'Did you see that idiot with his shirt hanging out?'. So, keep your jacket done up if you want total, rather than partial, acceptance from your trainees. For women, unless the jacket is tailored not to be buttoned, it is more acceptable to leave it unfastened as this tends to have little or no effect on the image being portrayed.

- **Pocket flaps.** Make sure that pocket flaps always remain outside the pocket rather than half in and half out. It seems a minor point but if, as can happen, you reach a point where you are not completely convincing, or holding the complete attention of your audience, their minds will start to wander and search for something of interest to focus on. Once their minds are focused on even such a small detail as a pocket flap out of place, a teaching point could be missed. One foolproof way of avoiding this problem is to sew up all jacket pockets.

- **Ties.** Keep ties under control. Ties, especially those made of silk, have an uncanny knack of slipping out of place. This is something we rarely notice in the heat of delivery but, again, is a potential distraction for trainees, giving them an opportunity to allow their concentration to lapse and perhaps miss an important learning point. Remember to check occasionally that the tie is still in place, but not in such a way that the action itself can cause a distraction. Check the tie as part of another movement – for instance, as you turn to face the flipchart – so that it does not become an obvious and noticeable habit. This way, you will maintain your professional image.

- **Loose change.** How often have you seen a lecturer or speaker jiggling loose change or keys in their pocket? No habit is more guaranteed to encourage trainees' minds to wander. It is usually an unconscious action and it is both distracting and annoying for anyone who is watching. Unfortunately, it is usually only the trainer who is unaware of the habit. So, before starting any lectures, training sessions or after-dinner speeches, always empty your pockets of anything that can jingle, rattle or bulge. Forestalling a potential problem before it can happen is a discipline worth cultivating.

- **Spectacles.** Spectacles can become a distraction if the wearer cannot leave them alone. Spectacles-wearers tend to suffer problems, particularly when the room is hot and they start to perspire under the intensity of delivery causing their glasses to slide down the nose. But, as with the silk-tie problem, you should adjust them discreetly. Many spectacles-wearers unconsciously push their glasses back into place with a finger each time they slide down, and this repetitive movement soon becomes a distraction. Even worse can be the annoying habit some people have of taking their spectacles off and putting them back on again when making a point, and even sometimes using them as a flipchart pointer. The more valid the point they make in this way, the more aggressive becomes their gesture, with the result that trainees begin to concentrate more on the possibility that the spectacles might snap in half than on the point that is being made. You can, and should, adjust your spectacles as part of another movement in order not to distract the audience. And *never* use them as a pointer.

- **Jewellery.** Avoid wearing any jewellery or earrings that jangle audibly every time you move. Again, trainees will listen for the distraction rather than to your point. Leave flamboyant jewellery at home. You can, of course, wear small items of jewellery that enhance personal image, but do not be excessive. Remember also that your appearance must match the trainees' perceived image of you, so look the part. Limit jewellery to items that would normally be worn by somebody doing the job your trainees are expecting to learn about. Don't overdo it, though – and don't be flashy.

- **Hair.** Some people, particularly men, have a problem keeping their hair from flying all over the place, especially when they become animated. We are all familiar with cartoons of politicians and public figures which accentuate their untidy hair. Their hair then becomes their 'trademark' and their words are soon forgotten. The same will apply to you if you are unable to keep your hair in place without making constant adjustments to it. If you have unruly or difficult hair, use a styling mousse or a good matt hairspray to keep your hairstyle in place. This may feel odd, if you are a man – but nobody need see you apply it! It is certainly better than running the risk of losing your audience's attention.

- **Make-up.** Before facing your audience make sure that your make-up is properly and neatly applied and that it will stay that way for at least a whole session until you have an opportunity to leave the room to make repairs. You will soon lose the trainees' attention if your eyeshadow, lipstick or other cosmetics start to run or smudge. As you cannot check it during a session, it is better to buy good quality make-up and apply it properly.

- **Eyebrows.** Again, there are some politicians who will always be remembered not for what they have said or done, but for their big bushy eyebrows. Eyebrows tend to become animated as you speak, so the bushier they are the more amusing they can look to trainees whose attention becomes readily diverted to following their movements at the expense of your words. If you don't like the idea of keeping your eyebrows trimmed to average proportions, then you will have to learn to keep them still. This may sound drastic, but it does prevent a further distraction for your audience.

- **Distracting words.** The constant use of meaningless words, such as 'basically', can be another source of distraction and ridicule. Trainees will wait for you to repeat your pet word or phrase and mentally count how many times you use it, rather than concentrate on the content of your presentation.

All the above factors, however trivial they may seem, are examples of simple potential distractions. There are, of course, many others than can contribute to destroying your image by becoming the focal point of your delivery. The fewer the distractions you create, the more professional you will seem and the more your trainees will respect you. The greater their respect for you, the better the initial learning criteria are met. That is one of the important aspects of this technique and of holistic teaching.

Avoid 'talking down'

If the trainer says, 'I am the expert and I am now going to inform you...', in the trainee's perception he or she is saying 'I am smart and you are stupid...'. This is known as a *talk-down statement* and should be avoided. It is unprofessional. For example, by saying something like 'I'm sorry, but you've got that all wrong – this is how it has already been explained...', you are making a classic talk-down statement that will not only embarrass the questioner but is also likely to alienate the rest of the group. If you are ever faced with somebody who is giving an uneducated or inaccurate assessment or opinion, or even if you plan to introduce a new topic which should be fairly obvious to most of the group, the golden rule is: **Give people the benefit of knowledge we know they *don't* have**. Accordingly, say something like 'I am sure most of us will have heard of this particular technique and will know about these ideas, but it is worth taking a few minutes just to run through them again....'

In this way you are giving people information you know they don't have without talking down or demeaning them at all. This will ensure that you don't lose respect and that you maintain your professional image. In addition, it is a further means of creating good bio-rapport between trainer and trainees.

Here are some examples of talk-down statements with examples of how to say the same thing in an acceptable way:

'You would not appreciate...' (bad)
'I am sure you appreciate...' (good)

'You are probably not aware...' (bad)
'I expect you are aware...' (good)

'What I'll tell you about now is...' (bad)
'The ideas we will now share are...' (good)

Never build self-importance

A trainer, coach or teacher should never build up their own importance or attempt to give the impression that they are the most important person in the room. It is essential to be held in high esteem by our trainees, but there is an art or skill in doing this in such a way that they will look up to us, believe what we have to say and act on it. We look at this in detail later but, for now, we must simply remember never to build up our own importance.

How many of you have ever encountered a speaker who is a member of the 'I' brigade – someone who always refers to themself, their achievements and opinions as a way of saying, 'Follow my example as a way of learning'. Typical of their statements are:

- 'I've done this'
- 'I've done that'
- 'In my opinion...'
- 'I believe...'
- 'I accept this argument...'

To their audience, they seem to be building up an image of being more important than the group they are teaching. However, when you are faced with such a person do you accept them? No! Are you impressed? No! More often than not, it has the opposite effect. Remember, trainees will soon become bored with self-importance, so make sure you eliminate all the 'I's'.

Never lie or exaggerate

Never resort to lying or making exaggerated claims in order to make a point, especially when trying to achieve trainees' acceptance of even a minor piece of information. The minute you make a claim that your audience knows to be exaggerated, all trust is lost between you and them. You know for yourself that, if you hear someone exaggerate you immediately cease to take that person seriously and become suspicious of them. Do not run the risk in front of your trainees. Never exaggerate or say anything that cannot be substantiated. To become a successful trainer you need, from your trainees, 100 per cent of their trust and 100 per cent of their confidence. You cannot expect this level of commitment from them if you make exaggerated claims to support our skill or our material. It is unnecessary.

Never attack the competition or competitive ideas

How do you feel towards somebody who continually attacks the competition? In business, it is generally regarded as unprofessional to criticize competitors as a means of winning an argument. Often, a trainee will raise an idea or make a statement with which you do not agree because it is against the principles or technique you are imparting. For instance, many people may have been trained or given information by others that may conflict with your own particular message. However, resist the temptation to be drawn into any form of criticism. It is easy to say 'That's no good' or 'That's out of date' or 'Haven't you got any better ideas?', but you should avoid this because it could easily provoke an argument which would be destructive for the trainee and could easily damage your professional image.

When faced with a competitive statement or argument, use the following sequence to handle the problem:

1   *Resist* the temptation to attack the competition.
2   *Praise* the competitor with a response such as 'Yes, I have heard of them and I believe they are excellent' or 'Yes, I have heard of that technique; it is well known...'.
3   *Dilute* the strength of the argument. For example, say: 'In fact, it was used some time ago and was quite effective then', which implies that it is based on an outmoded idea. Or, if there is some reasonable argument for the competition, say: 'Yes, I understand it is effective as well...', which implies that your idea is equally effective.

Resist attacking competitors or competitive ideas. *Praise* and *dilute*. It is much more professional – and much more effective.

Avoid criticism

Never criticize any trainee for any reason whatsoever, be it their attitude, timekeeping, lack of ability or anything else. Whilst criticism is an essential part of personal development it should never be used to embarrass a trainee in front of their peers because, whether the criticism is real or implied, it can alienate. We will examine later, how this vital area of training should be conducted because, as with any other form of communication, there is an art in doing it right without making enemies of our trainees or risking our professionalism.

Be beyond reproach

As professionals we must always be beyond reproach in every way, both as trainers and as individuals. The following guidelines will ensure this:

- **Never apologize.** The normally courteous act of making an apology implies that you have done something wrong so, as you must always maintain your professional status, it is better never to put yourself in the position of having to apologize. However, given that things can go wrong, which would normally cause you to apologize out of courtesy, how do you circumvent this?

    The answer is simple. One reason you might need to make an apology is because you are late for a session. This should not happen, but car problems, traffic hold-ups, delayed trains, business distractions and other such occurrences sometimes hinder punctuality. Even then, rather than start a session by saying 'Look, I'm sorry I'm late but...' and try to make excuses, it is much more powerful to say 'Thank you for being so patient' or 'Congratulations to everybody for being so early!'. If you begin by being apologetic, your group will immediately gain the upper hand and the session will start on the wrong footing. This is an important part of establishing and maintaining your professionalism.

The following mishaps are amongst those for which you do not apologize:

- being unprepared
- being called in at the last minute
- being asked to cover a new subject
- losing your place in a script
- forgetting details of a new subject.

You should always maintain your personal authority as the true professional your trainees will expect to admire and hold in high esteem.

- **Always be alert.** You have to remain alert at *all* times, which means that, as you will be setting a very professional standard whilst you are at the front of the room, you must not let those standards drop when you are mixing with the trainees outside the teaching environment – for example, at coffee or lunch, or even when the course or seminar is over. The time to relax a little will be when the last of your trainees has headed out of the door on their way home.

    Many of us have our own role models – those professionals we admire or aspire to. Would we be impressed if as trainees who respected our trainer as a truly professional person and as a model of perfection, if, in the bar after the session, we saw our role model drink too much, initiate a smutty story session and make loud sexual innuendoes about the barmaid? Suddenly, every vestige of respect we had for that trainer would dissipate – and wouldn't we then view them as a two-faced fraud? Clearly, then, as trainers, we must remain alert at *all* times in the company of our trainees. As we develop this technique and become completely immersed in the practices, remaining totally alert becomes an automatic process.

To remain beyond reproach is the only way to command respect. Many people involved in personal development prefer to pursue popularity rather than respect, but personal popularity will, at best, be short-lived. It is far better and far more effective, if we want to be successful trainers, teachers or coaches, to be respected. When people respect us, they will do as we ask them. To win that respect, follow the advice given and acceptance will be gained through bio-rapport.

Checklist: winning acceptance as a professional

1   **Matching the image.**
2   **Maintain the image.**
3   **Avoid talking down.**
4   **Never lie or exaggerate.**
5   **Never build up self-importance.**
6   **Never attack the competition.**
7   **Avoid criticism.**
8   **Be beyond reproach.**

2 Winning acceptance as a trainer

Trainer = instructor in a skill or practical education in any profession.

The previous chapter dealt with how to present ourselves as professionals but it is equally important that trainees accept us as trainers – people who practise their art and who command people's respect not only because they are professional, but also because they are fully skilled and knowledgeable presenters. Experience gained with groups in many different parts of the world confirms that the most obvious similarity between audiences of every nationality is that they judge trainers by what they *do*, not by what they *know*. The following techniques and guidelines, which are explored in detail below, are designed to achieve acceptance of us as trainers.

- Know the presentation equipment.
- Use the correct equipment technique.
- Don't waffle.
- Have a clear objective.
- Don't dry up.

Know the presentation equipment

Make sure that the equipment you use for making visual presentations is in good working order before starting the programme. If it does break down, your trainees will blame you, not the equipment. They will rightly think that you should have made sure it worked for their course – and this affects their judgement of you.

Sometimes, especially if you run your session on unfamiliar ground, such as in a hotel or an outside training venue or even on the client's premises, you may be provided with hired or in-house equipment that might have seen better days or has been abused by previous users. In such cases – and it is equally important to remember this when using your own equipment – check it thoroughly *before trainees take their place in the room*. It looks unprofessional when trainees arrive to find their trainer in shirt-sleeves trying to fix a piece of equipment which should have been set up, checked out, tested and ready to go before they arrived. Of course, the best laid plans do go wrong, and equipment may fail in the middle of a session. It can happen to us all. Much as we may laugh and shrug it off, our professionalism will still be affected unless we know how to handle the situation. Remember, don't apologize. Just arrange for the equipment to be replaced or repaired and move on to the next part of the course in which the equipment is not required. You can always go back to it later. Don't blame the hotel or facility and don't blame the equipment. Just pass it off by saying something like 'These things happen. We'll go straight on to the next part of this presentation and come back to this point as soon as the equipment is replaced/repaired'. Maintain professionalism at all times. Don't panic and always be seen to be in full control of the situation.

Use the correct equipment technique

Another important aspect of equipment usage is knowing how it works – a surprising number of speakers don't know how to use their equipment. Once again, check everything before the session starts. If provided with a projector or video playback of a type you have never used before, make sure you familiarize yourself with all the controls, power switches, focus control, connections and everything else you need to enable you to use the equipment without having to think twice about it. Always keep alert to any potential unnecessary and embarrassing mistakes that will threaten your professionalism. It is all part of achieving the all-important bond – the bio-rapport – you need to establish in order to be accepted by your trainees.

Another key factor in ensuring the maintenance of a professional image is knowing how to present material in the best possible way. The points that follow, although some might seem obvious, are often overlooked by trainers, yet contribute significantly.

Overhead projector

Nothing is more distracting to an audience than to see the presenter struggling with the OHP. Images can come out partly on and partly off the screen, crooked, out of focus, in the wrong order – all signs of an inexperienced or unprepared speaker who is making very hard work of what should be a very easy and, if used properly, very effective way of showing visuals. The secret of successful OHP use is simple. Switch the machine *off* when changing a transparency.

There is a four-stage technique for ensuring a perfect OHP presentation:

1 Switch the projector *off*.
2 Remove the previous transparency and *replace* it with the next.
3 Check that it is the right way up and is *straight*.
4 Present it by switching the project *on*.

Reveals are also an important feature of OHP presentations. As its name implies, a reveal involves keeping a section of the transparency hidden so that it can be 'revealed' at the appropriate time to add punch to the presentation. This can be done by using a piece of card, or cards if there is more than one reveal to make, to cover the part or parts of the page you wish to hold back. At the right moment in your delivery, take the card away, being careful not to misalign the transparency, thus revealing the additional feature. When setting up the page on the projector, make sure that the card is neatly placed so that the divides between the first, second or subsequent features are neat and tidy. Cut the cards to fit the image to make sure this is professionally presented. Most importantly, make sure that the point is not revealed until you are completely ready to refer to it. Synchronization will be covered later on.

This may all take a few moments longer, but it is time well spent. Work with hundreds of organizations and tens of thousands of people worldwide over many years has established that our audiences never notice when we get it right, but they most certainly do if we get it wrong! It is then that they start to doubt our professionalism. The key is *never* to get it wrong. This may be a bold statement, but we are setting very high standards here, which, once they are attained, will bring tremendous results as a trainer.

Flipchart

The flipchart is the most basic, and probably the most abused, piece of presentation equipment. Even with this simple means of presenting charts, graphics and, more likely, our own handwritten key points, there is an art and skill in achieving good professional standards.

One of the most common mistakes in the use of flipcharts is to talk about subject X and illustrate the points made on that subject, then start another topic, subject Y, while leaving the page about subject X in view. This creates a conflict in the trainees' minds as to what they are supposed to be concentrating on and thereby adversely affects their judgement of the trainer's professionalism. Remember, it was suggested earlier that, as professional trainers or coaches, our own reputations and livelihood depend not on what we know, but on what we *do*. We are judged by our actions.

Film projector

You are less likely to use a 16mm film projector nowadays as most training programmes are on video. However, if you have a very large audience of, say, a hundred plus, a 16mm film, if available, is better than video because it can be projected on to a large screen that can be seen by everyone. Although large-screen video systems exist, with a very large audience you would probably need to place a number of these at strategic points around the room so that everybody can see the programme clearly.

When using a film projector, make sure it is laced up correctly, that it is in focus and that the throw is contained within the screen without 'bleeding' off at the edges. As suggested earlier, ensure that you know how to work the machine and have it set up for use before the trainees take their places. If you want to use only part of the film make sure also that it is spooled up to the actual point from which it should run. It all contributes to your professionalism as a trainer or presenter.

Slide projector

Normally, you would use a carousel-type slide projector and will have made quite sure that your slides are in the correct sequence, the right way up, right side out and that the projector, and remote control if one is fitted, work well before your group enters the room. If you are using the type of slide projector that has to be loaded manually as you proceed, check to make sure that your slides are in order and that they can be picked up (in the dark) and inserted so that they are projected the right way up and the right way round. Your audience will ridicule any slides that are upside down and back to front, so be sure to be in total control. Failure to observe these simple rules will make you look like an amateur. Haven't we all, on some occasion, sniggered or joined in the ridicule when a presenter has got it wrong?

Video playback

Now very commonly used for informal presentations, video can be very effective. But make sure:

- you know how the playback unit works
- you know how to turn the monitor on
- that it is correctly connected
- that it is ready to switch on so that it instantly works, thus enabling you to switch it on discreetly without interrupting your flow
- that the programme is pre-wound to the beginning of the section you want to show before the group arrives. You will look unprofessional if you have to wind the tape backwards and forwards to find the correct starting point. Preferably, use a remote control if you need to find a second or other sequences that do not naturally follow on from the one just shown and, again, wind the programme backwards and for-wards as discreetly as possible. Know where the subsequent sequences start and don't allow your management of the programme to distract from the main point of the lecture.

Don't waffle

Effective training means delivering the message effectively – not filling time. Although very few trainers would ever admit to waffling, it is a com-mon fault. After all, if we can tell when someone else is waffling we can rest assured that trainees can tell if we are lapsing into the habit. One effec-tive way to avoid the risk is to stop as soon as you have finished your session. Have a break, hand over to someone else, call an exercise – do any-thing except pad the session out. The secret of good presentation is to know how to convey a clear, concise message – absolutely waffle-free! That is what this technique addresses, and the following tips will ensure that you keep to the points and so make sure that your trainees are with you all the way.

Have a clear objective

This subject is covered in depth in Part II of this book, but can be briefly described for our purposes here. Before you decide how you are going to present your programme, you should determine exactly what sort of reaction you will be seeking from your trainees. For example, will you want them to:

- enjoy themselves?
- laugh?
- immediately go away and practise what you have taught them?

In short, what do you want them to feel, to experience, to do?

Having determined exactly what *reaction* you want from your trainees, you should undertake the relatively simple task of deciding what *action* you need to take to achieve that reaction. This may appear to be an obvious and logical step, but too many trainers who spend a great deal of time designing a programme and preparing their material then wait until after they have presented it to see how well it has been received. The common reaction is: 'I thought it would go down much better than that!'

This outcome principally results from failing to prepare in the right way. You must assess your group first, and then consider how you intend to present your material to make sure you get the reaction you want. This may sound difficult, but the secret of assessing your group and presenting a clear objective will be passed on later (see Chapter 5). The object of this brief reference to such an important topic is to concentrate the mind on avoiding waffle – something we will be perceived to do if we attempt to train or coach anyone without first having defined a very clear objective. The steps, therefore, are to:

- assess the group
- determine their reaction
- gather your material
- decide on your approach.

Don't dry up

Research has shown that one of the biggest fears people suffer is the fear of speaking in public. Of course, it is just incorrect to say that people fear public speaking as it is to say that 'people are afraid of flying'. Aerophobics do not so much fear flying – it's the possibility of an air crash that scares them. They would love flying if they could overcome the fear that the aircraft wouldn't lift off at the end of the runway, or plummet earthwards at any moment during the flight, or burst a tyre and ignite in flames during the landing. In the same way, people do not really fear public speaking. It is the thought of drying up that creates the fear. That fear might arise when we are unexpectedly asked to present a brand new programme, teach a new class or stand in for somebody at short notice. It is only human to worry about drying up in such circumstances. The problem with drying up is that panic sets in, our trainees sense it and their respect for us, as trainers, diminishes.

How do we overcome the fear of drying up? Our technique shows how to avoid this extremely embarrassing and potentially damaging experience. It is, like most other solutions, quite simple.

The technique is to learn a joke or an analogy parrot fashion until it can be recalled at will – whatever the circumstances, even if you were suspended upside down and being hosed with freezing cold water! Learn this story word-for-word until it is embedded in your memory. It must, of course, be the sort of story you can relate to any type of audience without embarrassing anybody. It need not be too drawn out.

It has been found that the more professional the speaker is, the better they have developed their escape routes. We have all been in an audience when the speaker suddenly says, 'Oh, that reminds me of a story...' and has then proceeded to relate a story that bears no relationship to the topic they have been discussing. The speaker has done this almost certainly because they have lost their way in their presentation and they have called up their escape route – their lifeline – while they reorganize the programme in their mind and regain their place. When a speaker puts themself in automatic mode until they have regrouped in this way, we can tell we are in the presence of a true professional. It is a completely automatic reaction which takes much practice but, once it is achieved, you will find it is a very easy way of avoiding drying up and thereby helping to make sure your audience maintains its regard for you. It is rather similar to driving along a familiar route in the car. How many of us have driven to a regular destination and, having arrived, suddenly realized that we can't remember the turns, the roundabouts or any of our automatic driving reactions? The same subconscious state also applies to this technique to prevent drying up. You know that while you relate your chosen story or anecdote, you can automatically switch your mind back to your notes, find lost script pages and put yourself successfully back on track. The secret of not drying up is not to panic. This technique allows both breathing space and precious time. It will also give you confidence because once your escape route has been established and perfected, you will no longer fear drying up and, indeed, will undergo that experience fewer times in the future.

Nevertheless, you may, at some time, still encounter a serious and complete mental block – on presentational material, script and even the lifeline story. If this ever happens, remember the points learned earlier – *don't waffle*. All you can do in this situation is to *close the session*. Organize a break – for coffee if available – but end the session right there to give yourself time to reorganize (see pp. 85–8 on how to close a presentation). On no account let your trainees know that you have a problem; it will drastically reduce their respect for you as a professional trainer.

Checklist: winning acceptance as a trainer

1   Know the presentation equipment.
2   Use the correct equipment technique.
3   Don't waffle.
4   Have a clear objective.
5   Don't dry up.

3 Winning acceptance as an individual

Individual = characteristic of a single person.

The key to effective communication is the ability to 'sell' ourselves. It is true to say: *people buy people first and whatever else second*. Therefore it is a fundamental requirement of this entire training technique that the group accepts us as people. This chapter will cover the following key ideas that will help us gain this acceptance:

- identification
- questioning techniques
- bonding.

Identification

Identification is developed from creating a natural affinity with another person. Being able to identify with trainees is a key component of bio-rapport. It is something we quite often do naturally with others in our social lives, but seldom do consciously so closely in our business lives. There are three distinct methods of establishing identification which can either be used independently of each other or, to gain maximum acceptance, together:

1 Share commonalities.

23

2   Share opinions.
3   Share inabilities.

Share commonalities

Have you ever been away on holiday, or gone to a pub or restaurant, or anywhere there are people whom you have never met before, then struck up a conversation with a complete stranger only to find that you both have something in common? You might even have been on holiday thousands of miles away from home and, as so often seems the case, met someone from your own home country, region or even home town and exclaimed, 'Isn't it a small world!'. Immediately you felt you had something in common with them and were automatically drawn towards them. You had a bond – a shared commonality!

As we train others we need to look for things we share in common. The more we can find in common, the more we will promote a 'me too' reaction – 'the trainer is just like me!'.

Effective communication is based upon action versus reaction. As already stated, identifying, through shared commonality, is something we unconsciously practise in our private and social lives and must now start to practise in our business lives too. As we present to our groups, consciously train them and include shared commonalities to achieve the reaction we are looking for – that is, trainee acceptance – our ideas are being accepted and the recipient will take action as a result.

So, for example, when you mix with trainees before the course, gather information about them and use it to get the best out of them during the sessions later on. The three main areas in which you and they may have something in common are:

1   **Circumstances:**

- marital status
- number of children
- education
- home town or region.

2   **Experiences:**

- business experiences
- countries visited for business or pleasure
- pleasurable activities.

3 **Pastimes:**

- hobbies
- sports.

The list is endless. Anything we have in common with our trainees will encourage rapport and the more we can include these common links within our presentation, the more we will be automatically accepted as individuals. Our trainees will subconsciously respond – this is known as a 'me too!' response – and the more frequently they experience that automatic response the more they will identify with us.

Share opinions

Sometimes we will find ourselves sharing ideas with people with whom we believe we have very little in common. For example, we may be asked to train people of higher status than ourselves, older people, younger people or people who are more intelligent and educated than we could ever hope to be. At such times we are bound to question what, if anything, we have in common with them. The answer may be 'not very much'. Nevertheless, we still have to create this 'me too!' reaction. How, then, can we identify with them?

When you find yourself in this position with trainees with whom you have little in common, move straight away into what is known as the 'opinion mode'. We all know people with whom we feel we share a 'like mind' – people who think the same way as us, have the same philosophies and with whom we are generally 'in tune'. Rapport, and hence bonding, is then achieved through shared opinions. However, as was stated earlier, we must never lie or exaggerate to our trainees. How, then, can we share an opinion if we do not agree with what the other person is saying? This is almost certainly bound to happen when we have little in common with the people we are training. The key, under these circumstances, is to agree with the *logic or thought process behind the opinion, not the opinion itself*. This can be handled by saying something like:

- 'I can see why you would feel that way.'
- 'I understand exactly why you would have said that.'

In this way, you are being perceived as agreeing with the opinion but are actually agreeing with the logic behind it.

Share inabilities

As mentioned earlier, it is a mistake to imply how good we are or how much better we are than our trainees. In fact, the opposite approach helps to create a rapport and develop the necessary bond between us, as trainers, and our trainees. The more we can talk about our own inabilities and about our own non-performance before we put the training concepts into practice, the more our trainees will accept us. If we insist on trying to establish how good we are, it will have the opposite effect on them. Avoid such phrases as:

- 'Now, I never made this mistake . . .'
- 'Of course, I am totally organized . . .'

It is far better to say: 'I remember all the mistakes I used to make before I was really organized'. People feel much more comfortable, and can relate to another person much more closely when they feel that they share an inability or failing.

The human mind likes to compare differences and similarities. This process of sharing inabilities, which is called PNP, creates similarities between people. Similarities between us and our trainees, for example, can be categorized as follows:

- **Physical inadequacies**

  –too short
  –too fat
  –hair too thin or bald.

- **Non-performance**

  –made mistakes in past
  –couldn't close sales or arguments
  –didn't understand.

- **Pent-up emotions**

  –angry
  –frustrated
  –annoyed.

There will be many other examples you can think of.

Questioning techniques

Another technique to win trainees' acceptance of us as individuals is to ask questions. This is a good way of encouraging both group and individual participation and developing rapport. However, the wrong questioning technique can alienate people. One such example is using the dreaded 'trick question' – one to which there is no clear answer – such as:

- 'Can anyone tell me what this means?'
- 'What is the definition of . . .?'

Rather than encourage trainee participation, this sort of question stimulates fear and creates exactly the opposite reaction. Their immediate inner response will be:

- 'Don't know.'
- 'What do they want me to say?'
- 'Am I going to get it right?'
- 'Am I getting it wrong?'
- 'Will I be made to look stupid?'
- 'Will they make an example of me?'

Because of these instantly created doubts, the trainees' initial reaction to this type of question will be a complete non-response. That puts us, as trainers, in a dilemma. Having evoked no response we tend to pick on an individual – or rather a victim – in order to reassert our authority: 'How about you? You must surely know the answer?'

However, if we put ourselves in the victim's place – use our power of empathy – we will see that, no matter how mildly we posed the initial question, the poor victim is by now suffering agonies. These agonies are being shared by all the other trainees who, by now, will be sitting with their heads firmly lowered, thinking, 'I hope the trainer doesn't pick on me'.

The more we dig our heels in and insist on an answer, the more we alienate the whole group and the more they begin to dislike us as a result. In short, we lose rapport. There is a professional way to ask questions – an art – which is very simple. First, give the answer in the question, or at least make the answer very apparent. A question to which the answer is apparent, provokes a response from everybody. Imagine, for example, that you are watching a TV quiz show in which you are not particularly interested. Suddenly a question is asked to which you know the answer. What is your immediate reaction? You immediately become interested and automatically shout out the answer. This is precisely how to stimulate a response from trainees – ask them questions which they can easily answer. The more of these types of question you ask, the greater is the response from the group and the more you are bonding with them because they feel involved, both within the group and with you as their trainer.

Bonding

Bonding is crucial to foster a group spirit. A great deal has been written about the bonding between parents and children, and doctors and psychiatric patients. In these situations it depends very much on encouraging a natural and unaffected tactile approach – touching hands, hugging, gripping and other similar friendly and personal gestures – all of which can play a central role in developing togetherness with other people.

However, in a trainer–trainee relationship, tactile bonding is often inappropriate. However, we still need to get as close as possible to our trainees in order to develop a rapport with them. How can we resolve this dilemma? There are two techniques to overcome this:

● bonding with words
● bonding through empathy.

Bonding with words

'Togetherness' denotes a sense of connectedness, or the categorization of another person as a member of one's own group. Bonding can be established by means of the words we use whilst talking to our groups. We call these 'team words', and they include the regular and natural use of:

● we
● us
● together
● all of us as a group.

Often, you will be the only trainer in the room and it will seem logical to use the word 'I'. However, 'I' creates a division, a barrier, an 'us and them' situation which should be avoided at all costs. There will be many times in the course of giving an instruction when 'I' automatically suggests itself, but you must still use 'we' rather than 'I'. Developing a sense of togetherness is essential.

The one situation in which the word 'I' can be used is when you are identifying – for example, 'I remember the time when I got this wrong' – but you should then quickly revert to a 'team word', adding, for instance, 'but we are now going to do it together'. Use as many bonding words as possible throughout any session. This is one of the most important areas for trainers to develop because failure to bond through the use of 'team words' creates a division between our trainer and trainees.

Bonding through empathy

Empathy is 'the power to imaginatively enter into someone else's feelings'. A more everyday definition would be 'the ability to put ourselves in the other person's shoes'. Often, we look at people and judge the situation as *we* see it, not as *they* do.

As individuals, we may have experienced much and enjoyed much success. Consequently, we often make judgements based on our life experience. This is frequently the case between parents and teenage children. Parents tend to look at situations affecting their teenagers through more experienced adult eyes and very often misjudge the situation because they can no longer remember what it is like to be a teenager.

So, as trainers, we should always look at the people we are dealing with and ask ourselves 'Where are *they* in life?' and 'What are *their* problems now?'. In this way, we will be able to bear in mind their viewpoints, as well as our own, when dealing with them. The more we practise this approach the more empathetic we will be and will be seen to be. We will be promoting togetherness – or bio-rapport – the art of getting people to relate to, and respect, us.

Checklist: winning acceptance as an individual

1 Identify.
2 Share things you have in common.
3 Share opinions.
4 Share inabilities (PNPs).
5 Ask questions properly.
6 Promote togetherness.

4 Body language

**Body language = the art of non-verbal communication –
transmitting messages without speaking.**

We are now going to examine the second key factor in bio-rapport – body language. Many trainers, teachers, coaches, counsellors and those involved in the art of communicating with others, are adept at reading the body language of the people they deal with. In fact, they frequently use this skill to decide on their own communication strategy.

However, observations show that it is quite common for someone who trains others to ignore their own body language. Often the verbal message and the body language can be at complete odds, with the result that the message becomes incongruent. The key is to ensure that our body actions, gestures and posture convey exactly the same message as our words. In this way, we will become extremely powerful communicators.

First we will examine the body language indicators that *detract* from our message. It is recognized that:

- 80 per cent of knowledge is a result of what is seen, not of what is heard – and that it stems from the five recognized senses
- 65 per cent of what is accepted is accepted because it has been seen, as opposed to having been heard
- 80 per cent of interpretations are governed by feelings that are generated by the five senses – sight, hearing, touch, smell and taste – not by logical explanation.

We have all heard people say, 'I believe it. I saw it with my own eyes!'. In reality, what we are saying is *we listen aurally, but **accept** visually.*

Why are non-verbal cues, or body language, so important? Imagine a situation in which a salesperson is trying to sell you something. He or she delivers a perfect presentation that is 100 per cent to the point. Yet, although you can't put your finger on it, something does not seem quite right. At such a point, you usually make an excuse to escape. Even though you want what they are selling, the price is just right and the quality is exceptional, you still feel the urge to back away from it and, perhaps, even to buy from someone else. Why, then, if the salesperson has stated exactly what you want to hear, do you not agree and buy from them? The reason is simple. The uneasy feeling you experienced derived from the fact that your visual senses picked up inconsistencies in the salesperson's body language and, when what is *seen* does not agree with what is *heard*, uncertainty is created. It is a natural subconscious reaction and illustrates why an understanding of body language is so important for trainers if they are to successfully deliver their message.

Everything we do is controlled by the mind. The mind controls both speech and movement.

Speech

The words that we speak are controlled by the mind. It is said that the average person has a vocabulary of approximately 2500 words – that's all. Many of us will know individuals with vocabularies larger and, sometimes, smaller than average, but the average vocabulary is remarkably limited. Since it is quite easy for the mind to control these comparatively few words, we can pick and choose the words to say – things we believe other people want to hear. How many times have we started to say something to another person and stopped, suddenly realizing that if we said what we intended they would be upset or take offence, and quickly amended our words? Of course, sometimes, we are too slow and say what we should not have said, but on the whole we can control what we say.

This, of course, means that it is very easy for people to lie.

Movement

Our minds also control every movement that we make. For example, when somebody tells us to stand up, then sit down, then stand up again and sit down again, why do we do it? Was it because of their command?

In theory, the answer to this is 'yes'. We have conducted this experiment during training sessions. Usually, on the first command, everyone stands up without thinking about it. On the second command, some people do not move at all. When the command is given for a third time, some of those who are still obeying take the 'hover pose' – somewhere between standing up and remaining seated. They are clearly not quite sure what to do. Even though the commands are given in an authoritative tone of voice, the more times they were given the less they are accepted and acted upon. Therefore, it cannot be the command that makes the trainees stand up. If somebody tells us that we are all going up to the top floor of a tall building where we will leap off and teach ourselves how to fly would we do it? No. It is our mind that takes the instruction on board and it is our mind that determines whether or not we will act on it. We have all heard the phrase 'make your mind up'. This is exactly what we do. It is the mind that controls every action we take. We cannot lift our hand until the message to do so comes from the brain. So we should remember that the mind controls all bodily movements.

However, according to research carried out in body language, the body gives off more than 400 000 different non-verbal signals. There are some 13 000 that can be attributed to the face alone. This vast number of non-verbal communication signs is far too much for the mind to control. It is easier to deal with a vocabulary of just 2500 words.

This is why, in the case of the salesperson we referred to previously, if they do not have 100 per cent *belief* in what they are saying, or *confidence* in themselves, the words that come out are acceptable, but the body actions or gestures 'leak' a *different* message, creating disbelief or uncertainty in the other person.

This all goes to show that we are governed by our senses – not by the words we hear. Often, trainers, in their effort to communicate, deliver a verbally clear and concise message, which is even supported by excellent presentation material, but with their own body language conflicting with what they are trying to say. This is something that we, as good trainers, must avoid. Always remember to back up what you say with the correct body language. An understanding of this will make the difference between being a good communicator and a truly exceptional one, and the key to this is to understand the importance and role of gestures.

Gestures

There are two types of gesture – intentional and unintentional:

1 **Intentional or deliberate gestures.** These are gestures which we are

aware of making and understand to be readily recognizable by others – for example:

- a smile
- a thumb in the air
- clapping
- a frown.

These are straightforward gestures which have a precise meaning and are universally understood by others. We will explain later how to use these conscious movements to add emphasis to your message.

2   **Unintentional or subconscious gestures.** Unintentional, or macro, gestures as they are known, are those that are subconsciously given but, more importantly, are subconsciously received. In the case of the salesperson discussed earlier, it was their macro gestures – those unintentional gestures – that created the discrepancy between the verbal and visual message they were putting across. *Remember, unintentional macro gestures will influence the message we are aiming to deliver.*

To be effective, you must constantly ask yourself:

- What am I doing?
- What mental and physical image am I projecting?

To avoid making unintentional negative gestures, we must first understand the six universally recognized categories which will cause loss of trainer acceptance:

1   domineering gestures
2   lack-of-confidence gestures
3   impatient gestures that show boredom
4   superior gestures
5   defensive gestures
6   indifferent gestures that reveal doubt.

Domineering gestures

When trainees are faced with a trainer whom they perceive to be of a domineering nature, they generally reject both the individual and the topic. The most common gestures that suggest domination are discussed below.

The pointing finger

An index finger pointing directly at an individual or a group can be construed as anger, rather than just to direct an instruction. In some countries, finger-pointing is regarded with horror and is a classic threatening gesture implying domination. It intrudes on personal space and introduces pressure on trainees to respond or make a decision. Although it may often feel natural to point a finger, you should never point at a trainee. Remember that you are trying to create a bond using 'we', 'us' and 'together' words. The pointing finger says 'I am the boss!', 'I am superior to you!', instantly making your verbal message incongruent and creating subconscious doubt and mistrust.

Pushing with the palms of the hands

Sometimes, when disagreeing, rejecting or repelling points made by the audience, the trainer might hold either one or both arms forward and make slight pushing movements towards the group with the palms of the hands facing them. Yet, the gesture, because it can be subconsciously read as pushing away or rejecting, is really saying '*stop!*'. Since one of the most powerful demotivators is the feeling that either one's self or one's ideas are being rejected, never use the palms of the hands in this way.

Finger beating

This gesture, in which the finger is waved to highlight a point, is often unconscious. It is associated with people in authority or who are in an authoritative mood and carries with it the impression of admonishment or of moderate threat. As any suggestion of threat can cause a barrier between trainer and trainees, avoid its use.

Straddling the chair

This position is often adopted when there is an apparent superior–subordinate situation, such as during questioning. Consequently, it has subconscious connotations of dominance. Many trainers adopt this position in an attempt to promote an informal atmosphere, but in fact it can have quite the opposite effect.

Arms akimbo

This gesture, in which both hands are placed on the hips, gives quite an aggressive and threatening impression to trainees.

Dominance through height

In an effort to promote togetherness or to emphasize a particular point, many trainers try to get as close as possible to their trainees by reducing the physical distance between themselves and the group. As the audience is usually sitting down, this seemingly harmless action can place unbearable pressure on them because they suddenly feel dominated by the comparatively towering height of the trainer. Because, subconsciously, we are conditioned to believe that we should 'look up to' important people, this action unintentionally creates a barrier by forcing the trainees to 'look up' to the trainer, with the result that any bond so far created will falter.

Gestures that imply lack of confidence

Nowadays, trainee expectations are very high, and they will want the trainer to be confident, knowledgeable and willing to help. If our body language gives them the impression that we lack confidence they will not accept the information and ideas we are discussing. Let's now examine the most common body gestures that suggest lack of confidence:

Hands by the sides

Some trainers have a habit of allowing their hands to dangle loosely by their sides, letting their hands swing back and forwards in response to the general movement of their bodies. This looks quite unconvincing and gives an uninspiring impression to those they are trying to convince.

Fiddling with the hands

Many people, as they speak, place their hands in front of them and then, through tension, stress or plain boredom, start to fiddle – picking skin off their fingers, twisting rings or bracelets around and around – until whoever they are trying to communicate with begins to suspect something is wrong. If you are training a group and fiddle in this way, you lose both the focus of what you are saying and your authority. Even if you suddenly realize what you have been doing and then control yourself, the impression you have already given may be enough to damage the group's confidence in you.

Poor posture

When someone walks into a room with their shoulders upright and a straight back, taking firm positive strides, we instantly recognize confidence, even without a word having been spoken. This is known as 'strong physiology'. Conversely, when somebody walks into the room nervously glancing around, looking almost apologetic, round-shouldered and hunched up, dragging their feet as though they wished they weren't there, don't we instantly feel we are in the presence of somebody who is shy, nervous and timid? Maintaining a positive and confident posture gives you a better chance of attracting the immediate and undivided attention of your group.

Lack of eye contact

How do you feel when talking to somebody who cannot look you in the eye? We naturally warm to people when they look at us as they talk and, conversely, do not trust anyone who avoids looking at us. How often have you seen trainers who look above head height, look below table level, concentrate on their notes or presentation material – in fact, look everywhere else except at the group? How do you feel when this happens? Do you feel part of the group or do you feel left out? Do you warm to the trainer or do you feel detached from what he is trying to do? The answers are obvious and should highlight the importance of consciously looking at every member of your group. Make the effort to constantly scan the room to include everyone, individually and collectively, in your gaze. Remember how you felt when you were being excluded from your trainer's gaze – as though they were teaching another group entirely!

Gestures that indicate boredom and impatience

Another way of alienating trainees is to give the unconscious impression that we are bored by them, or that they are making us feel impatient. The gestures that can imply this are detailed below:

Head in hands

This is one of the most obvious boredom signals and should never be used in any of your dealings with trainees.

Hands behind the head

Sitting in a chair and clasping your hands behind your head tells your audience that you feel superior to everyone else in the room and are, accordingly, bored with everything and everyone in it. Use of this gesture will destroy the bond you should be establishing with your trainees.

Drumming the fingers

This is probably the most universally recognized gesture of impatience or boredom. Drumming the fingers unconsciously on a table or other hard object whilst, for example, a question is being answered, is not the way to win over either a group or an individual.

Supporting the chin

Whilst this gesture can sometimes be interpreted as demonstrating thoughtfulness, it can also imply boredom. If, as a trainer, you give *any* hint that you are bored with the proceedings you will soon lose the respect of your trainees, so this gesture is best avoided.

Ankle tapping

Sitting with one leg crossed over the other, moving the foot in a slight kicking motion as though tapping the other ankle with the heel or side of the foot also denotes boredom or irritation. Again, this gesture should be avoided.

Gestures that imply superiority

As discussed earlier, creating a sense of equality with your trainees is paramount. As we have also seen, body language can imply many things in direct contrast to what is being said and it can therefore be quite easy to unconsciously give the impression of being superior to your group. The following gestures fall into this category.

Hands behind the back

It is quite usual to feel an uncomfortable awareness when you do not know what to do with your hands. One option is to place them behind the back. Whilst this is certainly a confident gesture, it is also a military one, customarily adopted by officers when addressing someone of lower rank, and is also a stance often adopted by male members of royalty. It is therefore perceived as a gesture which denotes superiority, so even if your words may be promoting a sense of 'togetherness', the stance will contradict them. What you will be actually perceived as saying is 'I am superior to you'.

Steepling the fingers

Steepling the fingers – forcing the palms together with the fingers out-stretched so that they form a 'steeple' – is seen to be a rather egotistic gesture that shows that the person concerned is very confident of what they are saying. This may well be the case but, as it also communicates superiority, it should be avoided.

Nose twist

In this action, the nose is unconsciously twisted to one side for a brief moment. This signifies that something has been seen or heard which is not liked or not believed. Using this small, but very noticeable, gesture implies that you feel superior because you know more than your trainees, so you should avoid it.

Nose up

This gesture is made obvious by tilting the head slightly backwards to raise the position of the nose and is used when somebody wants to re-inforce their superiority by raising their height. Its universal interpretation is well illustrated by the phrase: 'He walks around with his nose in the air'.

Peering over the top of spectacles

Some spectacles-wearers, especially those who only need glasses for reading, often peer over the top of them when they need to see further than their lens prescription will allow – for example, while looking at notes and simultaneously trying to focus on whoever they are talking to. It is not only an annoying habit from the viewpoint of anyone who is being peered at in this way, but it also gives the impression of superiority on the part of the spectacles-wearer. If you wear spectacles bear this in mind at all times.

Defensive gestures

Defensive body language implies that we are worried about being made to look wrong. How can we, as trainers, convince our trainees to accept our message if our bodies are saying 'I'm not sure whether what I am saying is correct?'. Defensive gestures to guard against are discussed below.

Clenching the fists whilst listening

Listening to somebody with clenched fists expresses a negative reaction and risks alienating the other person. If you are listening to a trainee who is proffering an opposing opinion, complaining or just waffling, relax and make sure you are not clenching you fists. Refer back to how to deal with opposing opinion, or competition, as discussed in Part I, p. 12. Remember, people interpret the signals from your whole body, not just your face.

Clenching the fists whilst talking

Clenching the fists whilst talking denotes passion and belief and is interpreted that way. However, whenever you use such a gesture in this way, make sure that your body and words say *the same thing*, otherwise you will introduce a conflict that will cause your trainees to wonder which to believe!

Folding the arms

This is a very common gesture that is generally used when wishing to rest but, because it effectively closes off the body, it also forms a barrier between you and your trainees and will be interpreted as defensive. It is a gesture best avoided.

Crossing the legs

Sitting with crossed legs signifies a need to shield oneself against what is being said. It is another form of barrier. Crossed legs denote that you sense competition and accordingly if you ever sit down to present your material you should never cross your legs. It is defensive and says *'Don't approach me!'*

Gestures that denote doubt or indifference

The body can transmit an indifference to other people or even that we sometimes doubt our own abilities. These particular messages can be sent out in a number of quite subtle and unconscious ways. They are so small that we may not even notice them, but they are noticed by others and will be taken to mean that we are uninterested in them, both as a person and as an opinion-former.

Scratching the head

This gesture is not the one used deliberately to settle an itch, but is an unconscious gesture, sometimes accompanied by a blank facial expression. In body language terms it demonstrates perplexity and could be interpreted to mean that the trainer does not understand the material, is confused, or finds the subject too complex. Using this gesture, in training, will hinder your ability to inspire confidence.

Covering the mouth whilst talking

It is generally accepted that when somebody is talking with their hand partly over their mouth they are not telling the whole truth. For example, if someone covers their mouth and says 'This training course guarantees that...' it probably means that either they are not happy with what they are saying or they are telling an untruth. We can all recognize the origins of this gesture: when we were children and were trying to conceal something we should not have done, what was our automatic reaction when we told a lie or said a forbidden word? We clapped our hand to our mouth, as though trying to push the lie or forbidden word back where it came from! As we become older and more sophisticated, we modify or attempt to conceal the give-away gesture but the subconscious message remains the same. Similarly, if we are not entirely comfortable about something we are telling somebody, such as passing on information that should perhaps have been kept confidential, we place one finger over our mouth. It's a perfectly natural gesture, but should be avoided if you want your trainees to believe what you are telling them.

Covering the mouth whilst listening

Covering the mouth with a hand whilst listening to someone's opinion conveys doubt as to what is being heard. This is yet another gesture that will detract from the rapport you should always be developing with your trainees.

Touching the neck

Telling lies generates a chemical reaction within the body which creates an uncomfortable tingling, usually around the neck. This is how the phrase 'hot under the collar' originated. Therefore, when you share ideas or techniques which you are not entirely sure of, or a trainee questions you on an area with which you are unfamiliar, and you are unsure whether your intended answer is correct, remember not to betray your uncertainty by touching your neck. The words you utter may be completely plausible, but the small gesture will give you away.

Rubbing the chin

Rubbing the chin with the fingers while listening means 'I do not believe you'. Any unconscious face-rubbing gesture demonstrates underlying disbelief. This is a quite complex piece of body language which can easily be unconsciously used when in the enthusiasm of training or coaching, and it will alienate any trainee who is trying to make a point. They will receive the body message, 'Do not tell me lies', when they may believe they are right.

Scratching or rubbing ears

Scratching behind the ear with a bent forefinger, denotes uncertainty about whether or not what is being said is true. This is an unconscious action which signifies puzzlement to the other person. Similarly, rubbing the ear lobe between the thumb and forefinger means that the listener does not particularly want to believe what they are hearing. Once again, any trainee will instinctively perceive that their point is being rejected and this can cause division, because they may well believe it is true.

Biting the nails

This unconscious gesture indicates that the nail-biter is under pressure and is therefore unsure of him or herself. If you, as a trainer, give the physical impression of being anxious in this way it will certainly be registered by your trainees and create immense doubt as to your authority.

Rubbing the eyes

In body language terms, anyone who touches or rubs the eye, or near the eye, is being deceitful or being deceived. The action is a displacement gesture indicating a suppressed urge to look away – to avoid eye contact when the truth is being bent. This can occur either on the part of a speaker who is not being entirely truthful or on the part of a listener who feels they are not hearing the truth. Either way, this gesture indicates doubt in the message.

Conclusion

Body language, and the understanding of unconscious physical reactions, plays a crucial role in training. When we can match what we say with confirming and appropriate body language, we will become powerful and sympathetic trainers. It stimulates the following reactions:

- 'I like this trainer'
- 'I can relate to this trainer'
- 'This trainer is just like me'
- 'I respect this trainer's knowledge'
- 'I understand this trainer'

'... *therefore I will listen to their message....*'

You have to practise to become a truly effective communicator and trainer. You do not become effective by accident but by design. By applying ideas covered in this chapter you will achieve that effectiveness.

Checklist: body language

1   **Understand the mind.**
2   **Avoid domineering gestures.**
3   **Don't let your body language imply lack of confidence.**
4   **Don't let your body language imply boredom or impatience.**
5   **Avoid gestures denoting superiority.**
6   **Avoid defensive gestures.**
7   **Don't let your body language imply doubt or indifference.**

PART II

Communication that works

Introduction

Communication = the means of giving and receiving information.

We have now covered the first criterion for effective learning: the need for teacher, trainer or coach acceptance through bio-rapport. Once our trainees have accepted us, we then have to convince them that our ideas make sense and that they are both practical and useful – if not immediately then at some time in the future. This process should involve both the left-hand side of the brain – the logical side that deals with *rational thought* – and the right-hand side of the brain – the emotional side that governs *creative thought*. In Part II we examine how to present ideas so that they will be perceived to provide sensible, practical and useful benefits by means of the next three criteria for learning:

1 *logical* presentation
2 *mental* stimulation
3 *subliminal* influencing.

5   Logical presentation

Logic = the force or effectiveness of an argument.
Presentation = the manner in which something is laid out.

To reflect the two components of logical presentation this chapter is in two distinct parts:

1   Thorough understanding
2   Presentation technique.

Both parts are concerned with the logical requirement.

Thorough understanding

To give a logical presentation first requires a thorough understanding of:

1   the material
2   the reaction
3   the group
4   physical realities
5   response techniques.

These elements are discussed in detail and learning the skills to master them will enable you to adjust your presentation to make it logical, practical and useful for the variety of trainee types you will, sooner or later, encounter.

The material

The first step in being able to provide and present ideas and techniques that trainees will easily understand and accept is to make sure that we are completely familiar with the subject and the manner in which we intend to present it. Although this may seem a rather obvious statement, there are good reasons for making it as there are several situations that occur which will serve to remind us, too late, that we should have known the subject and the material much better.

Occasionally, for example, we may be asked to deputize for a colleague at short notice and find ourselves presenting material with which we are not fully conversant. Second, as trainers, many of us will be constantly searching for new areas or subjects to train in order to increase our repertoire and add to our own value. These are likely to be topical subjects that may seem more easily marketable than the old 'tried and tested' programmes. Extensions of our own core skills are relatively easy to manage, but we may be faced with the opportunity to challenge or expand outside our specialist area – and herein lies the potential problem. This can lead to situations in which we may be tempted to conduct sessions without having full command of the new subject which in turn leads to the temptation to involve the group more as a means of developing the material than as a means of developing the trainees themselves. Consequently, we can find ourselves presenting new material whilst keeping our fingers crossed in the hope we are not asked too many detailed questions!

Have you ever sat through a session or seminar in which it has become painfully obvious that the presenter did not really fully understand the material they were presenting? What was your, and the group's, reaction to that material? Questions were raised and doubts implanted, eventually resulting in the death-knell statement 'Well, that's OK in theory...'. Trainees do not expect mere theory from trainers. They expect a good, cohesive, sensible, practical and logical technique which is demonstrably superior to any alternatives. As trainers, we must take great care not to risk overstretching our abilities in this way.

Third, many trainers inherit their teaching material from their predecessors. This often means that they present this material without question, but with little enthusiasm, belief or understanding of it. Even the most polished presentation is no substitute for a thorough understanding and acceptance of the material. *If we don't understand or believe in our own material, how can we expect others to?*

Understanding the reaction

The second stage of giving a logical presentation and ensuring that our trainees understand our material is to predetermine the *objective* of the training session. In other words we must establish what type of *reaction* we want from our trainees. For example, do we want our presentation to:

- inspire thought?
- impart knowledge?
- generate consideration and analysis?
- impress people?
- amuse or create laughter?

or do we want it to:

- motivate people to act?
- inspire people to change?
- improve their results?

Inspirational training means that we are motivating people to *act*, to *perform*, to do *something* as a result. By defining the result or the *reaction* required, we can identify exactly what we want them to do. Often, the result sought from a training session is influenced or dictated by the client, management, or even the trainee objective, but whichever is the reaction we wish to obtain it should be clearly defined *before* we start the programme.

The reaction we want from trainees will automatically determine the action we need to take, and this, in turn, will govern the way in which we present our material.

Assessing the group

To determine what action to take in order to obtain the desired reaction, we will first need to identify the group's expectations, needs, goals and aspirations. Only then can we deliver a message which, to that particular group, is clear, concise, logical, easily assimilated and readily acted upon. There are five recognized categories of information that must be established before an assessment can be made:

- physical information
- background information
- professional information

- reasons for attendance
- feelings and expectations.

Physical information

By establishing such physical criteria as the age, the sex, or the mix of the group, you can plan specific generalities that will create interest and awareness. The physical composition of the group can affect the vocabulary and style of language you choose to use for the presentation, and this information will also influence the type of stories and analogies that can be brought into play. All the issues and references used will be governed by the physical make-up of any particular group. Remember also that the age of the trainees has a bearing on their attention span. For example, a very young group, say six years old, will be able to remember your message for about ten minutes. A teenage group will remember what they have been taught until something more interesting enters their minds. A group in their thirties will remember the points for as long as they need to retain them. The older the trainees, the greater their attention and memory span. The younger they are, the less they will assimilate and remember.

Background information

The method of training, the techniques employed and the concepts shared are often dictated by the background of the group or its individual members. Such factors as their level of education will have a profound effect on the way in which you address your group. Whilst you should not assume that the group is more intelligent than you – remembering also that there is a distinct difference between a person's intelligence and their actual common sense – you should not try to talk up to people whom you assume to be highly intelligent any more than you should speak to a supposedly less intelligent group in an oversimplistic way. To find out what level of address is acceptable to the group you must, however, understand their background not only because an obvious discrepancy will affect their acceptance of your message, but also to establish what action you need to take to obtain the desired reaction. For example, you should establish:

- their marital status
- their earning capacity or income group
- whether or not they are home owners
- what sports, hobbies or pastimes they enjoy.

These factors will all ultimately have a bearing on their thinking processes and what they will find acceptable, thereby determining the method of your presentation.

People with a high level of education or with a 'higher learning' background are more readily prepared to accept more complicated or more detailed explanations, whilst those at the other end of the scale – for example those from a 'lower learning' background with less education – will expect a more practical and down-to-earth method of presentation.

Have you ever arrived at a training venue only to discover that your carefully prepared programme became less and less relevant as you began to understand the background and level of intelligence and learning that your trainees had achieved? Or, have you ever been in a situation in which you found that your stories and analogies, that were fully accepted by a previous group, fell on stoney ground? The importance of understanding your trainees cannot be overemphasized.

Professional information

The different levels of experience, management levels, corporate positions or business acumen represented in a group will also affect the teaching methods you introduce in the session. For example, introducing a role-playing exercise may be intimidating for a relatively inexperienced member and too simplistic for another. When planning a programme that is based on professional information, you should be influenced not by the trainees' work titles but by the activities they perform within their jobs. Never fall into the trap of feeling at all subservient to your trainees. Always remember that you are professional – in what you do, in what you perform and in yourself. When you project this, your trainees will never doubt that you are in total control.

Reasons for attendance

Many of the people you train will already be familiar with the subject. However, it is still necessary to ask the reason for their attendance and why they have decided, or been asked, to attend our session in particular. Their reasons will affect the learning process and, consequently, the method, style and content of the programme. There are three reasons why people attend training programmes:

- because of their interest in the subject
- because of personal interest
- because of necessity or because they are required to attend.

Subject interest

The first recognized reason for attendance, and another factor which will influence the preparation of our material, is a particular interest on the part of trainees in the subject we are presenting. Trainees with an avid interest in any subject will be looking for an in-depth, knowledgeable, comprehensive and well presented session. Have you ever invested in a training programme purely because you are particularly interested in the subject matter and its attraction from either a professional or personal point of view? When this has been the case, you will remember how your personal expectations were raised before the session.

Nevertheless, a particular interest in a subject does not necessarily mean that there is a shared interest. Many people will have an interest in the same subject, but from a different viewpoint, and will attend a session to argue their viewpoint with others during that session. When you have prior knowledge of this possibility, you can prepare the presentation with this particular point in mind.

Personal interest

The second reason for attendance is that, quite often, delegates are inspired to attend a programme because they particularly want to hear a presenter who has a special reputation. Good trainers or presenters often develop their own following, either as a result of good public relations, by word of mouth or because they have a great deal of experience in their subject or present an interesting viewpoint on the subject. In these circumstances, a heavier emphasis on the personal point of view and references to personal success will enhance the programme, and it is acceptable to take a more personal approach.

No interest

While it is always pleasing to train people who are keen to share your ideas, there will always be the situation in which training holds very little, or no, interest for trainees. The reasons for this will include one or more of the following:

- Some trainees will attend because they have been told to or because it is expedient for them to do so. There may be some, especially those seeking promotion, who feel that it will be good for them politically if they are seen to attend and there may be others who are not so much interested in the benefits of the course other than that their attendance will look good on their CV in any career move.
- Some trainees will attend because, for them, a regular series of training

sessions is mandatory. They may be busy people who consider that attendance is an intrusion on their normal routine.

- Sometimes your training session may form part of an overall event, such as a conference or convention, in which a number of sub-events is included. In these circumstances some trainees may attend your particular session because they are expected to attend, although they would not, under normal circumstances, bother.

In all these cases, as long as you know the reasons why people have no particular interest in attending your session, you can prepare your presentation accordingly, to take them into consideration.

Feelings and expectations

You should also know how trainees feel about attending your session, especially if they are there because they are obliged to attend rather than because they actively want to be there. Generally, such trainees display one or more of the following characteristics:

- they are resistant
- they feel passive
- they wish to feel anonymous
- they want to be affiliated
- they suffer in silence
- they feel relaxed
- they are tense
- they have an open or closed mind
- they are suspicious about the whole event.

The techniques presented in this book will show how to overcome these feelings but it is important, in the first place, to understand the trainees' various emotions.

Their expectations of the subject, the session, the entire programme and the trainer will either be high or low. There is no middle ground. You should therefore try to discover and understand what areas of resistance you are likely to confront so that your presentation can be modified to correct as many of them as possible.

Physical realities

Having considered the status and emotions of the trainees, another factor must be checked and you should now pay attention to the physical realities they will have to face in the training environment. When you have the use of a room that is designed for training purposes you know that every requirement is catered for, but when you find yourself in a hotel or a client's premises, any problems created by the practical nature of the venue will affect the way in which trainees receive your message. Any problem in this area will reflect on your professionalism, because you, as the trainer, will be blamed if trainees feel that any physical comfort they are suffering is impeding their progress. Make sure that the training environment, the room and the surrounding areas, are as practical and comfortable as can be arranged. Check, for example, the following:

1   **at a hotel venue:**

- Is the room large enough?
- Is it the correct shape?
- Are the seats comfortable?
- Does everybody have somewhere to write?
- Do any pillars obstruct their view?
- Is there a signboard to guide delegates from Reception?
- Are there any noisy corridors nearby?
- Are there any distracting cooking smells?
- Is it constantly noisy outside?
- Is the lighting adequate?
- Is it too hot or too cold?
- Is the parking and access easy?

2   **at an office venue:**

- Is the room conducive to training?
- Is it situated away from telephones and noise?
- Are there note-taking facilities?
- Are other staff aware that training is taking place?

If conditions are not ideal for training, adjust and prepare the presentation to take into consideration the physical realities with which your trainees have to cope while trying, at the same time, to maintain your message.

Response techniques

Truly professional training means knowing the answer to any question you may be asked by your trainees. A nonsensical response to a question does not promote a 'that makes sense' reaction. Here, we look at ten ways to master the art of answering the type of questions likely to be asked by trainees:

1 **Admit you don't understand the question.** When you don't understand a particular question and cannot give a sensible answer, be honest and say so, and ask for clarification. Never attempt to answer a question you do not understand.

2 **Admit you don't know the answer.** When you understand the question but have no sensible answer, once again, do not attempt to respond or make a guess as to what that answer should be. There are two ways in which you can deal with this category of question:

   ● offer to research and report the answer later
   ● refer to the group to see if anyone else has the answer.

3 **Acknowledge a good question.** When you are asked a question that you are able to answer, tell the questioner that it is a good question. Thank them for raising the point and compliment them for thinking about it.

4 **Never interrupt.** When a trainee is asking a question, even if you have heard it many times before, allow them to finish it in full before responding. Remember that the other trainees may never have heard this question before and will not understand your answer if you interrupt the question or pre-empt what the questioner wants to say.

5 **Don't belittle the questioner.** Even if the question does not make sense or is irrelevant, never embarrass the questioner for having asked it. This will alienate the group.

6 **Repeat the question.** It is helpful to repeat a question after it has been asked, both to clarify your own understanding of it and to ensure that the group understands it as well.

7 **Give yourself time to answer.** When you are asked a question that is difficult to answer, first ask the questioner to repeat it or rephrase it in another way. This may make it easier for both you and the rest of the group to understand it better – and it will also give you time to think of an appropriate answer!

8 **Take particular care with foolish questions.** Great care is required when answering 'stupid' questions. They are raised for one of two reasons: either the questioner believes the question to be a serious one or the questioner is deliberately asking a silly question to create a lighthearted situation or to show off in front of friends. You have to be able to determine which! Care is required in answering a question which is meant to be serious because the questioner, in realizing that it was foolish, may defend themselves by generating an argument

rather than admit the stupidity of what has been raised. Deal with the question quickly to prevent this happening. The best way of dealing with the 'show-off' question is to make the questioner believe that we have not taken their question seriously by saying to them, with a polite laugh, 'Is that right?', and then immediately asking for a question from a different part of the room. This will prevent the trainee from making themselves look even more stupid in front of their group and stop them from developing an unpleasant scene to cover up their stupidity, thereby avoiding what might otherwise develop into an awkward situation.

9   **Deal effectively with insults.** You may sometimes encounter a trainee who tries to assert superior knowledge by goading or insulting you. The way to deal with this is either to ignore them, or rather more effectively, to stop the proceedings and ask them to repeat what they have just said. This is usually sufficient to stop them from persisting because you have quickly reasserted your own authority, letting them know that you do not fear them and that you will resort to embarrassing them in front of their group if they persist.

10   **Give a simple response to the heavy question.** Sometimes you may be faced by a trainee who insists on showing off by asking complicated questions just to assert their superior knowledge or education in your subject. The best way of dealing with this sort of question, which usually bores the other members of the group, is to give a really simple response that does answer the question but in a way that would be understood by somebody who knows nothing about the subject. This lets the 'show-off' trainee know that you are one step ahead of them and that you are not prepared to let them try to sabotage your authority in this way. You must have encountered the type of person who breaks in to reveal the punchline when someone is telling a good joke? It is this type of person who tends to ask such questions.

Checklist: thorough understanding

1   Know the material.
2   Establish the desired trainee reaction.
3   Assess the group.
4   Assess the physical realities.
5   Know how to respond.

Presentation technique

In the last section, we covered the value of gaining a thorough understanding of our trainees. We are now going to examine the logical, or rational, way to present the ideas we want them to accept through:

1   Transferable workable ideas (TWIs)
2   Simplicity
3   Avoiding jargon
4   Determining the action requirements.

Transferable working ideas (TWIs)

Textbook training is almost entirely theoretical and, whilst our sessions must inevitably include a certain amount of theory in order to develop the points for discussion, the objective of the training technique we are discussing here is to inspire others to develop, or improve, skills in such a way that they will leave the session with *practical* ideas that they will act on. This means that we, as effective trainers, must spend time converting textbook theory into TWIs – logical, useful, practical ideas that make sense. Theory is of little use unless it can be turned into something of positive and practical benefit and that is why we, as inspirational trainers, should provide our trainees with as many TWIs as possible. Inspiring others is not just a case of motivating them, but also providing them with practical, workable tools.

Simplicity

The best way to give a logical and easily understood presentation is to make it as simple as possible. Many trainers take full account of the age, ability and experience of their trainees and plan their presentations on the basis that the older and more experienced the trainee, the more complex should be the presentation. This practice seems to be adopted because the trainers concerned feel that the higher up the career, professional or educational ladder their trainees are, the more complicated and information-intensive they will expect their course to be. But, in reality, no matter how well educated, experienced or successful people may be, when they are bombarded with too much information too quickly, like everyone else, their minds switch off due to overload. The solution is to keep presentations simple, irrespective of the status or standard of the trainees involved. The following tips will be helpful in this respect.

Lists

Schoolteachers are trained to write lists of the points they are covering on the board so that children, of any age, will learn them quicker, in 'parrot' fashion. This is a tried and tested method of teaching that goes back many years. We have all learned our school subjects in this way, yet many adult trainers ignore this basic art of teaching because they seem to feel that adult trainees are more experienced and more intelligent and expect to be treated in a way that does not insult this intelligence. In reality, whatever the age, status or intelligence of trainees from all walks of life, they will learn much more when the salient points under discussion are written on the board in the form of a list, just as it was when they were at school. Nevertheless, you should make sure that you always list bullet points, rather than full texts, and that you list points using a structured approach, such as the following:

1 **Main point**

   a. sub heading 1
   b. sub heading 2.

Also, break the information down into single, easy-to-follow components by listing, for example:

1 who?
2 what?
3 where?
4 why?

This enables trainees to more easily learn the points under discussion and also makes note-taking much simpler for them. Never be afraid of presenting in the most simplistic way – even when you are training people who may seem to be more intelligent, more experienced or of higher status than you are.

Slides

The most effective slides are produced as a reversed-out negative – that is, with a black background and white lettering. This is far more powerful than a black or coloured text on a white or coloured background which appears psychologically less clear by comparison. Another important consideration is never to cover too many points on one slide. When presented with several lines of listed points, trainees tend to scan the list, focus on the one in which they are particularly interested and then ignore the other points. On page 17 we discussed OHP 'reveals' – using overlays to reveal points as you come to discuss them – but this is not possible with slides. It is therefore better to invest in more slides that show fewer points.

Avoiding jargon

Avoid buzzwords and jargon. Whilst some people in the group may understand what is being said, those trainees who do not understand the jargon will rarely ask for its meaning for fear of being ridiculed. There is little point in trying to appear to be up-to-date and trendy in your speech if some people do not understand what you are trying to communicate. If they do not understand you, they will not listen. If they do not listen, they will not learn. Speak to trainees in a language you know they will understand and, to make sure that they *always* understand you, keep presentations simple.

The key to logical, practical and useful presentations is simplicity. *The more important the message, the more simply it should be presented.*

Determining trainer action

The method we choose to present our material will depend on what sort of reaction we want from our trainees. The material we use may be constant, but the delivery or method we use should vary, depending on the action we want the trainees to take.

There are six different elements to training:

- the lecture
- the syndicate group
- the forum session
- the individual presentation
- tests or exams
- homework.

Advice on when and how to use these different elements and tips to make sure they run smoothly are given below.

Lecture

A lecture is really an ideas platform from which many trainees can be trained at the same time, without any trainee participation. Use the lecture when you want to disseminate as much information as possible in a given amount of time and in circumstances where your trainees are seated in classroom or theatre style, that is, sitting in rows facing the front of the room.

For maximum effect, the room layout should be set up with:

- the entrance at the rear of the room, ensuring that, as trainees enter the training area, the correct image is portrayed;
- no centre aisle. Most trainers present from the 'front centre' of the room, which means that they continually project left and right over the most effective area – that is, the centre of the room.

Tips

- Make sure each trainee has a table or writing tablet.
- Make sure there are soft drinks and water on each table.
- Make sure there is no centre aisle.
- Make sure each trainee has a pad and a pencil or pen.

Syndicate groups

A syndicate group will contain no more than eight trainees and should be arranged when you want to analyse and discuss the topic in detail.

Tips

- Give clear instructions to the group.
- Set a time limit.
- Assist trainees as necessary.
- Come to a definite conclusion.

Forum session

A forum session comprises a small group of trainees and should be organized when you wish to encourage creative thinking and participation to discuss and agree a particular point.

Tips

- Always maintain full control.
- Prevent 'limelight hogs' and disruption.
- Make sure that *everybody* participates.
- Form a definite conclusion.
- Obtain group agreement on the point under discussion.

Individual presentations

Individual presentations should be used to present ideas by individuals, either singly or as members of a small group. Use this training format when you want to build an individual's skills and build their confidence, and to develop a team spirit.

Tips

● Make sure there is *total* participation.
● Give a fair analysis of the proceedings.

Tests or exams

This is a training format in which trainees give their own answers to a set of questions. Apply firm parameters and time limits.

Tips

● Play background music. This helps to relax trainees.

Homework

This is where trainees are asked to go away to consider the points discussed in the session in order to produce their own individual thoughts for assessment later.

Checklist: logical presentation techniques

1 **Convert theory into practice with TWIs.**
2 **Keep presentation simple.**
3 **Avoid jargon.**
4 **Determine trainer action.**

6 Mental stimulation

Mental = relating to the mind.
Stimulation = increasing or exciting vital action.

The third criterion for persuading people to accept our ideas is to make the training interesting. This can be tackled in two ways. First, it can be achieved by the use of interesting facts, information or subject matter that can provoke thought or conflict. However, this alone is not sufficient.

The mind is an active muscle. It is impossible for it to be absorbed in something for too long. It craves stimuli, and the simple presentation of information is not usually significant to provide this because the mind is capable of operating faster than we can speak. People are able to think at the rate of approximately 400 words a minute compared to the average speaking rate of about 200 words a minute. Thus the brain has spare time capacity and, if there are too many facts or the presentation is not sufficiently interesting, trainees' minds will start to wander and search for anything else that will provide a stimulus.

Since we have already adjusted and corrected our own personal image (see Part I), the trainees' minds cannot concentrate on us as their focal point. Because the room is also laid out in a professional manner, nor will this provide any alternative points of interest. Therefore, in the absence of an external diversion, their minds will become *internally creative* – in other words, trainees will start to *daydream*. They will conjure up images of past holidays, future holidays, situations at the office, previous conversations or arguments or pleasant memories – in fact, any thoughts that will satisfy the creative aspects of the right-hand side of the brain. As a result, crucial teaching points can be lost. The solution is to keep the creative side of the mind busy by absorbing it in the message being delivered. We must:

- make it sit up
- jog it
- astound it
- startle it
- instruct it

and, in so doing, build and maintain interest levels during each training session. Before we look at how to do this, again it is necessary to fully understand the process and the psychology involved. So, let us look at what we are attempting to achieve in the minds of the trainees.

In Figure 6.1 the vertical axis represents the *interest level* of the trainee, while the horizontal axis represents the *time factor*. The objective of any training session is to take the trainee step-by-step through each session and to steadily initiate, raise and maintain interest throughout until the

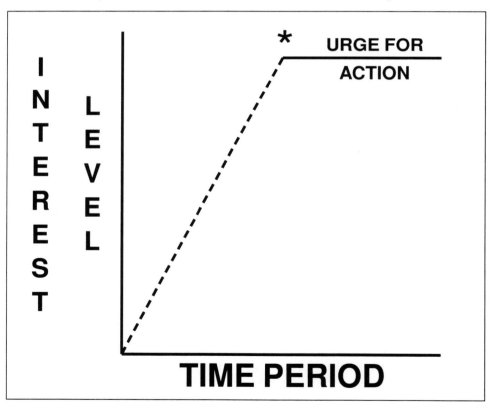

Figure 6.1   Session psychology

close of the session when interest levels reach their peak. Then we can effectively close the session with an *urge for action*.

This represents the key for effective training for, as mentioned earlier, the Advanced Training concept detailed in this book provokes trainees to *do something* or *take action* as a result of training.

It is this objective that we will be examining in the three stages of mental stimulation, which are:

1   scene-setting
2   the session
3   closing the session.

Scene-setting

Before the session starts, our own actions and our trainees' perceptions of those actions will either raise interest or cause it to fall. The following ideas will help to *raise* initial interest.

Music

Music (and rhythm) is one of the earliest known stimuli. It is often used prior to psychotherapy or counselling sessions to create a calming influence. By the careful use of music, it is possible to mentally prepare trainees for the forthcoming session. Music is seldom used in a formal training environment but, by understanding that the mind is a mass of pre-programmed images, imposed mainly by the media we are exposed to on a daily basis as well as by association, we can use these images and associations to create the correct intellectual environment.

Below we suggest some music titles and themes that cross many cultural boundaries and can therefore be used universally:

Relaxing themes

● **Telemann**

–   Largo from 'Concerto in G Major for Viola and String Orchestra': Wurtemberg Chamber Orchestra (Turnabout, Vox Records).

● **Vivaldi**

–   Largo from 'Winter' (*The Four Seasons*): Loa Bobesco (violin) with the Heidelberg Chamber Orchestra (Peerless Records).

- Largo from 'Concerto in D Major for Guitar and Strings' from *Baroque Guitar Concerti*: Konrad Ragossnig (Guitar) with The Southwest German Chamber Orchestra (Turnabout, Vox Records).
- Largo from 'Concerto in F Major for Viola d'Amore, Two Oboes, Bassoon, Two Horns and Figured Bass', 'Three Concertos for Viola d'Amore', 'Two Concertos for Mandolin': The New York Sinfonietta (Odyssey Records).
- Largo from 'Flute Concerto No. 4 in G Major' – 6 Flute Concerto Opus 10: Jean-Pierre Rampal (Flute) with the Louis de Froment Chamber Ensemble (Turnabout, Vox Records).

Stirring themes

- *Fanfare for the Common Man*
- Sousa Military Marches (any)
- Theme from *The Dam Busters*
- The Halleluyah Chorus
- Theme from *Chariots of Fire*
- Theme from *Star Wars*.

Motivational themes

- Theme from *Rocky III (The Eye of the Tiger)*
- Main theme from the 'James Bond' films
- Theme from *2001 (Thus Spake Zarathrustra)*

Room setting/layout

This is another factor that is rarely considered when preparing for a training programme. Yet, as a trainee first enters the room, the manner in which the seating has been laid out beforehand, the equipment visible and the general ambience create an instant mental picture and assumption as to the type of programme that is to follow. We can either use room layout to our advantage or, as with other areas of preparation, ignore it at our peril! The following factors should be considered.

Seating arrangements

Classroom style

A training room set up in traditional 'classroom' format will either generate relief because the session is probably taking the form of a lecture and the trainee will therefore not feel expected to be asked to participate, or it may provoke the expectation of boredom – a legacy from school or college days.

U-Shape with tables

When the training room is set up with tables and chairs in a U-shape format, trainees will immediately know that discussion is highly likely. They will prepare themselves to stimulate thought and participate.

U-Shape without tables

This layout may intimidate a trainee entering the training room for the first time because chairs arranged in a U-shape usually evokes a mental image of therapy groups, or self-confession, and could be interpreted to signal a 'self-confession' session or some form of pressure relief, unless clear objectives have been established in advance. This interpretation also depends on the circumstances and the style of the room itself.

Audio-visual equipment on display

This generates the obvious assumption that a 'show' will take place, followed by possible group analysis.

Video recording equipment on display

This instantly shows that there will either be tutor, group or self-analysis, which can instil a sense of panic or pressure, even amongst the most enthusiastic trainees.

Lectern on display

A lectern gives the impression that the session will take the form of a lecture. Since most people have experienced boring lectures, the trainees' enthusiasm levels could immediately start to decline.

Tidy, organized room

Anyone entering a tidy and well organized training room will immediately receive an instant impression of professionalism and discipline – without even a word having been spoken.

Opening gambits

How we start any training session will determine the outcome. Having set the initial scene by the careful choice of music and room layout, you now have to increase expectation levels and proceed along the 'interest' scale in two areas:

- your physical presence and confidence
- your opening statements.

Your physical presence and confidence

There are schools of thought that suggest that it is not *what* you say that really counts, but *how* you say it, and this certainly applies to the start of any training programme. If you are perceived as lacking in confidence, nervous or ill at ease, then whatever the trainees' expectation level it will soon start to diminish. Therefore you must *appear* to be totally confident. However nervous or tense you feel, if you look confident, this confidence will soon transmit itself to the group.

Although it has been established that it is better to experience 'nervous tension' before a training session than it is to be overconfident, the way you feel can very easily be misinterpreted by the group. Therefore, before you start the session, you should:

- take deep breaths
- tense and relax the muscles
- give positive 'self-talk'
- stride purposefully to the front
- step out from behind the lectern.

(See also 'Relaxation techniques' in Chapter 9.)

Your opening statement

Having presented a confident image, make sure that your initial words incorporate an 'attention-grabber'. The most powerful way to generate interest is through the use of a technique known as *the initial benefit statement*. This is a statement designed specifically to raise trainee expectations with regard to the promised *outcome* of the training – not just the programme or its content. A better idea of its power can probably be conveyed by describing it as an *opening hot-button statement*. It is generally recognized that everybody has their own particular 'hot-button' which, when pressed, stimulates an automatic interest. A hot-button represents what every individual wants more than anything else. It could be the house of their dreams, the car they would love to own, the holiday of a lifetime – any one of those things that, when they think of it, generates excitement and anticipation.

How, then, can you use this hot-button to win the full attention of your trainees? To illustrate the point, concentrate fully, for two minutes, on the particular hot-button that inspires you. When it is firmly in mind, imagine that a salesperson says:

'Good morning, sir/madam. What I am going to do is spend the next three minutes showing you exactly *how you can get* that thing you want more than anything else. I am going to show you how you can have it right now!'

Now let's ask the question:

'Would you necessarily believe this salesperson?'

Probably not. So, let's ask another question:

'Would you listen to them?'

Probably yes.

That is the power of this type of statement. Obviously, in training, you should relate it to trainee result expectations. For example, if you were conducting a Negotiation Skills programme for key account executives whose corporate payment structure was based on a large and generous commission element based on sales generated, the objective of the programme would be to increase skills to obtain more new business and, as a result, increase their personal earnings. Thus, a possible *initial benefit statement* could be:

'... for the next two days, we will be covering every aspect of negotiation skills and techniques designed to increase your effectiveness as a businessperson and, ultimately, to *increase your earnings....*'

Suggesting a *result* – that is, increased benefits for them – gives the opening statement a great deal of 'you' appeal. This is another irresistible lure to the trainee because, ultimately, every trainee is interested in *what the training **will do**, not what the training **is**.*

Although the use of the initial benefit statement is undoubtedly the most effective method of winning attention, when running a programme with a varying number of sessions, you will vary your opening statement. Other ways of raising initial interest include the following:

Arouse curiosity

Everyone is naturally curious, and, once that curiosity is aroused, will mentally 'lean forward' in anticipation. For example:

'... there is one mistake that nobody can make. We can make every other mistake bar this one. We can even invent mistakes of our own – but never, never ever make this one....'

Being curious, you will almost certainly be wondering by now what this mistake might possibly be! The answer is, of course, 'We must *never* quit!' However, the answer is actually irrelevant in terms of the 'curiosity factor' raised.

Shock tactics

One way to gain a group's attention is to make a sudden noise. This does not necessarily mean shouting at them, but perhaps, banging on the flipchart stand, or slamming a book down on to a table. It is surprising how effective a sudden noise can be in gaining attention! Another option is to make a shocking statement, for example:

- '... we have just experienced the *worst* results ever recorded by this company....'
- '... the value of this company has *plummeted*....'

This is guaranteed to make people sit up and pay attention!

Unusual facts

Known as the 'would you believe it syndrome', the occasional use of inconsequential, but factual, information also stimulates the thought process. For example:

'Can you imagine thirty litres of milk on a table? Where did it come from? It could have come from just one cow after one day of milking!'

This ploy, by giving the mind something to wonder about, is an effective focuser of attention.

Exhibits

By using the visual aspects of our own communication skills, it is also possible to create immediate mental arousal. For example:

'... this small piece of engineering I have in my hand is designed to revolutionize the....'

Faced with such a statement, the mind is forced to focus intently on the displayed object, thereby ensuring its attention.

Rhetorical questions

A simple but powerful way of obtaining mental participation is through the use of rhetorical questions – questions that do not require a verbal reply, but automatically stimulate mental response. For example:

● 'How many people here have...?'
  brings the mental response: 'I have!'
● 'Have you ever wondered...?'
  brings the mental response: 'Yes!'

Quotations

The use of philosophical or well known quotations also stimulates thought, either by causing the mind to consider the quotation or by remembering it. For example, '... a man going nowhere usually gets there...' will certainly provoke thought or, alternatively '... a horse, a horse, my kingdom for a horse...' will be easily recognized by most people.
    The key is to use well known and familiar quotations.

Historical facts

Putting a date to an item of information will add to its interest factor. For example:

● 'This novel idea actually dates from 1928...'
● 'The company was established a century ago...'
● 'The design hasn't changed for over ten years...'

Identification

The value of identification has been discussed in Chapter 3 'Winning acceptance as an individual', and the same concept is included here as a means of securing initial interest. For example:

● '... I remember when I was in a similar situation to yourselves...'
● '... I wonder what's going through your minds now, because I can still remember clearly what my thoughts were when...'

Sometimes known as the 'levelling approach', this technique also generates the reaction we sought in Part I of this book (Bio-rapport) in which the trainee believes of the trainer: 'This person is just like me – therefore it will be worthwhile listening to what they have to say.'

Topicality

By relating the session opening to an important local current event or to a corporate occasion, it is possible to demonstrate an unexpected, impressive awareness of local situations which automatically hits trainees' 'interest buttons'. This ploy is sure to impress, especially when the trainer is from outside the company or locality.

Instructions

By giving specific instructions with regard to the rules and regulations, we can set the tone and also generate interest. For example:

- 'Open your mind...' tells trainees to remove any preconceived ideas and points of reference whilst simultaneously implying that new innovative ideas will be shared.
- 'Take copious notes...' implies that much relevant information will be supplied and that, if full attention is not maintained, important teaching points may be missed.
- 'Feel free to ask questions at any time...' generates the expectation of a highly participative programme.
- 'Save any questions until the end...' indicates that a lack of attention during the session could prove to be embarrassing later.

Informality or humour

Informality and humour can be excellent ways of breaking the ice, or even setting the tone of the forthcoming session when opening a programme. However, beware. This also represents a potential danger, because if you obtain the wrong response, even worse, if the humorous comment or joke meets with a stoney silence, then the session will have started off on the wrong footing. Be humorous by all means, provided you are an accomplished raconteur of amusing stories, but beware the danger of telling jokes or establishing humour with an audience that may resent it. Some people have no sense of humour, and there are some who may find the use of humour about certain topics personally distasteful. It goes without saying that humour about race and religion must always be avoided.

Having now looked at eleven acceptable ways to open a session, we should also look at the following five ways of how *not* to open a talk:

Making apologies

There may be various circumstances in which you may feel it is necessary to apologize to trainees, or to adopt an apologetic manner. However, this can create entirely the wrong reaction. For example:

- 'I won't keep you long...' will generate the mental response of 'Oh no, here we go!' rapidly followed by a mental shutdown.
- 'I'm not very good at this...' or 'I'm not really prepared for this...' will elicit the mental response: 'This is going to be amateurish!', usually followed by an immediate and severe drop in expectations. In any case, why bother to warn them when they will find out sooner or later anyway?
- 'Unaccustomed as I am...' will meet the silent response. 'Not that old line again! The rest of the programme is going to be equally outdated.'
- 'They dragged me into this...' will stimulate the mental response: 'The trainer doesn't really want to talk to us', followed by a loss of all interest on the assumption that the programme will be badly prepared and presented with little or no conviction.

Listing everyone present

Many trainers believe it is important during the introduction to a session to mention everyone present. This is a legacy from official functions where it is often protocol to make everyone known to everybody else. However, in the training environment, it is not only unnecessary but boring.

Building suspense

Although building suspense is also a recognized way of gaining interest and is acceptable provided it is not overdone, the rule of thumb is never to allot more than 10 per cent of the introductory talk to the suspense factor.

Building self-importance

Although we have already covered this particular aspect in Part I, it is necessary here to re-emphasize this point, since many trainers still unwisely become self-centred which, at the entry to a session, can work against them. Remember, the use of 'I' gives trainees the impression the trainer is full of self-importance and is, accordingly, likely to be rather more interested in the sound of their own voice than their response.

Using tasteless humour

Even though we have already considered humour as a good way of opening a session, it is included again here because it is so easy to misjudge. What may be a perfectly acceptable piece of humour in a social situation can often have the opposite effect in the training room. There is nothing worse than starting a session with something that is intended to be funny but falls flat. If this does happen, do not let it diminish your image. Let the onus of the joke pass to another by saying, for example, 'Mr Jones told me that. I didn't think it was funny either...'.

How you say it

The first few moments of a training programme determines the trainees' receptiveness and interest level. Trainees instinctively notice, assess and respond to personal style, which is governed by the manner in which the message is put over. Certain 'perceived qualities' can inspire interest, whilst others can promote an instant 'turn-off'.

Interesting qualities

How you project yourself to the audience can instantly capture interest and make trainees *want* to listen. For example:

- An *exciting and creative* approach promotes a feeling of anticipation.
- A *knowledgeable and confident* approach is instantly reassuring.
- A *warm and friendly* approach is comforting.

'Turn-off' qualities

The following qualities are barriers to listening and, when opening a session, there is a much greater opportunity to create these barriers than there is of building a rapid rapport. For example:

- Being *monotonous and lethargic* fails to raise interest.
- Appearing *formal or pompous* immediately creates a 'them and us' situation.
- Delivering *complex or irrelevant* material generates anxiety and boredom.
- A *stuffy* approach indicates a complete lack of empathy with the group.
- Being *overmotivational or overintense* at the opening of a session leaves the audience behind because they have not yet been able to raise similar passion.

Summary

All the above ideas are of great importance, because it is essential to be able to open sessions in such a way that ensures you have the full attention of trainees at this point. Without it, there is little hope of proceeding into the detailed training programme with any conviction.

The session

As stated at the beginning of this chapter, the brain is an 'active muscle' that requires constant stimulus. Research has shown that listening requires as little as 15 per cent of brain capacity. This means that about 85 per cent of our trainees' brainpower is left idle, searching for something to focus on. The fact that we have contrived to grasp their attention at the session opening is no guarantee that trainees will automatically continue to listen throughout each session. Therefore, we must now fight all the distractions that are competing for our trainees' attention.

The most effective way of stimulating or attracting attention is to use *visual reinforcement*. By using visualization – either physical visuals such as slides, handouts and exhibits or mental visuals, by encouraging the creative side of the imagination to conjure up mental pictures – we can decrease the likelihood of boredom and disappointment setting in. The most powerful way to stop attention wandering is to *show* trainees what we are talking about by harnessing the power of their own minds through the following methods.

Use stories and analogies

The structured use of stories, preferably based on real-life situations, helps to engage the right-hand side of the brain and stimulate creative recall. However, as with all the techniques, there are pitfalls. To avoid such pitfalls, note the following guidelines:

● **Restrict the length.** Because stories and analogies generate a greater response from the learning group and because many trainers are frustrated entertainers who relish the opportunity to perform, the presentation often turns into a 'show'. Some trainers become so involved and adept in relating the scene they are presenting that the teaching point often gets lost – both by the trainees and the trainer! How often have you heard a lecturer say '... let me see, where were we...?', purely because they have become so engrossed in their own rhetoric. Therefore, whenever relating a scene to a teaching point, keep the session short and to the TWI that is intended (see 'Presentation' p. 58).
● **Restrict the number.** The whole purpose of using any type of story or analogy is to help the trainee to create a mental picture that they can relate to within the teaching point being made. Once that reference point has been established, the mind is then refreshed sufficiently to allow the acceptance of the next piece of information. Again, many trainers overuse this technique by calling on too many illustrations per

teaching point. For effective training, incorporate only one or two stories for each point.

- **Restrict the content.** The point of using stories or analogies is to keep the trainee mentally alert, not to entertain nor to turn the session into a cabaret act. However, the rules of entertainment *do* apply inasmuch as there are subjects that are taboo in *any* mixed or single-gender audience, these being:

  - sex
  - religion
  - politics.

It is very easy to assume that because you are addressing an all-male or all-female group there is greater licence to use sexual references or innuendoes than would be the case with a mixed group. This is not the case. Moral standards vary enormously between individuals, groups and cultures. It is said that if you are looking for an argument, talk religion or politics and if you are looking for a fight, talk both! Many comedians use these subjects for their 'cheap laugh' value, but here we are talking about the professional skill of training, and a professional trainer does not need to resort to cheap tricks to maintain interest.

Use games

The use of 'games' during certain types of training session is an ideal way to develop and maintain interest. Many trainers believe that the use of this technique – often referred to as *infantalization* – is ideally suited to younger groups or even the 'less intelligent'. However, it is a powerful way of maintaining mental awareness for all ages and education levels, and it can be used in the development of teams or cohesive units. In this case, the games – even though they take place in an artificial setting – by stimulating the players' 'creative imagination' with realistic situations, can be used as teaching points in the subsequent debriefing sessions. Some examples of trainee games follow.

- **Round Robin sessions.** Ideal for introducing a 'fun' element, whilst simultaneously developing quickness of thought and reaction.
- **Building Props.** Introduces problem-solving disciplines and also highlights the value of teamwork and communication.
- **Charades.** Fun sessions with the serious purpose of encouraging total participation.

Use role plays

Role-playing works on the principle that 'the mind of man cannot tell the difference between that which is real and that which is imaginary'. Research into the human mind has discovered that, even in the most obvious classroom environment, students, when put into role-play situations, will automatically assume the role they were assigned. From a teaching point of view, this is invaluable for it provides a training environment that is second only to a real-life situation. From a trainee point of view, it is also invaluable because it provides the stimulation the brain requires to maintain learning interest levels. The more challenging the role play, the more effective it will be. By 'challenging', we are not referring to the acting ability required, but rather that the more 'confrontational' the situation that is set up, using trainees in all roles, the more the participants will assume their roles. For example:

- **Management role play.** In a situation where a manager or supervisor reprimands a subordinate for a serious misdemeanour, both characters would very soon assume the roles they were assigned, including all physical actions (body language would be totally congruent), and the emotional intensity equivalent to that in real life.
- **Selling or negotiating role play.** In a situation where a salesperson negotiates with a buyer, and in which both parties are given clearly defined responsibilities and guidelines on how to obtain the best deal, the players would soon become almost indistinguishable from real-life characters.

One word of warning, however. The purpose of role-playing is, as already stated, twofold – first, to help identify areas of trainee development and, second, to create and maintain the 'interest factor' throughout each session. In order to do this, we must look at how to conduct a role-play session in such a way as to achieve those aims.

Conducting a role play

Many trainees fear role play – possibly because of first-hand experience but often as a result of hearing about another person's ghastly experience. The following five steps are the most effective way to conduct a role play, both to ensure benefit to the participants and to maintain the interest of those observing it.

1   For the participants, set the scene, the parameters and suggest a time limit to reach the conclusion of the exercise. Because role play can be

boring for those not participating, involve the onlookers as observers, setting them points to comment on at the end of the session and thereby also ensuring their maximum attention.

2   At the end of the session, ask the leading role-player how well they thought they had performed and what conclusion, if any, they have reached. This gives an opportunity to individuals for self-assessment.

3   Next, ask the other participant(s) what their feelings and observations are. This gives the other role-player – the main participant – first-hand information on the results of their own actions.

4   Praise both people for their appraisals and add your own comments and relevant teaching points. This will dilute any criticism directed at the participants by the observers – which is often more destructive than constructive and can lead to trainees entering a 'payback' situation so that, when it is their turn to comment, personal feelings, rather than professional observations, come into play.

5   Now allow the group to make observations and comments. Praise each comment made and either endorse or sweeten the comment as appropriate.

Build anticipation

One of the most accurate definitions of *effective training* is: 'training is a sales process'. That is, training requires the constant 'selling of ideas' to trainees. One of the factors in maintaining trainees' interest is to constantly raise anticipation of each training segment before the session begins. For example:

● 'The next point we will be covering is, without doubt, one of the most crucial we shall be discussing. . . .'

● 'This particular technique often makes the difference between success and failure in. . . .'

Promote each segment as and when it happens, building upon each point in turn to culminate in the final section of the programme.

Make constant 'them' references

It has been said that being able to gratify self-interest is one of, if not the, greatest motivators available and that the pursuit of pleasure outweighs many of the restrictions that hold people back. The *initial benefit statement* (see p. 70) raises interest, initially. Constantly linking the training to the results promised during each session guarantees maintained interest. Linking can be achieved by an understanding of individual or group requirements. For example:

- **General interest subjects:**

  - themselves
  - personal relationships
  - the opposite sex/relationships
  - toys and gadgets
  - sporting achievements
  - shared experiences
  - success stories
  - money and power
  - bad news.

- **Specific interest subjects:**

  - managing directors: maintained or increased profits
  - financial directors: cost reduction or savings
  - sales directors: increased/more profitable sales
  - production directors: increased efficiency/quality
  - junior/middle managers: corporate climb
  - commission staff: increased income
  - academic students: certification/qualification
  - sports students: medals
  - poor economic climate: keep job
  - good economic climate: get better job.

Whilst the message or objective of the programme may not be individual-oriented – for example, it could be about team development, staff improvement or be customer-related – nevertheless each TWI (see p. 59) should always ultimately finish with an individual benefit. For example:

'When we achieve this the company will profit, our teams will communicate better and it will result in increased efficiency which will ultimately reflect on us and enhance *our own prospects for promotion...*'

In the absence of specific outcome requirements, relate to the title of the programme and/or general results. For example:

'by doing this, we will become much better organized [*time management programme*], have more time available to develop other projects [*benefit statement*] and ultimately achieve whatever our own individual aspirations are [*general result – individual-oriented*].

Use embedded commands

By the subtle use of words and phrases, we can constantly nudge the mind and also give hidden instructions that the mind *has to obey* – thereby keeping it active. These words and phrases are known as *embedded commands* – hidden messages to the subconscious mind, or instructions that are given without being obvious. The technique includes the use of:

● individual names
● reverse activity instructions
● suggestive instructions.

Individual names

It is recognized that an individual's name is one of their most valued possessions. In many cases, our name is *us*. It is our identity, it is who we are, it is individual, it is personal, it is inseparable from ourselves – it is a very powerful attention-grabber. Imagine that, standing in a crowded airport terminal your name is announced over the public address system. What is your reaction? Instant alertness! It is an automatic response. How many films have shown fugitives revealing themselves when they hear the casual mention of their name? The constant use of the detainee's name to extract information during interrogation is a well known technique which is also used in many therapies that instruct the subconscious to recall past experiences.

Use the technique in training as follows:

● When [*trainee name*] takes notes, he/she retains more information....'
● [*trainee name*] could return to the office with a completely new outlook on business...'

By using an individual name to stimulate a 'mental sit-up', you also prepare the mind for action by issuing an activity command.

Reverse activity instructions

This is a casual way of instructing which does not resort to the normal trainer/trainee relationship in which one dictates and the other pretends to follow. For example:

- 'Don't relax [*activity instruction*] too quickly...' implies 'It will ultimately happen, so do not fight it.'
- 'Try to resist the temptation to look [*activity instruction*]...' implies 'I'll try but will be unable to'.
- 'You don't need to understand how it works [*activity instruction*] in order to use it...'. Superficially this is a true statement, but underneath is a hidden instruction to understand.

Suggestive instructions

Suggestive instructions are indirect suggestions which automatically cause the brain to mentally focus on the point instructed, such as:

- 'You might notice...'
- 'As you focus on...'
- 'Sooner or later, this will...'
- 'Eventually, you will...'
- 'Sometime you're going to...'

Two fuller examples are:

- 'You might notice the feeling of comfort as you begin to relax your whole body...'
- 'At this stage, readers will probably become aware of the time and start to wonder whether this book can be...'

How many of us have ever looked at our watches as a result of such an indirect suggestive instruction?

Use powerful vocabulary

The trainee's mind responds to imaginative, colourful messages. It takes the trainer's words and transforms them into images which, in turn, should inspire its creative side. It is our role as trainers to make sure that the images evoked are positive and rewarding. By controlling the use of our vocabulary and using the words below, we can lead the imagination.

Special/specially

As mentioned earlier, trainees' thoughts mainly concern themselves so, by the use of either of these words, you can make them feel good. When people feel good about themselves, they produce better results. How do you feel when you go to a restaurant and are told they have prepared a *special* dish? 'Special' is a very powerful word that generates the feeling of wellbeing: '... what we are going to cover now has been designed to deal with your *special* requirements – *especially* for you.'

Normal/normally

Although people like to be thought of as being 'special', they still, naturally, have a herd instinct. Rather than attempt something new, people are much happier doing something they believe others have done before. 'Normal' is a powerful word which encourages action through the inference that what is being asked is quite normal and standard practice. For example:

- 'What *normally* happens now is...'
- 'The next step, *normally*, is...'

The mental reaction to statements such as these is:

'Well, if others are doing it, then I don't mind having a go myself...'

Imagine

This is one of the most powerful words to use when conjuring up mental images of success or promised results. It is regarded by the brain as an *automatic instruction* which cannot be refused because it bypasses the logical side of the brain and engages its creative side. For example:

- '*Imagine* now that you are the confident person you wish to be...'
- '*Imagine* how good you'll feel when you have made these improvements...'

The main point to understand here is that the subconscious mind cannot tell the difference between what is real and what is imaginary so, accordingly, both the mind and the person start to experience the mental picture. To test the power of this, imagine picking up a lemon and taking a knife in the right hand. Now imagine cutting slowly through the lemon, taking in the smell at the same time. Put the 'knife' down and now place one half of the 'cut lemon' next to the knife. Take the remaining half of the lemon in your hand and place it in your mouth, sucking gently at the flesh of the fruit. If your mouth isn't watering at this stage it soon will be! That is the power of imagination. There was no lemon and no knife, yet, because of this word *imagine*, the creative side of the mind took over so that the relative senses of taste and smell automatically came into action. It could not tell the difference between the real and the imaginary situation. Stories abound about the power of the imagination; it is reported to cause illnesses, blisters and even 'freezing to death'.

Suppose/supposing

As powerful as the word 'imagine' is for creating a mental image of success, the words 'suppose' or 'supposing' are equally as powerful for painting pictures of doom and despair. For example:

- 'Just *supposing* we don't improve our skill level, where will that leave our career prospects?'
- '*Suppose* things carry on as they are now, what will eventually happen?'

The negative image being created is obvious. The same can apply to you as a trainer: suppose you don't constantly upgrade your communication techniques, how will you fare in the increasingly competitive field of training?

Emotive words

As discussed in the Introduction to this book, the brain is split into two distinct halves. The right-hand side handles the emotions whilst the left-hand side deals with logic and reason. To *instantly* appeal to the creative side of the brain, use the most effective vocabulary to ensure that you *eliminate logical words and instructions*. Two examples of logical words/instructions are:

- 'What do you *think* so far...?'
- 'What do you *reckon* the next step should be?'

Such questions cause the trainee to think, to consider and to ponder rather than give a more immediate response. Instead, use emotional or visual words to engage the right-hand, creative, side of the brain, such as:

- 'Are you *happy* with everything so far?'
- 'Can you *see* why we are taking this step?'

By comparing the above statements, can you see the value of using emotional or visual words? They evoke an immediate response from the trainee – telling you that you hold their interest. See also page 99, 'Subliminal influencing and Influential words'.

Closing the session

Having first won and then raised trainees' interest, close on a high note. As the entire objective of any training is, through the transference of information and skills, to generate action and ultimately increase results, it is the trainer's responsibility to make sure that this objective is achieved. The way sessions and programmes are closed determines whether this happens or not.

Many sessions finish on an administrative note with:

- the completion of delegate opinion forms
- the distribution of course notes
- the distribution of handouts
- the provision of extra documentation
- the distribution of sales literature.

Nevertheless, the trainees should leave the training room with an inspiring message still ringing in their ears!

The solution is to deal with the administrative matters *before* starting the finale. This can be communicated, for example, as follows:

'Just before we finish, could everybody please complete the programme assessment form, hand it in at reception, where your course notes and other literature is waiting for you, and then everybody can go home. However, just before we hand the forms out, let me say...'

Then close the session in any of the following ways:

- **The Urge For Action.** Without doubt the most effective way to close is with an urge, or request, for action, such as:

  'Take the ideas we've shared, practise them, develop them and – more importantly – use them, and you will achieve the results you are looking for!'

- **The Alternative Close.** By giving a choice of non-action and its results or action and the benefits of that action, no choice is actually being offered at all. Such a close could be communicated, for example, as follows:

  'Are we going to do nothing and accept mediocrity, or are we going to prepare for a change and strive for excellence?'

- **The Quotation Close.** Once again, the use of accredited statements to inspire people at the end of a session is an extremely effective way to motivate both thoughts and action. For example:

  'Winston Churchill once said that "everybody stumbles across opportunity at least once in their life. Unfortunately, most just pick themselves up, dust themselves down and carry on as though nothing has happened." What will you do with this opportunity?'

- **The Summary Close.** Summarizing all the facts given *plus* all the benefits will reinforce trainee understanding. For example:

  'We have covered the fundamental aspects, developed them over the past two days and shown exactly how each one of us can be better organized as a result.'

- **The Fear Close.** The second selling psychology is 'fear of loss'. Whilst promoting benefits and results is ultimately more motivational, the occasional use of the Fear Close can be equally as effective. Overuse of this negative can lead to indifference, so it should not be used frequently. An example of such a close could be:

  'Ladies and gentlemen, we need these traffic lights if we are to limit the number of accidents at this spot. John Smith was killed here last week – it may be one of our children next. . . .'

- **The Question Close.** The use of a rhetorical question generates 'action thoughts'. For example:

  'The question we must all ask is – what will be the cost if we don't go ahead?'

- **The Story Close.** Often a favourite when addressing larger groups, for example at conventions or conferences, a story, provided it is relevant, can be very motivational. Such stories should be highly polished in terms of presentation technique.
- **The Drama Close**. By using the voice in a more theatrical fashion it is possible to create a sense of drama – for example, by *lowering the voice, raising the voice* and *pausing for effect*.
- **The Sincere Compliment.** Thanking the group and showing sincere appreciation is a useful self-marketing device which also reminds trainees of the value of the training they have just received. For example:

'Before we finish, I would personally like to thank everybody for their involvement and participation and, more importantly, for helping to make this programme the success it has been.'

- **The Poetic Close.** By introducing poems and/or quotations, it is possible to add colour to the final address. Whatever poem or quotation is used must, however, be relevant to the subject of the training.

The above ideas for closing the session can be used in conjunction with each other in any sequence that feels comfortable. However, *never* finish:

- on a weak note
- using weak words
- with an 'I, I, I' routine
- by clearing up while trainees are still in the room
- by beating the trainees out of the door.

Checklist: ways of creating mental stimulation

1 Set the scene properly.
2 Create the appropriate room setting.
3 Start the session on the right foot.
4 Create interest.
5 Keep them interested.
6 Close the session strongly.

7 Subliminal influencing

**Subliminal = being or acting below the threshold of conscious perception.
Influencing = producing an effect.**

We earlier made the point that the human mind controls everything, be it thoughts, words or actions. Most training techniques rely on the trainer's ability to communicate with that area of the mind we call the conscious mind. The conscious mind then decides whether to accept what is presented to it, or not. The technique we describe in this book goes far deeper – into that almost hidden area of the mind that is universally known as the subconscious. Certain hypotheses suggest that external stimuli presented *below the level of conscious awareness* can, and do, affect human behaviour.

Subliminal influencing is *the ability to influence others* by making use of their subconscious minds to accept the ideas presented to them or the results promised from the use of these ideas.

First, why should it be necessary to even attempt to implant ideas in the subconscious mind of somebody else? Why not just explain the ideas or lecture about them and leave it at that? To answer that, we need to ask another question: when somebody says, 'Do that, it's good for you', do we? Of course not! Nor do others accept what we say when we make such a statement. For example, we are all told that smoking is bad for us. If we are smokers, do we stop? Not if we don't want to! We are all told that certain foods are bad for us. Do we give them up? No! Human psychology is very simple. Whatever doubts we have, somebody else also has those doubts. Whatever processes we go through, somebody else goes through them. So why should we expect people to unquestioningly believe everything we say? They don't! If teaching or training was just a matter of giving instructions, it would be easy to develop people. There would be no need for highly skilled communicators and, for example, all children would behave well, study and learn simply because their parents told them!

Accordingly, whenever we present a new technique, we must always anticipate doubts on the part of our trainees. No matter how convincingly we tell them how valuable the point is, there will be natural barriers to the external messages we give them.

So how do we change this situation? How do we stimulate their perception of what we say and convince people that our ideas are something they will be able to use? There are ten areas we should develop that will affect this perception:

1   subconscious affirmations
2   physical leading
3   peer group acceptance
4   reference stacking
5   accreditation
6   coordinated movement
7   influential words
8   third-party critique
9   repetition
10 conscious projection.

Subconscious affirmations (SAs)

Personal affirmations – sometimes known as *self-talk* ('I can', 'I will', 'I shall') – are used in the sporting arena to develop confidence. It is a recognized performance-enhancing tool. The same psychology can be applied to the teaching process and is one of the keys by which we can influence a trainee without their conscious knowledge. Psychological investigations have shown that, whilst trainees may not necessarily agree with what we say, they *do* believe what they say themselves. SAs can be used to create mental agreements within our trainees' subconscious minds. Here we describe how to enter our trainees' subconscious minds – a powerful means of winning their acceptance. Remember, it is not what we tell the trainees that is important, but what *they tell themselves* as a result of what we say to them. That is the key to SAs which are almost irresistible positive responses to requests for their agreement. SAs are obtained with such questions as:

- '... isn't it?'
- '... couldn't it?'
- '... wouldn't it?'
- '... wouldn't you agree?'
- '... isn't that right?'

all of which promote an *automatic agreement*, such as:

- 'Yes.'
- 'Yes, it is right.'
- 'Yes, I do agree.'
- 'Yes, it can be done.'
- 'Yes, I do understand that.'

Each time a trainee says 'Yes', either in the form of a physical nod or by a mental agreement, they are positively reinforcing their acceptance of your point in their own subconscious. The power of this technique will become more apparent as we run through the following various ways we can use SAs:

- **Conventional SA** is promoted by making a request for agreement at the end of a sentence. For example:

  Trainer question: '... that makes sense, *doesn't it*?'
  SA response: 'Yes, it does!'

- **Inverted SA** is promoted by making a request for agreement at the beginning of a statement. For example:

  Trainer question: '*Can't you* see how powerful that technique is?'
  SA response: 'Yes, I can!'

- **Intermediate SA** is promoted by making a request for agreement in the middle of a statement. For example:

  Trainer question: 'When you do this, *can't you see* how effective it will be?'
  SA response: 'Yes, I can!'

- **Confirmation SA** is where a trainee spontaneously says, for example, 'That makes sense!' Subconsciously, they are already telling themselves that they have accepted the topic in their own mind. However, a confirmation SA gives you an opportunity to obtain two agreements, rather than one, by confirming the point and adding as follows:

Trainer statement: 'It does, *doesn't it*?'
SA response: 'Yes, it does, *doesn't it*?'

These four methods of using SAs seem, and are, relatively simple but, as with most things, they are not as easy as they may first appear, for this technique does not come naturally. Our natural inclination when teaching is to tell people how important the point is, rather than, as the SA technique demands, ask for their agreement on that point, so the technique will take much practice. However, once mastered we will have developed the ability to enter another person's subconscious with such conviction that we will obtain agreement on any point we wish to make. This applies to all situations – one-to-one training, one-to-one coaching or presentations to ten, a hundred or a thousand people.

Practise the SA technique by using it as part of your everyday style of conversation. Every time you want to make a point, try SA to obtain mental agreement from the person you are talking to. You will immediately notice that they listen, agree, accept it and act on it as a result – which is the whole purpose of training.

Physical leading

The second way to obtain subliminal or subconscious agreement is to lead the person or group we want to influence with a *physical* sign or body movement. By this means, we can suggest to somebody else how we want them to respond. Politicians often use this technique to great effect by following a verbal instruction with a physical lead that subliminally tells an audience to give a favourable response. When they give a verbal instruction, such as 'All those in favour raise their right hand', whilst at the same time giving the physical lead of raising their own right hand, the audience will invariably raise their right hands in agreement. This is a classic example of physical leading.

You can use this same psychology by giving a conventional SA, when you say, for example, 'Now that makes sense, *doesn't it*?' and ending the question with a slight nod of the head, which is a physical lead. The reason for this is that it is impossible for another person to shake their heads negatively when you are nodding positively. You can practise this quite easily. When at home, for example, ask if somebody wouldn't mind making a cup of tea and use the slight nod at the end of the question. It works! They won't notice the physical lead given by the nod, but it will have registered subliminally. This is a powerful way of accessing the subconscious, obtaining agreement – and getting a cup of tea!

Peer group acceptance

The third way to influence somebody else through their subconscious is known as peer group acceptance – that is, receiving a favourable reaction from a group of people equal in age, rank, merit and/or status. The more people there are in a peer group who have stated that the message they are receiving is correct, the easier it is to influence any others who are not quite sure of the value of that same message. For example, let's say there is a member of our group who still doubts the topic or the suggested result. If we ask for – and receive – acceptance from other group members who have accepted the idea, they begin to discover that everyone else in the group is in accord. That realization alone will influence them to accept it.

In summary, first obtain the agreement of as many people as possible and then make use of peer group acceptance to subliminally influence any members of the group who doubt the message.

Reference stacking

Apply this technique when you have been able to gain a universal positive reaction to the three techniques covered previously. In training, individuals are often being developed for a change of career path or are being introduced to entirely new skills. Normally, when you present an individual with facts or circumstances, or when you ask them to make an assessment of a point being made, their automatic reaction is to search through the memory for similar situations, circumstances or a previous experience so that they have a 'reference' on which their assessment will be based. However, when trainees are learning about a topic with which they are not familiar, they may not be able to draw on any earlier experience and therefore cannot use a reference to make a sound personal judgement or accept the point being made. The solution is to provide that reference by using a technique known as reference stacking in which the experience of others are used as points of reference. The more references that can be provided, the higher becomes the stack and the more readily they are accepted.

Use this technique when you, as a trainer, have failed to get a positive response from SAs, physical leading and peer group acceptance. The sequence will therefore be as follows:

1   **Subconscious Affirmation (SA)**
     Trainer action: As discussed – ask questions aimed at generating a
                          'Yes' response.
     Trainee reaction: No response.

2 **Physical Leading**
Trainer action: Repeat the question and add the lead, or direct the response required – that is, nod.
Trainee reaction: No response.

3 **Peer Group Acceptance**
Trainer action: Direct the question at the group whilst continuing to lead.
Group reaction: Acceptance.
Trainee reaction: Uncertainty.

4 **Reference Stack**
Trainer action:

a) Identify an individual within the group whose personal or business profile matches that of the doubtful trainee and who has already agreed on the point being made.

b) Ask this person how they believe the particular point can help them and how.

If the trainee is still in doubt after this, select another good match from the 'stack' and repeat the process until they understand and accept the point. Since the success of this technique depends on making *as close a match as possible*, make sure you give a great deal of thought to the selection process, otherwise the trainee will be unable to recognize the reference. Examples of good and bad matches would be:

Doubtful trainee	Good match	Bad match
Male	Male	Female
35 years old	30–40 years old	25 years old
Recently appointed manager	Fully experienced manager	Sales representative
Admin. background	Accountancy background	Sales background

The wrong match will result in the subconscious reaction: 'I can see why they accept the point being made, but they are less experienced than me, come from a different background and discipline and, therefore, *it will not apply to me*. The correct match and the object of reference stacking is to gain the opposite reaction: 'If it works for them and they can see the value of it, then I will accept it because I believe *they are just like me.*'

Accreditation

In the process of influencing people to accept ideas, we need to add authority to our words so that they more readily accept the points we are making. This is known as accreditation, and there are two distinct areas in which this is applied:

1   accrediting the teaching points
2   accrediting the trainer.

Accrediting the teaching points

There are a number of subtle, but effective, ways to add value or weight to a particular teaching point. Trainers, when they want to add weight to a point, will very often refer to themselves as the accreditation. For example, they might say:

● 'I accept this particular point of view.'
● 'This is a subject that I personally endorse.'
● 'I can tell you this is absolutely correct.'

Going back to Chapter 1, you will recall why you should avoid the use of the word 'I', or appear to be self-congratulatory in any way, because your trainees will lose respect for you if you try to impress them with how clever you are. Similarly, if you accredit the point to yourself you assume responsibility for the issue itself and run the risk of your opinion, rather than the actual issue, becoming the subject of debate. Remember that you are only the *bearer* of the message; you are not the message itself, which is why you should always add weight to that message. Described below are some ways in which you can subliminally press home teaching points by accreditation, thus adding weight and authority to your argument.

Famous people

When you accredit a statement or a fact to a famous person or to a reputable source, you are giving known authority to that point and will impress your trainees far more than if you had taken the credit yourself. Experience and research from all around the world has shown that when teaching groups comprising people of any type – young, old, professionals, managers, clerical, skilled, semi-skilled or unskilled workers – are split into two and *separately* given exactly the same teaching points, in separate rooms, results vary. But when a teaching point accredited to an authoritative figure is introduced into one part of the group but not the other, the members of this part of the group invariably retain more information than those who were not given the accredited point. From this, we can establish that people accept a statement far more readily when it is accredited to an individual or body of repute. Given this fact, you should research quotations that are relevant to the points you wish to make and introduce them, for example, in the following ways:

- 'The famous statesman, Winston Churchill, once said...'
- 'President John F. Kennedy, when addressing Congress, stated...'
- 'According to Stephen Hawking, the world's greatest physicist...'
- 'Sir John Harvey-Jones, the business guru, suggests that...'

When you accredit a famous person with the teaching point you are making, your trainees will more readily accept it.

Third-party accreditation

If it is impossible to give specific accreditation to an idea, adopt what is known as a *third-party accreditation*. This is a technique to give credibility to the point without resorting to accrediting yourself. Here are some examples of the right and wrong statement techniques:

Wrong	Right
'I have found that...'	'*It has* been found that...'
'I have said...'	'*It has* been said...' or '*They* say...'
'I have researched...'	'*Research* has shown...'

Third-party accreditation means just that. Always add weight to any point you want to emphasize by referring to it in the third person or referring it to a third party. This is sometimes known as *proof support*.

Accrediting the trainer

As trainers we often have to add weight to ourselves to establish our own, or extra, credibility. In so doing, many trainers make the mistake of referring to themselves in the first person as a means of establishing early accreditation for their particular knowledge on a subject. They say, for example:

- 'I have studied this subject for 20 years...'
- 'As a leading expert in this subject, I will tell you...'
- 'My vast experience enables me to share my ideas with you...'

As explained earlier, this actually has the opposite effect on people by introducing the impression of trainer superiority. However, there are two alternative techniques that will allow us quickly to establish ourselves as an authority in our trainees' subconscious.

Having yourself introduced

To add to, or build, your reputation as a trainer, you should, whenever possible, have somebody else introduce you to your group. Apart from the fact that it should be easier for someone else to build you up in front of others, it also gives you added credibility when, for example, the MD of a client organization gives the introduction. However, remember that when you ask somebody to introduce you, always tell them what to say in order to maximize the effect!

Gaining recognition through a third-party reference

Often it is not possible to have somebody else do the introducing – for example, when you are holding your programme at an outside venue where there is nobody who can help. The way to add weight to yourself in these circumstances is to refer to a third party in order to establish your credibility and reputation with the group. This can be quickly achieved through giving yourself *third-party accreditation*, for example, by saying:

● 'The ideas we are going to share now were handed on to me by the most eminent of all specialists in this field . . .' or
● 'I consider myself lucky to have been trained by the person who evolved this idea . . .'

In this way you are not just building up the person concerned as an expert whose ideas you are passing on, but are also adding to your own reputation by your association with that person.

Using the two above techniques adds weight to both you as a trainer and to what you are saying and thus influences the trainees' acceptance of your ideas.

Coordinated movement

Coordinated movement, or synchronization, means making sure that everything we do is in harmony – that our body actions are in tune with our words. Research has shown that when the eye sees a fully coordinated movement of the hands, for example, the message that is being received by the ear is accepted, or implanted, much more effectively. In the context of reaching the subconscious the concepts of coordinated movement ensures that our hands, in particular, are at one with the voice. The following hand movements are the most influential in this respect.

- **Numbering.** Using your fingers to emphasize points that are being made will focus the attention on those points and influence the subconscious. When listing three points, for example, hold up three fingers. Then, as you run through those points one by one, first hold up one finger to emphasize the first point and use the forefinger of your free hand to tap the first finger. At the second point, keep the first finger in place and raise a second finger, tapping that with the free forefinger. Likewise, at the third point, keep the first and second fingers in place and hold up the third finger, tapping that with the free forefinger. This subliminally emphasizes what you are saying and enables the points to be more easily registered by your trainees.
- **Hand chop.** Holding one hand palm upwards and using the edge of your free hand to strike the upturned palm, as though chopping wood, gives a very powerful subliminal emphasis to your point.
- **Vertical hands.** By holding both hands vertically in front of the body with the palms facing each other and then moving them apart to widen the gap between them, you convey the subliminal message that the promised result will grow bigger and bigger, thus indicating to our trainees' subconscious minds that the point you are making will be beneficial to them.
- **Horizontal hands.** A similar subliminal message to that above is conveyed by holding the hands horizontally, one over the other, with one palm facing upwards and the palm of the uppermost hand facing downwards. By increasing the distance between the hands to emphasize your words, you will subliminally imply that your message contains an increasing scale of benefits.
- **Pointing to the board.** When using a flipchart or a board to present points, the spoken message will be subliminally implanted if you point to the key words written on the board as you say them.

These techniques guarantee that the eye will feed the subconscious at the same time as the ear receives the conscious message. The coordinated movements will require practice but, once you have perfected and used them, you will know that your trainees are receiving the message through 100 per cent of their minds – both the conscious and the subconscious.

Influential words

To maximize the power of the subconscious through the spoken word, we must choose the right words to use. While some words in particular are very powerful subliminal influencers there are also many weak words that create a barrier within the subconscious mind. The words to avoid are:

- change
- disappoint
- hopefully
- guarantee
- supposing
- maybe.

On the other hand, there are powerful words which we should use as an aid to reach the subconscious. These are:

- special, or specially
- normal, or normally
- imagine
- emotional words.

Special/specially

Each of your trainees will feel that all their own particular problems and situations are unique to them and that nobody else suffers from exactly the same thing. This, of course, is never true but, because we all feel we are special, or that there is something special about us, the use of the word *special* emphasizes that you, as a trainer, recognize this and that you are interested in them. This registers with the subconscious and creates more interest in what you have to say. For example:

- 'This particular point is aimed at your *special* situation.'
- 'This is a *specially* powerful point for you.'

Normal/normally

Even though people like to be thought of as being special, they are much happier visiting places and doing things that they believe others have already done. Few people are natural pioneers; most instinctively wish to be regarded as normal – that is, not to be seen to be outside life's accepted parameters. Therefore, using the word *normal* encourages reaction or action through the subconscious. For example:

- 'This would be a quite *normal* reaction from anybody.'
- 'What *normally* happens now is...'

Imagine

The word *imagine* gives a powerful automatic command to the subconscious which it cannot ignore because it bypasses the logical side of the brain. When you say to somebody 'Imagine this...' it is impossible for them not to switch to the creative side of the brain. Therefore, for example, if you want to paint a picture of success in a trainee's mind, say, 'Just imagine how much better you will be as a salesperson once you have perfected this technique'. The trainee will automatically attempt to visualize their future results and success.

Emotional words

As we have already discussed the human brain has a logical side and an emotional side. It is also recognized that, in the decision-making process, it is generally the emotional side of the brain that says 'yes', whilst the logical side considers and ultimately 'rejects'. Logic is often required for justification purposes only. Therefore the more we can utilize the power of emotional words the more likely we are to gain acceptance of ideas rather than assessment and judgement. Most trainers approach the logical side of the brain to gain acceptance, but this technique, as we have suggested before, goes much deeper than that and we should use words that appeal to the subconscious to accept our message. As an illustration, the following requests reach only the conscious and logical side of the mind and are therefore not correct:

- 'What do you *think* of that?'
- 'What do you *reckon*?'

Conversely, the following requests contain emotional words which will address and reach the right-hand or emotional side, thereby eliciting an automatic response:

- 'How does that *feel*?'
- 'Can you *see* why we recommend this?'
- 'Are you *happy* with what we've covered so far?'

Third-party critique

Criticism is often an integral part of the training process. However, in the face of real or imaginary criticism of themselves, people's natural reaction is to become defensive. When, however, others are criticized, their natural reaction is to agree with that criticism. Bearing this in mind, we can use a technique known as *third-party critique* to win agreement in situations where there may be resistance to the point we are making, because, for example, the trainees do not want to appear to have made a mistake or an error of judgement in the past. There are three steps to this technique:

1   **Imply criticism of others** – a third-party critique. For example, say 'It has been known for people to do this in the past...', to which the group reaction will be *acceptance*.
2   **Introduce a first-party reference** – a critique of yourself. For example, say 'In fact, I myself have often made the same mistake...', to which the group reaction will be *identification*: 'Me too!'
3   **Introduce a personal reference** to win acceptance of the point. For example, say 'Let's be honest, if the truth be known, haven't we all made similar mistakes?', to which the group reaction will be *agreement*.

In this way we can obtain an unchallenged agreement with the criticism. The group have now acknowledged that a problem exists.

Repetition

Learning 'by rote', or repetitive learning, is recognized as one of the most effective methods of training a larger group of individuals. It is especially effective in the teaching of children because it gives an opportunity to introduce a 'fun' element and because of the group activity that it makes possible.

When training adults, however, the concept of learning by repetition can have entirely the opposite effect, as the process will often act as a barrier to the assimilation of information in the adult human mind. Nevertheless, it is a very effective method of learning, and you should still use the concept in a different format when you want to ensure that a particular teaching point is 'driven home'.

Having identified the main teaching point, you should develop the skill and have the confidence to continually make, or repeat, that point in as many different ways as possible. So you should:

●   refer back

- summarize
- obtain agreement
- repeat the phrase

and repeat it all again if necessary.

Apart from making sure that the particular point is made, there is another reason for repetitive quotation. In general, about only half the audience pays full attention to what is being said for half of the time, so repeating the point ensures that everybody hears the message and that, at the same time, their subconscious is being bombarded by the transferable workable idea (TWI) that we covered in Chapter 5 (p. 59).

Conscious projection

We have already covered unconscious body actions – those unconscious bodily gestures that deter people by subconsciously showing them that we are bored or impatient with them, feel superior to them or don't believe what they are saying – in Chapter 4. Now we come to *conscious projection*, both in the way we present ourselves to others and in the way in which we can, through conscious acts of body language, communicate non-verbally, or support what we are saying positively to gain acceptance of ourselves and what we communicate.

With the exception of some cultural or regional expressions, many of our conscious body actions are naturally understood by all people worldwide whether or not we are able to speak each other's language. We all know, for example, that when somebody rolls their eyes towards the heavens that they are exasperated or when they set their mouth in a grimace and scowl that they are angry. We do not need to understand what they are saying to appreciate what is being communicated. Because this bodily language is so obvious, we should use conscious expressions and body actions to enhance our communication with trainees, all of whom will naturally understand them.

The eight areas in which we consciously project ourselves in a positive way are as follows:

1   eyes
2   smile
3   chin stroke
4   listening
5   stance
6   conscious hand movements

7   voice intonation
8   dress and image.

Eyes

The eyes of men converse as much as their tongues with the advantage that the ocular dialect needs no dictionary and is understood the world over. (Ralph Waldo Emerson)

It is said that when conversing on a one-to-one basis, if eye contact between the two parties conversing is not maintained for 80 per cent of the time, then proper communication will not be established. People communicate with their eyes. When we meet somebody whose eyes do not hold ours, we instinctively think of them as shifty – somebody not to be trusted. The same would apply if we were unable to maintain eye contact with any person we communicate with. We would lose their trust very quickly, and they would not accept, or register positively, what we have to say.

We have all been in an audience, listening to a speaker who failed to look at us as part of that audience. It leads us to consciously and subconsciously feel that we are being 'talked at', not 'talked to'.

When training, make eye contact with the people or person you are communicating with to emphasize your verbal message. Make a conscious effort to look at *all* trainees, even when addressing a large group. In fact the larger the group, the more you should give the impression of looking at everyone as frequently as you can. You may not be able to fix your gaze on every individual, but you must certainly make everyone feel that you are looking at them as individuals as well as members of a group. Everyone must feel involved with you as their trainer, and you can achieve this through eye contact.

How do you make your trainees feel as though you are looking at them? First, you must understand the *eye zone* – the specific area of the face at which you should be looking. The eye zone comprises:

- the eyes
- the eyebrows
- the bridge of the nose
- the cheekbones.

Whenever you look anywhere inside the eye zone your trainees will believe that you are looking at *them* and communicating with *them*. There is no need to stare eyeball to eyeball – just look within their eye zone.

Smile

A smile typically expresses pleasant feelings of approval and shows a
favourable disposition or aspect. (Ron Cartey)

Extensive research into *conscious*, rather than *unconscious* expressions of
the face, head and body has revealed that there are no less than 135 distinct
gestures, of which 80 involve the head and face. It is therefore perhaps
surprising that there are only nine different types of the usually most
pleasant and acceptable facial gestures – the smile – and that, of these, only
three evoke a sense of pleasant feelings of approval, a favourable disposition or aspect.

These three, then, are the ones to use in training, and they are:

- the *simple* smile
- the *upper* smile
- the *broad* smile.

The simple smile

This is a conscious smile in which the teeth are not shown. It is otherwise
known as the self-smile and it shows that the person is pleased with themselves or pleased about what they are seeing or hearing. You can usually
recognize a trainee who has understood the teaching point when they
smile to themselves in this way and, likewise, when you use this simple
smile they will recognize that you are pleased with them.

The upper smile

This, too, is a conscious smile but, here, the upper teeth are exposed and
there is usually eye-to-eye contact at the same time. It indicates a good
rapport between the two people concerned. When a trainee smiles at you
in this way, you generally feel they have a high regard and warmth for you
as their trainer. Therefore, the same applies when you smile in this way at
a trainee – they will feel at ease with you.

The broad smile

This is the most conscious and contagious of all smiles, commonly used
when people are enjoying themselves. If a trainee smiles broadly, he or she
feels very involved with you as their trainer. When you smile in this way
at your trainees, they will feel very involved with you and in what you are
saying.

It has taken thousands of years of evolution to develop the smile, which is one of the characteristics that separates humans from the rest of the animal kingdom. It is said that the smile is the shortest distance between two people. A smile can make up the differences between friend and enemy, yet it is seldom practised in the business environment. Always remember how important a smile is to the recipient when dealing with your trainees.

Chin stroke

A gesture that signifies a wise man making a decision. (Henry Siddens –
Rhetorical Gestures)

When someone slowly and gently strokes their chin with the forefinger and thumb, it is generally accepted that they are thinking about, or evaluating, a point. This is known worldwide as a 'thinking' gesture, and you should use this gesture consciously during trainee observations or verbal assessments to emphasize or give the impression of interest in what is being said.

Listening

Listen with your heart and you will find understanding. (Jim Bishop)

People will feel more relaxed with us and relate to us more closely when we can show we are naturally interested in what they are saying or doing. This is all part of 'body language' and bio-rapport (see Part I), and the following non-verbal signals, which indicate that we are listening attentively will help promote a 'togetherness' through the subconscious:

- **Lean forward.** When we are naturally interested in something – for example, the announcement of a result – we naturally lean forward. The same applies when you want to demonstrate your interest in someone – lean forwards towards them.
- **Shift your weight to the front.** Echoing the principle above, shifting your weight on to the front foot when someone is talking, or when you have asked for an opinion, shows that you are concentrating on the point being made.
- **Smile and nod.** These are both conscious gestures that convey a subliminal message that you are listening to what is being said. Most trainers believe that, to be interesting, they need to impress with the volume or extent of their knowledge. This puts people off. *Listening involves being seen to listen. To be interesting, we must first be seen to be*

interested. The value of listening in a training context is that it provokes the following subconscious reactions from trainees:

- 'I like them.'
- 'I can get on with them.'
- 'They are just like me.'
- 'I respect their knowledge.'
- 'I understand them.'

When we achieve this, we can say we have achieved true bio-rapport.

Stance

> *An upright 'angular' posture represents a sharper, more dramatic image.*
> *(Mary Spillane)*

The more confident your posture, the more subliminally impressed people are with you. A positive posture is to be upright, with a steady breathing pattern. Confidence breeds confidence. Stance is extremely important and the following points will be useful:

- If nervous, maybe because it is your very first session, or there is some pressure from the group, plant your feet in a confident stance and *do not move them.* This does call for a conscious effort, but do not move or walk about if nervous.
- If confident, move around as it suits you, but *avoid repetitive movements,* as this can distract. Some trainers continually walk around whilst delivering their material. This results in the group not knowing where to focus their attention.

Conscious hand movements

> *Learn to read hand movements. You will be reading the truth.*
> *(Stanislavsky:* The Method*)*

Even though our trainees will spend most of their time watching our faces for reactions, our hands will also be on show for the entire duration of every training session in which we are involved. We should therefore consciously use our hands to influence the message and also to emphasize teaching points and statements. Discussed below are several hand movements which we can use to emphasize the degree of importance of what we are saying or doing.

- **Rubbing the hands together.** This indicates excitement, a sense of satisfaction or pleasurable anticipation. The speed at which the hands are rubbed together is important: the faster the action, the greater is the emphasis. However, take care for, if you rub the hands together too slowly, it can also indicate indecision, doubt or greed.
- **Open palms.** Palms can be used in the most expressive way for a variety of conscious gestures. Showing two open palms indicates complete honesty, and it is very difficult to lie when using this gesture. A more emphatic gesture is to move one hand to cover the heart, leaving the other open palm displayed, indicating that you are speaking the truth 'upon your heart'.
- **The horizontal downward-facing palm.** This gesture creates a sense of authority. Use it, for example, to indicate that you wish your audience to sit down or to reduce their level of noise.
- **Hands pressed together.** Pressing the hands together, as in prayer is a conscious way of indicating a desire to persuade or gently reinforce a point.

Handshakes

It is often possible to learn a great deal about a person by the manner in which they shake hands, so we will briefly look at some of the most common handshakes, not just to learn about the correct form, but also as a guide to assessing or 'reading' trainees at the first encounter.

Normal

Interlock the hand firmly and make three or four pumping movements with the palm in the vertical plane. This indicates that you are in charge of the proceedings.

Hand loose with palm facing down

This type of handshake invites the other person to take the hand and shows a superior attitude – particularly useful for women in a male-dominated environment.

The palm-down thrust

This is the most aggressive way of offering to shake hands and gives a definite message of 'I'm in charge here!'.

Finger tip grab

Just holding the finger tips whilst shaking hands keeps the other person at a safe spatial distance. This method is used by members of the Royal family when being introduced to people who are not close to them.

The stiff arm thrust

Extending the arm forcefully and rigidly is an aggressive handshake which will make the other person keep their distance.

The two-handed handshake

This is the warmest and most friendly form of handshake, which should only be used when both people are well known to each other or have struck up a good rapport quickly.

Voice intonation

> *Your voice is the message and it is the message that controls actions. (Marshall McLulan)*

Many people speak in a monotone which soon bores an audience and loses their attention. Voice intonation is an important element in gaining trainees' interest. Expressive and appropriate intonation can be learnt from hypnotists, stress counsellors, motivational experts, professional speakers and actors, all of whom rely on the voice to direct attention to the points they are making. The golden rule is to vary the tonality of the voice in such a way that you enhance your message.

Dress and image

> *Managing and Personnel Directors consider a good image more important than holding a Postgraduate Degree! (MB Image Consultants)*

In Chapter 1 (pp. 6–8) we discussed the importance of presenting ourselves to our trainees by being suitably dressed, looking the part and avoiding a variety of distractions in order not to ruin our perceived image. This section shows you how to consciously project yourself in order to create the right image.

Dress

● **Top garments.** Whether you wear a suit or smart casuals (slacks and a blazer or sports coat for men and a two-piece for women, depending on the image you wish to project) a sober colour and style are best. Although fashion trends often lean towards more colourful attire, always remember that, if you are training others in business skills, you should maintain the image trainees would expect of the profession or position you are training them in. The rule of thumb is if an executive in the discipline in which you are training would not wear the clothes you plan to wear at a training session at work, then your choice of clothes is wrong. Always dress to match the *perceived image* (see Chapter 1, pp. 6–7).

- **Ties.** The above is particularly true of ties which can be extremely colourful and at the same time be fashionable. A sober tie pattern may seem boring, but if you would not expect a respected senior executive to wear a gaudy tie in the office or boardroom, you should not expect your trainees to accept it either.

- **Crease-free clothing.** Whether you choose, if you are a male, to wear a suit or smart slacks and a sports coat or blazer or, if you are a female, a neatly presented suit or two-piece outfit, they should be crease-free. If, for example, you have to drive some distance to your venue, arrive early and change into the clothes in which you will be making your presentation.

- **Dust, fluff and stain-free clothing.** Similarly, clothes should be hair, dust, fluff or stain-free. How often have you seen an otherwise immaculately dressed presenter with dandruff or hairs on their shoulders or, even worse, the tell-tale white stains of overgenerously applied deodorant spray under their arms? It is details like this that ruin self-projection. For the same reason you should also make sure that ties are clean, neatly pressed and knotted. It is very embarrassing to have somebody walk up, study your tie and identify the soup you enjoyed for dinner the night before!

- **Shirts and blouses.** The no-crease rule also applies to garments worn under jackets. Although jackets should ideally be kept buttoned up, it is sometimes permissible and necessary to remove it – for example when the room is too hot.

- **Belts and braces.** Braces or belts should be of good quality and not brightly coloured. If your trousers are fitted with belt loops, always wear a belt, whether or not it is needed.

- **Shoes.** Many people who are otherwise immaculately presented are let down by the standard of their footwear. Do not forget that when you are in front of a group of people you are open to scrutiny and that it is often an apparently small detail that can ruin the effect. Make sure that your shoes are not down-at-heel, are polished and that the toes are not scuffed. If you are female and are wearing open-toed shoes, make sure that there are no holes in the toes of tights, that toenails are trimmed and clean and, if nail polish is worn, that it is evenly applied to all the toes that show.

We have actually seen presenters who have not only worn odd shoes, which can be especially embarrassing if one heel is leather and one rubber so that a 'thump-clack' sound accompanies their walking movement, but also a presenter wearing one black shoe and one brown shoe! Such presentational errors give a trainer no chance of establishing any credibility whatsoever.

Image

As stated in Chapter 1, it is inadvisable to wear personal accessories that can cause distraction. This section contains a number of ideas as to the correct items that you should be seen to use so that you consciously present the right image. When dressing to fit your trainees' perceived image of, for example, a sales director, senior personnel manager, chief accountant or a senior executive in any discipline, remember also to use an equivalent standard of accessories. The following hints will be useful.

- **Watches.** Always wear a watch that at least appears to be of a good and reliable quality. An obviously cheap plastic analogue watch from a market stall or a highly coloured watch is not the type of accessory that would be worn by a senior business executive, so make sure that the watch to which you may refer several times during a session appears to be of equal quality to that perceived to be worn by a top business person.
- **Pens.** A company director about to sign an order or a contract would hardly take a cheap ballpoint pen out of their pocket to complete what may be an extremely important transaction. You would expect them to use a good-quality fountain pen. Similarly, our trainees will also expect you, in your perceived role, to own a good-quality fountain, fibretip or ballpoint pen.
- **Briefcases.** Similarly, when you see an immaculately dressed senior executive, you are impressed. If, however, that executive carries a particularly well-worn briefcase with the lid secured by an old belt, you would begin to wonder whether or not the image you perceive is actually correct. The same would apply if you were ever seen with a personal accessory which did not match your otherwise polished image.
- **Cuff links and jewellery.** You may have noticed that people who have reached the top rung of the ladder never wear ostentatious items of jewellery to work. This does not mean they don't enjoy wearing diamonds and platinum whilst socializing, but, for work, their choice is rather more modest – no heavy gold bracelets, no dangly bejewelled

earrings, no expensive-looking diamond necklaces – in fact, nothing that is likely to distract the people they deal with during the working day. Emulate their example by consciously choosing to wear modest, tasteful items of jewellery, selected to fit your image but not overpower it.

The above ideas will subliminally influence your trainees' subconscious image of you. This is an important aspect of your education as a trainer if you are to break through the natural barrier every trainee will automatically build until you have won their confidence. Until you know how to break that barrier by using the techniques presented above, you will not easily become a successful, fully skilled, trainer.

All these subliminal influencing techniques and ideas will require practice to perfect. The following notes are therefore most important.

Practice makes perfect

We can all learn to control our physical messages to influence people and their perception of us. Most people look at body language as it relates to others, but very few actually look at themselves in the same critical way. To cultivate conscious gestures with which we can influence others, we must perfect them. That means practising them and observing experts to see how they convey non-verbal messages. The following ideas are also worth adopting.

Watch TV

Actors are schooled in projection, and we can learn a great deal from their methods. Actors cannot act until they have developed the ability to convey obvious messages without speaking. Watch TV productions and turn the volume down to see if you can pick up the message or plot through the physical projections of the cast rather than by what they say.

Watch people

People are great fun to watch. You can almost get to know them by their mannerisms and can learn a lot about people simply by watching passers-by from your seat in a café, at the railway station or at the bus depot. Use the ideas outlined in this chapter to practise understanding what makes people 'tick'. See how easy it is to be influenced by body actions and to subsequently place our interpretations on them – correct or not! It is an invaluable exercise that will help you to 'read' your trainees so that you can subliminally influence them to accept you and what you say.

Use a mirror

Always ask yourself what your own particular habitual gestures actually convey to others. It is a good idea to practise them in front of a mirror and to criticize what you see. Smile at yourself to find out whether your smile is really warm and welcoming or whether it is unconsciously offputting. Two types of smile that will alienate people are the *sneer*, which is when the lips are pulled back and turned down at the corner, and the *oblong smile*, which is when the upper and lower teeth are exposed with the lips drawn back in an oblong shape. This smile is used when someone is making a conscious effort to be polite. Will your smile encourage rapport? Practise, also, coordinated hand movements, boardwork technique and leading gestures. Practising in front of a mirror is a good way of eradicating any habits you have that others could interpret as creating a conflict between what you say and what you are physically projecting.

Use a video camera

A video camera is an invaluable aid for teaching yourself the skills of conscious body language. Practise in front of the camera, then evaluate the performance. Repeat the exercise until you feel confident that you have mastered the techniques.

Use guinea pigs

Practising these techniques does make perfect and, when you have perfected them, try them out on unsuspecting close family and friends who know you well. When you can subliminally influence them, you will know that you have mastered the technique and are well on the way to becoming a very powerful communicator and trainer.

Checklist: how to influence others

1   Encourage subconscious affirmations (SAs).
2   Give physical leads.

3   Make use of peer group acceptance.
4   Stack references.
5   Use accreditation
6   Coordinate your movements.
7   Use influential words.
8   Make use of third-party critique.
9   Use repetition.
10 Consciously project.
11 Practise, practise, practise.

PART III

Helping trainees to learn

Introduction

We have now discovered two key elements of becoming inspirational trainers, teachers or coaches. Part I of this book dealt with ideas and techniques that will enable us to gain our trainees' acceptance as professionals, as trainers and as individuals. Part II showed how to win trainees' acceptance of our ideas. These two elements combine to give the fundamentals of this training technique.

We now turn to the third element, developing trainee confidence or the principles of personal motivation – the action that trainees must take to develop their self-belief and motivation to take the ideas they have accepted, act on them and, in so doing, create success for themselves.

Whereas both Parts I and II concentrated on what the trainer should or shouldn't do, the techniques to add weight to the messages and gain acceptance, Part III examines the *messages to convey* that will develop self-belief, rather than the *actions to take*. It concentrates on awakening the potential from within – helping the trainees to push their own 'confidence button' to develop their own enthusiasm for *their* job, *their* career or to inspire *themselves* to use the ideas and new skills taught.

8 Attitudinal development

Attitude = a state of mind or feeling with regard to some matter.
Development = the process of growing or gradually progressing.

In studies carried out by the University of Columbia in collaboration with successful staff employed by a wide variety of industrial organizations, it was established that whilst enormous sums had been spent on important aspects of personal training to develop their knowledge of the industry they worked in and their products, together with their skills and sales techniques, there was a third factor, unrelated to specific industrial information, which determined the difference between those at the pinnacle of their profession and those who, whilst performing reasonably well, could never quite compete with these top performers. This vital factor was the *motivation to succeed* and, indeed, research into highly successful people shows this factor accounted for a much greater proportion of their success than their industrial and product knowledge, or skills.

Motivation, or the will to succeed, comprises three distinct attributes – **D**rive, **A**ttitude and **C**onfidence – known as the DAC factor and briefly mentioned in the General Introduction to this book. It is the key to self-belief and should be communicated to trainees as follows.

These three factors will enable us to motivate others to succeed. The first of these is to instil in them the will to win, which is built on the foundation that they must, first and foremost, have something to aspire to.

Drive

Drive = energy, ambition or initiative.

The first, and crucial, step in becoming successful is to help trainees decide what they really want to achieve – that is, to have a personal goal. In selecting this goal always bear in mind:

It is desire, not ability, that determines success.

It is impossible to have desire until it is known in detail what it is that is desired. Remember the well known saying: 'Nobody plans to fail, but most people fail to plan'. Without planning, circumstances control destinies. People then find they are living *'under the circumstances'*, rather than dictating the circumstances under which they wish to live. Successful people live *'above the circumstances'*.

Let us look at goals in detail. It is by having a goal and building a desire for its achievement that we create *drive* in our personalities. Throughout its evolution the human race has been striving to improve. Without goals, or targets, there would have been no progression from the primitive to the sophisticated. Without the desire or drive of certain individuals, humankind would have made no discoveries nor achieved advancement. Psychologists tell us that the human brain, nervous and muscular systems combine to form an automatic goal-seeking mechanism. This means that everyone possesses the will to succeed if they want to. All that is needed to take advantage of this mechanism is the provision of a target that it can work towards.

For the brain to work towards targeting a goal, the goal must be precise – not one shared by everybody else, such as happiness, health, fitness, money or success. About 95 per cent of all people, when asked, state common aspirations such as these as their chosen goals in life.

As goals *they will not work*. They will create neither drive nor ambition. To be one of the 5 per cent who aspire to greater things, we must first know *exactly what we want* that is over and above the goals that everyone else hopes to achieve.

The ultimate steps to the successful attainment of goals, which are tried, tested and unbeatable, are outlined below. These steps have stood firm against the test of time and have been proven throughout history. They are based on the undeniable premise that *people have control over their own destinies*.

Each training session should include an element of goal-setting and/or discussion on the value of goals. The steps towards teaching trainees to set and successfully attain goals are as follows. These can be used either as a whole or in part in training sessions.

Step one: Decide to be in control

Most people are other people. Their thoughts are someone else's opinions, their lives a mimicry, their passions a quotation. (De Profundis)

The first step in effective goal-setting is to decide to be in control or to regain control of one's own destiny. Many people, when starting out on a working career have a clear idea of where they would like to go – what successes they would like to achieve. Yet, often, through circumstances outside their control, they find their careers heading in an 'unplanned' direction, and find themselves fitting into other people's plans rather than their own. Therefore the first step is to decide to 'take charge' of the career. This does not mean 'being the boss' but being in control.

All the goals or setting of goals your trainees wish to aspire to will be fruitless if they are controlled by other people, by circumstances or by time. They must commit themselves to the belief that they wish to be controllers, or achievers.

Step two: Determine life's purpose

The second step in goal-setting is to determine one's purpose in life.

A simple exercise is to allow trainees some time for uninterrupted thought to answer the following questions:

- 'What am I here for?'
- 'What would I like my obituary to say?'
- 'What would I like to see written on my tombstone?'

The answer, or answers, to such questions begin to clarify 'purpose'. Most people's response, when asked these questions in relation to business or financial success or in terms of career path, are 'success', 'health', 'wealth' and 'happiness' – generalities that have little or no real meaning.

What is success? What is health? What is wealth? What is happiness? Because these are difficult to define they are both difficult to achieve and difficult to measure in terms of achievement – which is why few people achieve. To effectively determine purpose we believe that an individual should set goals in three categories:

1	Business Objectives	Income, career path, profit, promotion – *where they want to go.*
2	Personal Development	Confidence, characteristics and qualities – *what they want to be.*

3   Material Wealth   To have, to own, to acquire
                                    – *what they want to have.*

Ideally, individuals should have objectives in each of these categories, and these then become their life's purpose or long-term goals.

Many people, having set themselves short-term goals, which they achieve, are still not truly happy. The reason for this is that their short-term goals take them away from their true purpose – away from their innermost requirements. This is why a long-term purpose is so important. Therefore, once your trainees have decided on their general purpose, they should outline:

● their 20-year plan
● their 10-year plan
● their 5-year plan
● their 2-year plan
● their 1-year plan.

By this means you are making sure that, at all times, they will remain on course to achieve their purpose. To have achieved their goal in 20 years, where should they be in ten years' or five years' time? To achieve it in five years, what should they be doing this year and next year?

Step three: Select a primary goal or goals

Primary goals are those short-term objectives that enable 'step-by-step' achievement of long-term goals. Everyone has dreams, aspirations, desires – a wish to achieve something – yet they look up to those lofty heights and say to themselves:

'I would love to have, own, be but . . . *I'm not sure whether I can.'*

With that simple thought, their aspirations are quashed, for it is said that:

'Whether we think we can or whether we think we can't, either way we are right!!!'

Therefore primary goals should be set in each of the three categories:

● business objectives
● personal development
● material wealth

and trainees' selection of a primary goal should take account of the following:

- It should be sufficiently ambitious to create excitement.
- It must be realistic and attainable within months rather than years. For example, the primary goal of owning an ocean-going yacht is not foreseeably attainable if the trainee only has £5 in the bank.
- It must be based on realistic financial considerations. If the trainee sets goals that are wealth-related but currently has debts, the primary goal should be to pay off those debts before attempting to achieve wealth.
- It must take into account the trainee's current position. If the ambition is to run a marathon, maybe the primary goals should be to run 100 yards, 200 yards, half a mile and so on.

Step four: Define the goal

Research has shown that the most successful achievers have *clearly defined* written goals that they carry around with them night and day. Goals have to be defined in comprehensive detail for someone's goal-seeking mechanism to work effectively.

If the business goal, for example, is to increase earning power then the increase has to be clearly defined, and the aspired corporate position clarified exactly in terms of title, package and benefits.

If the personal goal is to become physically fitter, trainees should determine by *how much*. Will they aim for 50 press-ups rather than the 10 they do now? Will they aim to swim 20 lengths rather than the 10 they currently achieve?

If the material goal is to buy a new car, they should define clearly *what car* – which make, model, engine size, colour and extras!

Clear definition of goals can be conducted as an individual or group exercise to show how it makes the goal more personal and to demonstrate that the more individually tailored or personalized the goal is the more likely is its attainment.

Step five: Believe it

A belief is not merely an idea the mind possesses; it is an idea that possesses the mind. (Robert Bolton)

As discussed, many individuals have aspirations but few have the conviction or belief that they can achieve them. An apt quotation, often used in the context of goals and goal-setting, says:

'What the mind of man can perceive, man can achieve.'

Psychologists have universally concluded that not only is this quotation true but that it should be expanded into an even more powerful message.

'What the mind of man can perceive AND BELIEVE it is FORCED to achieve'.

Once there is an unshakeable belief in place the outcome is inevitable. Show trainees through examples, comparisons and discussions how people with fewer talents and lesser skills than they have overcome tremendous odds to become life's achievers and encourage them to consider what they can do with their own skills, knowledge and talents.

Desire becomes stronger when trainees work on their personal belief that they can achieve it *for themselves*.

Step six: Want it

Having decided to take control, define purpose and identify goals, the key questions for trainees to ask are:

- 'Do I really want it?'
- 'Is it a passing fad, a whim, an "on the spur of the moment" wish or is it a *deep-down burning desire to have, own, be or do*?'

Again, surveys have shown that it is desire, not ability, that determines how successful we are. While knowledge and skills are obviously important elements in personal development, in the search for achievement it is *desire* that is the key element.

There are many stories of men of limited ability, who were consumed with desire to become leaders in the world of commerce. They had the dream but surrounded themselves with people of ability to perform the necessary tasks. Desire breeds determination.

'Obstacles are things you see when you take your eye off your goal'

Step seven: Imagine it

The power of imagination should never be underestimated and, to keep alive the burning desire to achieve, trainees should be encouraged to imagine that they have attained their goal. For example, they should:

- *imagine* being completely physically fit
- *imagine* living in that new house
- *imagine* driving that new car
- *imagine* no debts and having money to spare in the bank
- *imagine* being more confident.

In 1979 Chicago University conducted an experiment in basketball. They put 30 boys together in a group in the sports hall and gave them all the equal opportunity of shooting into the basket. Then they split the group into three teams of ten and gave each team the following instructions:

Team A: Return to the sports hall every day for one month and prac-
            tise shooting into a basket for one hour every day.
Team B: Go home and forget all about practising basketball.
Team C: Go into a lecture room for one hour every day for one
            month and *imagine* they are practising shooting into a
            basket.

After one month, all 30 returned to the sports hall and their success rate was monitored – with the following results:

Team A: 24 per cent improvement through actual practice.
Team B: No improvement through no practice.
Team C: 23 per cent improvement through *imagined* practice.

Why did Team C do so well? Because *the mind cannot tell the difference between reality and imagination*. This is why imagining that you have attained your goal is such an effective technique.

Run the following exercises with trainees to show them the power of the imagination.

Exercise 1

Ask the trainees to close their eyes and take them through the imaginary scenario of picking up a lemon, holding it and feeling its weight. Then, tell them to take an imaginary knife, slowly cut through the lemon and then place one half in their mouth, sucking strongly.

Even though there is obviously no fruit, the trainees will experience extreme salivation – a testament to the power of imagination.

Exercise 2

Ask the trainees to close their eyes and imagine that they are the confident, decisive person, bursting with energy and vitality, they wish to be. How would they sit? How would they breathe? How would they hold their bodies? Within seconds, trainees will be experiencing physical changes brought about by simply using the imaginative power of their minds.

These two simple exercises are fun to do and create an awareness of the power of imagination and its value by highlighting the fact that:

'We become what we think about.'
'We are the sum total of our thoughts!'

Step eight: Set deadlines

Any goal without a time limit set for its achievement will not have the sense of urgency required for attainment.

Any goal without a time limit becomes a wish, or a pipe dream only. By setting a deadline a sense of urgency is automatically put into place – the nearer to the deadline the more urgent we become. Imagine a football match with no time limit. One team scores and the referee says, 'Carry on playing, lads. I'm sure we've got a lot more time available – I'll let you know as the day goes by!' Where is the urgency? In reality, knowing that there is only 10 minutes of playing time left, the losing team would launch an all-out assault to salvage a point before the whistle goes. Is there a sense of urgency? Of course there is!

Step nine: Write down all goals

It was mentioned earlier that successful people have clearly defined *written down* goals that they carry with them night and day. This simple step of committing dreams to paper is often omitted from most goal-setting exercises because its value is not fully appreciated. Advise all trainees to write a master list, and explain that, by writing down their goals, they will:

1 **Create constant focus**. It is often stated that the human mind is a *goal-seeking mechanism* – whatever we *focus* on we are forced to achieve.
2 **Visually commit to attain goals.** It is easy for people to lie about their goals – that is, they mentally set a goal and mentally agree the objectives necessary to achieve it. When they fail to achieve the agreed objectives their usual response is 'Well I didn't want it anyway' and, because there is no written record of the goal, they do not need to justify themselves.

3 **Provide constant reinforcement**. It is very easy for people to be distracted from their purpose when immensed in day-to-day business or corporate activities – to become sidetracked into activities that do not contribute to the attainment of their goals and the achievement of their purpose.

By carrying a reference card stating their purpose and regularly referring to it, trainees will:

- inject purpose into their everyday activities
- find it easier to make extra effort
- create enthusiasm for the task at hand
- ensure they remain organized
- differentiate between activity and real achievement.

Step ten: Establish starting position and develop the plan

Having established goals in each of the varying categories, clearly defined them and set target dates for the achievement, the final stage in goal-setting is putting the plan together – precisely identifying the activities and achievements necessary.

The first step in establishing the starting position is to take into account some of the following:

- time constraints
- resources
- skills
- current performance
- external influences
- market forces
- potential liabilities
- expectations
- primary goals.

With the starting position established, and a time limit set for the attainment, it is now possible to plan for achievement. The planning stage continues until a workable, achievable plan has been worked out. If this is found to be difficult, or even impossible, the solution is simple – either change the time period, change the plan or, if necessary, change the goal.

These ten steps, when practised and applied, will help trainees to decide on their own goals – the fundamental requirement of creating the *drive* they must adopt to achieve success through self-motivation.

Attitude

Attitude = mental view or disposition.

The second stage of motivation, or will, to succeed, is governed by the way in which every individual thinks. This element is called *attitude*, and it is the most important of all personal attributes. There is no action that can be taken by the body unless the mind decides that action must be taken. It is attitude of mind that determines what that action will be and the manner in which it will be taken. The mind is many times more powerful than any manmade computer but its output, like any computer, is only as good as what is put into it – and that is governed by *the way people think*.

Most people have heard of *positive thinking*. It is the subject of numerous books and it is a topic that frequently comes up in discussions and training. Nevertheless it is a fact that 95 per cent of all people in the Western world are habitual negative thinkers. The law of conformity states that people conform to their environment, whatever their environment may be. Therefore, if people constantly associate with a negative environment, they will become negative themselves. Because 95 per cent of all people are negative about business and financial success, it is 19 times more likely that they will mix with negative people rather than positive people and it is therefore 19 times more easy to be negative rather than positive. This is why they are negative about their work careers and why 95 per cent of all people, after a lifetime's work, have virtually next to nothing to show for it.

Everybody is positive about their hobbies or pastimes. Many football supporters, for example, know much more about football, the players, the team manager, their teams' rivals and football statistics than they do about the industry in which they work, their colleagues, the boss, the market competition and their organization's performance. Similarly, a person whose hobby is gardening is positive about their hobby and is usually very good at it, compared to somebody who looks on gardening as a chore. If we regard our job as a chore, we will never succeed at it.

Positive thinking isn't magic – all positive thinking does is alter the way we view things. And the way we view a situation determines the action we take. No one will every achieve positive results from a negative attitude. The people who are most damaged by their negative thoughts are themselves. To become positive, positive habits must be adopted and there are 12 of these which, if practised (both by you and your trainees), will guarantee results.

1 Smile

. . . the shortest distance between two people

. . . the curve that makes everything straight

People who smile tend to manage, teach and sell more effectively and to raise happier children. (Professor James V. McConnell)

A smile has been defined in many ways and each definition extols its virtue. The smile is uniquely human and has evolved over millions of years as a means of expressing inner joy and happiness to others. It is spoken about in customer care programmes, in relationship-building and in sales and communication techniques. People naturally warm towards people that have a 'happy disposition' – it breaks down barriers of resistance and brings about inner warmth – and yet most people don't smile enough.

> It costs nothing, but creates much.
> It enriches those who receive without
> impoverishing those who give.
> It happens in a flash and the memory of it
> sometimes lasts forever.
> None are so rich they can get along
> without it and none so poor but are richer
> for its benefits.
> It creates happiness in the home, fosters
> good will in a business and is the
> countersign of friends.
> It is rest to the weary, daylight to the
> discouraged, sunshine to the sad and
> nature's best antidote for trouble.
> Yet it cannot be bought, begged, borrowed
> or stolen for it is something that is no earthly
> good to anybody till it is given away.
> If people are too tired to give you a smile
> may we ask you to leave one of yours.
> For nobody needs a smile so much as those
> who have none left to give. (Anon)

2 Look for the good

This second of the suggested positive habits is to 'look for the good' rather than the normal practice of 'looking for the bad'. Sometimes referred to as the *outlook habit* we must explain to trainees the value of being in control of:

- situations
- people
- themselves.

Let's have a look at each in turn.

Situations

Everybody is hit by adversity at some time. Most lose their self-control and wallow in self-pity, seeking sympathy for their misfortune. Many use it as an excuse for non-achievement or non-performance. However, achievers see adversity as a stimulus for achievement. A positive reaction to such situations is to realize that 'out of every adversity lies the seed of an equal or greater benefit'. Develop the habit of asking one simple question: 'How can I turn this situation to my advantage?'

People

It is almost part of human nature to discuss other people in disapproving terms. It is said that people with small minds talk about people, people with medium-sized minds talk about politics, and people with large minds talk about the universe. Expand the mind and look for the potential in colleagues, subordinates, managers.

Themselves

Most people lack confidence both in themselves and their ability to succeed – they tend to concentrate on what they haven't done or what they can't do. Learn to acknowledge your past accomplishments and achievements. Look at other successful people, compare their qualities and attributes with your own and discover your own potential.

3 Compliment people

One of the most positive habits to develop is that of delivering sincere compliments. The reasons for this are threefold.

1 By giving genuine sincere compliments to people who we believe to deserve compliments *makes the giver feel good*.
2 The recipient of any compliment naturally feels good and *people that feel good produce better results*.

3   One of the principles that governs existence is the *law of sowing and reaping* which states that whatever we give out, we get back. Therefore, the more compliments we give the more we receive – and, again, *it makes us feel good*.

However, take care with compliments for, as with everything else concerning business, it is an art. Listed below are three tips for giving effective compliments:

1   Make sure that the compliment is sincere and genuine.
2   Make sure that the recipient believes that the compliment is sincere.
3   Don't dilute the value of the compliment. For example

●   'You look good today.' . . . (implied meaning: 'makes a change!')
●   'Had your hair done?' (implied meaning: 'looked a mess before!')

4   Treat people with respect

Treat people as if they were what they ought to be and you help them become what they are capable of doing. (Goethe)

The simplest way to determine how to treat an individual is to ask ourselves one simple question 'How would I like to be treated?' and to treat others accordingly. It is no accident that truly successful people have the uncanny knack of making people feel good. Also, the more we treat others with respect the more we are treated with respect. It is said that respect is very similar to sex:

1   Those that talk about it the most get it the least.
2   Everybody wants it.
3   You can't get it if you don't give it.

5   Eliminate negative language

Recognized as one of the most important of the positive habits is the ability to eliminate negative language. Negative language comes in two forms:

1   verbal messages
2   self-talk.

Verbal messages

When addressing others or responding to requests for action eliminate from your vocabulary all such words as:

- 'can't'
- 'won't'
- 'maybe'
- 'if only . . . '
- 'I'll see . . . '.

Never think or speak in negative terms for it is said that:

> Words become thoughts,
> thoughts become actions,
> actions become habits,
> habits become characteristics and
> characteristics become destiny.

Self-talk

Most 'self-talk' is known to be negative, thereby limiting the individual's actions and, ultimately, their achievements. The story of Roger Bannister highlights this more than most. In the mid-1950s it was said to be impossible to run a mile in under four minutes. This wasn't just the opinion of the day but medical opinion. It was believed that the human heart could not stand the pressure and that it would explode with the additional strain placed upon it. It took not just a superb athlete, but a doctor of medicine, to explode the myth. Roger Bannister stated that he didn't know whether he could run a mile in under four minutes but what he *did* know was that he *could* run a quarter mile in under a minute – and, of course, the rest is history. Dr Roger Bannister became the first man ever to break the four-minute mile barrier. However, what is not generally known is that, within six months, *seventeen* other athletes had also run a mile in under four minutes. What had changed? Only one element. Instead of saying to themselves 'It can't be done', they now said 'It *can* be done'. They had eliminated their negative and limiting self-talk.

6   Look for the common success denominator

An excellent habit to get into is that of finding and associating with 'like-minded' people. As already stated, there are many laws that govern human existence, one of the commonest being the *law of conformity* which states that:

**Man (or woman) conforms to his or her environment *regardless*
of what that environment is.**

Having identified your life's purpose, search for people with similar goals, outlooks and objectives and mix with them. Observe their actions and thought processes and copy them. It is impossible to achieve your goals if you associate with people who have different values. If you can't find a successful person to associate with, identify people whom you would consider to be failures, study them, see what they do and then, quite simply, do the opposite.

7   See the oak tree in every acorn

Positive people look for every opportunity rather than 'loss-making' situations. This is a healthy attitude to adopt with regard to business clients. Often the smaller customer is overlooked in favour of the larger, established client, forgetting that today's 'one-man band' is tomorrow's corporation. Although realistically, not every acorn can become an oak tree, it is also true that every oak tree was once an acorn.

8   Paint positive pictures

Everybody automatically creates images in their mind, provided they have a personal or related reference to the subject. However, if they have no reference and they are facing a completely new situation, the normal mental procedure is to imagine the worst – the negative side of the creative imagination takes over, generating fear at worst, uncertainty at best. Use the power of the creative side of your imagination by mentally placing yourself in various situations and imagining the very best outcome.

When communicating, always use words and phrases that evoke a positive picture. Imagine a managing director addressing a meeting and saying, 'Whether we like it or not, we have a job to do' or, alternatively, 'We are confronting a tremendous opportunity'. Which of these statements paints the more positive picture?

9   Recognize the dangers of external negatives

One of the most significant causes of failure is to succumb to the negative thoughts or opinions of others. Many people believe that they are mentally strong enough not to be affected by external influences but

The negative is more powerful than the positive.

For example, if we introduced a single drop of writing ink into a bottle of natural spring water, what would happen to the contents of that bottle? *Contamination.* So it is with the mind – the most seemingly trivial negative will dilute the positive thought. The only solution is therefore to guard the mind: only allow positive influences in.

10   Be a 'how can I do it better?' person

To grow as an individual you need to be on a constant self-improvement path – to develop the attitude of wanting to improve. Constantly assess performance, activities and motives. Conduct a regular *self-audit*.

Identify strengths and weaknesses. Suggested areas are:

- skills
- personality traits
- physical characteristics
- knowledge
- education.

Whilst it is important to work to existing strengths, long-term success depends on the ability to turn our weakness into strengths. This is an ongoing, never-ending process – adopt the attitude:

'Every day in every way *I* will get better and better and better.'

11   Don't worry

Worry is another significant factor in lack of success. Often, the principal cause of worrying is problems, be they work-related, of a personal nature, real or even imaginary. Therefore a solution to worry is to develop a positive attitude towards problems.

Share methods or techniques with trainees on eliminating worry. Two possible suggestions are to prioritize activities and to rename the activity.

Prioritize activities

Order all personal activities in the following way:

1   striving to achieve goals

2   training for improvements
3   handling problems.

Most people have their priorities in reverse order – first, spending time on problems, then trying to develop new skills and finally taking action to achieve results.

Develop the maxim 'No problems until after 3pm'. This frees up mental energy for achievement rather than concentrating on reasons for non-performance. In many cases, problems that are seemingly insurmountable problems in the morning have faded away by the afternoon.

Rename the activity

One of the principal causes of worry lies in the actual word 'problem' and its associations. The dictionary definition states that a problem is '. . . something hard to understand or accomplish or deal with' and therein lies the crux of the matter. People don't like 'hard' things. When faced with something that appears to be problematical, the body automatically responds in a stressful way. Stress levels are dependent on aptitude and ability and therefore, if the individual believes the task at hand is difficult or hateful, the greater will be their stress level.

The simple solution therefore, is to 'reframe' the problem – give it a different set of references by calling it something with more pleasant connotations, such as a 'situation'. Because a situation is merely a set of circumstances that can generally be handled, it is a much less stressful response and eases the 'worry' factor.

12   Have a purpose in everything you do

Everything you do must have a purpose. For example, if your goal is to increase sales of a room heater, it would be a negative and purposeless action to make a sales trip to the Equator. A more positive action, for the purpose of attaining the goal, would be to set off on a sales trip to sell room heaters to countries closer to the Arctic circle.

Practise these 12 positive habits. They develop a positive attitude that will contribute towards success – through self-motivation.

Confidence

Confidence = belief in one's own abilities, self-assurance.

The third and final element of the DAC factor is confidence. It would be difficult to maintain drive and a positive attitude without it. It is the trainer's role to develop both individual confidence in the ideas and additional skills being imparted during training sessions and trainees' confidence in their own ability to perform. This particular training activity, often referred to as the coaching element, can be broken into two activities:

1 preparation
2 technique.

Each of these is now discussed in turn.

Coaching preparation

The preparation for any coaching session is similar to the preparation techniques already discussed, and can be defined in four stages.

1 Understand the purpose

The purpose of any coaching session falls into five categories:

1 to agree areas of improvement with trainee
2 to gain the trainee's commitment to improvements
3 to show how to make improvements
4 to inspire confidence in ability to improve
5 to motivate to act.

The purpose is *not* to impress trainees with the trainer's expertise or quickness of mind.

2 Determine the desired outcomes

The desired outcomes in terms of skill improvement should be determined prior to any coaching session. This can be done by the trainer alone or in conjunction with the trainee. Marking out a clear path for the improvement of skills is, in itself, confidence-building for trainees who lack self-belief in their knowledge or skill base.

Take the following steps to identify the desired outcomes.

1 Identify the achievement required in terms of 'immediate' results.
2 Identify the achievement required in terms of 'long-term' improvements.

3   Set realistic timescales to ensure achievements.

3   *Determine the coaching strategy*

As with all training activity the strategies should be predetermined, taking into account all of the criteria discussed in Chapter 1.

Confidence is best built by activity, so that fears can be overcome through constantly performing whilst under pressure. The feeling of euphoria experienced once 'action' has taken place and the thrill of achievement replaces the fear of failure. Careful thought should be put into the 'activity' to make sure that it is both relevant and realistic, and it should have carefully thought-out time limits and guidelines.

4   *Focus*

Coaching success lies principally in the effectiveness of the trainee assessment – the degree of detail and relevance in the analysis. Trainers with experience in a given area of expertise will have already established areas of potential ineffectiveness and should therefore, prior to each session, be able to:

1   decide what 'teaching' points need to be endorsed, practised or emphasized
2   limit improvement points to a maximum of two to three per session
3   identify one or two good points for praise
4   ideally look for areas for improvement and confidence-building in the three following areas:

- skill analysis
- behaviour analysis
- attitude evaluation.

This enables the trainer to focus on particular points during the coaching period rather than try to improve a number of various areas at once and consequently failing more than succeeding. This approach also ensures more effective lectures and trainee assimilation.

Coaching technique

The objective of coaching is to bring out the best in trainees, and it is a much more effective way of developing trainee confidence in the application of skills and in individual ability than simple 'instructive' training.

Successful coaching encompasses all the communication techniques discussed in Chapters 1 to 4 but it is delivered in a more informal, 'hands-on' way. The emphasis should lie not in the use of 'formal lecture' techniques but more in the 'personal skills' covered earlier:

- empathy
- listening skills
- patience
- understanding.

The seven-step technique for effective coaching

Coaching is another tool that trainers can use in a wide variety of situations to build attitudes, skills and, most importantly, confidence.

However, as with all tools, there is a way of using it to make it more effective. Here is a suggested seven-step technique to improve coaching effectiveness.

1   Show appreciation

At the end of the activity and prior to assessment thank all the trainees for their effort and participation. This is an essential part of coaching that is often omitted.

2   Outline procedures

Having shown appreciation inform trainees of the structure of the coaching session. All sessions should be analysed in this format:

- Stage 1:   Trainee assessment
- Stage 2:   Trainer analysis
- Stage 3:   Agreement to act.

3   Carry out trainee assessment: part one

This step enables the subject of the coaching session to assess their own performance. Whether the trainee assessment is of an individual nature or even the summation of a team assessment, either way we refer to this as self-assessment. Although many coaches omit this important area, it is recognized as the *most productive form of assessment*. External or trainer assessment is often merely regarded as feedback, whereas self-assessment bypasses the possible negative effects of criticism.

The points to remember during this self-assessment period are as follows:

- **Don't interrupt.** An interjection from the trainer causes trainees to stop their analysis.
- **Encourage trainees to talk**. Make encouraging noises and agree with observations.
- **Take notes.** Not only is this a professional practice but it also shows that you are taking notice. In addition, it serves as an aid to memory.
- **Lead if necessary**. The use of leading questions can encourage the trainee to 'open up' and reveal feelings and emotions.

4 Carry out trainee assessment: part two

Having encouraged the self-assessment the trainer should now comment on it. This should be done in three stages:

1 **Comment on the assessment**. Comment in the form of praise if you are impressed with the analysis. For example:

'You have certainly given it a lot of thought.'

'That was an excellent analysis.'

If you feel that the trainee explanation was not sufficiently detailed say so. For example:

'Thank you – although we've known you to assess better in the past.'

2 **Recap on purpose**. Recap on focal points. For example:

'However, what we are specifically looking for in this session is to improve . . .'

3 **Clarify the benefits**. Restate the benefits. For example:

'. . . because by improving this particular area it will enable you to do . . . !'

5 Commence trainer assessment

The next step in developing trainee confidence is to show how improvements can be made simply and effectively.

1 Run through each of the focal points in turn.
2 Praise for delivery, effort, preparation and content.
3 Suggest new techniques or improvements, giving clear examples of how and when it would have improved the activity.

4   Gain agreement on each teaching point being made.
5   Move on to the next 'focal' point.

6   *Summarize the session*

Each coaching session should be summarized to make sure the teaching points have been accepted and that trainees feel comfortable with the new techniques. The summary should be in a three-stage format:

1   Recap on each teaching point.
2   Summarize the benefits of the improvements.
3   Gain agreement to the following questions:

   ● 'Has this been useful?'·
   ● 'Can we all see how it can help?'
   ● 'Wasn't that easy to do?'

7   *Commit and motivate*

Coaching, as with all training activities, is ineffective unless we gain commitment from trainees to take action. To take the initiative:

1   Set the next task – 'Would like you to do this?'.
2   Set a time limit for improvement – '. . . and have it ready by . . .'
3   Send a motivational message – 'Keep up the good work'.

Applying this seven-step sequence to coaching activities ensures the building of confidence in both the skills shared and the use of those skills, but more importantly in the individual ability to improve.

Conclusion

With the will to succeed, combined with positive thinking and confidence, anyone can motivate themselves to become exceptional in whatever they do. It requires discipline, common sense, dedication and desire. It does not require any special qualifications, advanced education or particular abilities. Practise delivering the DAC factor, using the various checklists and questionnaires given in Appendix II of this book, and your trainees will soon join that 5 per cent of all people who *will* succeed.

9 Relaxation for 'super-learning'

Relaxation = the state of being less tense or rigid.
Superlearning = enhanced acquisition of knowledge or skill.

Any trainer wishing to teach new information, techniques or ideas must be able to ensure that their trainees concentrate fully on the training presentation. Some people have a natural ability to 'switch-off' distractions and completely direct their minds on the proceedings, but many allow their minds to wander – especially if they are mentally or physically tired – and, in so doing, will miss an important teaching point.

The solution to this problem is to teach relaxation. We cannot expect trainees to be able to maintain a high level of concentration unless we can show them how, and allow them, to relax. There are many textbooks on mental and physical exercises to help achieve an ideal state of mind, and it is not the objective of this book to explore this subject fully. However, the following points will serve as an introduction to this subject and enable us to provide simple, workable strategies to attain the perfect 'learning state' in our trainees.

Relaxation techniques

The key to 'superlearning' is relaxation. People learn much faster when in a slowed down physical state. Experiments have shown that the rhythms of the body, the heartbeat and brainwaves tend to synchronize themselves to the beat of music. Indeed, music-induced relaxation produces similar psychological changes to meditation – slightly lower blood pressure, heartbeat slowed down by five beats per minute and brain waves indicating increased mental alertness.

'Superlearning', or the holistic approach, was discussed in the General Introduction to this book. It was first developed in Bulgaria and has been adopted widely in the Western world. The method makes use of breathing, rhythm and sound to stimulate the ability to achieve a remarkable memory and abilities that are far beyond our normal comprehension. For this reason, conduct relaxation exercises to music – some suggested pieces are listed later in Appendix III.

Users of this learning system found that, in today's harassed environment, it took between a week and ten days of relaxation training to completely relax, so it is very important to realize that many exercises will not have an immediate effect. It can take a number of attempts to reach a state of complete relaxation. Since most trainers do not have that length of time available, we detail below some simple everyday exercises that you can use to promote physical wellbeing in any training programme:

Breathing

Encourage trainees, instead of breathing haphazardly, to breathe to a regular rhythm. By holding the breath for a few seconds in between inhaling and exhaling, mental activity stabilizes so that the mind will sharpen automatically and be able to focus on a single point or idea. To reach the perfect learning state, the breathing must be harmonized with the pulse and with the beat of the music. Moslems have been breathing in rhythm to chants for centuries in order to control stress and induce relaxation. In some programmes, you may find it possible to introduce the concept of 'mantras' but, in the main, teach trainees to concentrate on pulse and heartbeat.

Music

The idea that music can affect the body and mind is not new. For centuries mothers have sung lullabies to soothe babies to sleep. In many parts of the world, including Asia, the Middle East, South America and Africa, people have used music for hundreds of years to induce unusual states of consciousness.

The music required for 'superlearning' has a specific rhythm of sixty beats per minute. Baroque music is ideal, as it often has a very slow bass rhythm like the human pulse. As trainees listen to baroque music, their bodies listen too and tend to follow the beat. Their bodies will relax and their mind will become alert in this most simple of all forms of relaxation. The music will eliminate the stress of hard intellectual work.

The music selected is very important and, as suggested in Chapter 6, pp. 67–68, to set a relaxed mood before the start of training sessions, we again recommend the Largo movements from baroque concertos composed by such masters as Bach, Vivaldi, Telemann, Corelli and Handel.

Exercises

No matter what your trainees need to learn, from languages to selling techniques, they will achieve better results if they know how to relax and enhance their positive abilities. For the exercises to be totally effective, they will need at least a week to practise them in their own time. Urge them to persist because it will pay dividends in terms of their future learning and will positively affect their entire lifestyle.

Relaxation

Talk through these exercises with trainees or read out aloud. They help to free the body of muscular tension.

Exercise 1

Make yourself comfortable – either in a chair or lying down on the back. With the eyes closed, take a slow deep breath. Exhale. Feel the tension float away and concentrate on relaxing. Repeat this exercise three times.

Exercise 2

Clench the toes as tightly as possible. Count to five. Relax the toes. Feel the difference!

Now repeat this exercise on other muscle groups, tensing and relaxing each in turn:

- the feet
- the calves
- the thighs
- the stomach
- the back
- the shoulders

- the arms
- the hands
- the neck
- the scalp
- the face

until the whole body, section-by-section, has been tensed and relaxed. Concentrate on the feeling of tension and then the feeling of relaxation when releasing the tension and always breathe slowly.

Then tense every muscle in the whole body, count five seconds and then relax. The body is now completely relaxed and you will be feeling a pleasant and enjoyable sensation.

Each time these relaxation exercises are practised, they will become easier and faster. A few minutes practising and teaching the above exercises is time well spent. They help to relieve tension and fatigue and help the mind to stay active, alert and better able to concentrate. Use them at any time during the working day. Nobody works efficiently when under stress and taking a few minutes to bring about a state of relaxation can crystallize thinking and help to clarify how best to tackle situations that are causing stress.

While they are in a relaxed state, encourage your trainees to affirm their own abilities. Affirmations work best while the body and mind are in a serene state. The following are good examples:

- 'I can do it!'
- 'I am confident!'
- 'Now I am achieving my goals!'
- 'I am calm!'
- 'I remember all I need to know!'
- 'My memory is alert!'

Mind calming

The best way to calm the mind is to visualize situations that are associated with pleasurable thoughts. For the following visualization exercise make sure your trainees are sitting comfortably with their eyes closed and read, in a measured tone, the following:

- You are on a beautiful beach. Feel the warmth of the sun on your skin.
- Walk along the beach and down to the edge of the sea. Feel the warm sand under your feet and the fine sand between your toes.
- Savour the blue sky and the blueness of the water.

- Feel the waves lapping around your ankles at the edge of the sea.
- Feel the light, cooling, breeze and feel your cares and worries gently drifting away.
- Listen to the call of distant seabirds. See the sparkling patterns of the sun on the sea. It is totally enjoyable and relaxing.
- You are completely happy and relaxed.

Advise trainees to visualize this scene as much as possible, then when they are preparing for a training session they can take a few seconds to imagine themselves in this calm place in order to soothe the mind and to release themselves from distracting worries, cares and pressures.

Learning to recall joy

Ask the trainees to remember a time when they felt good about a particular success. They should then recapture that moment, remembering all the details, remembering how they felt. Perhaps it was a simple achievement, such as solving a crossword puzzle or it may have been a more difficult achievement such as passing an important examination. The important thing is that they should recall the emotional excitement of that moment as a means of achieving a good, relaxed state of mind.

Body rhythms

Read through the following exercise to teach trainees how to achieve a state of relaxation. Its objective is to learn how to breathe in rhythm and, thereby, to relax, slow down the mind and body rhythms.

- Close your eyes and relax.
- Take a very slow deep breath through the nose, inhaling as much air as you can comfortably hold. Now take in just a little more.
- Exhale slowly and when you feel you have exhaled completely, exhale just a little more.

Repeat this sequence several times and then continue as follows:

- Inhale to a count of four in a very even, continuous breath.
- Hold to a count of four
- Exhale to a count of four.
- Pause to a count of four.

Repeat this sequence four times, ask them to relax briefly and then continue as follows:

- Inhale 2–3–4–5–6.
- Hold 2–3–4–5–6.
- Exhale 2–3–4–5–6.
- Pause 2–3–4–5–6.

Repeat four times and then run the whole exercise again to the count of eight, also repeating four times.

All the above exercises for relaxation, mind calming, learning to recall joy and breathing to a rhythm, will bring anyone into a harmonized state of body and mind which is conductive to learning.

Simple 'anytime' exercises

Of course, it may not always be possible to conduct the above exercises, either through lack of facilities, time or general convenience. The following simple exercises take just a few seconds and can be completed virtually anywhere, as and when we feel the need arises to revitalize the body:

Neck

Exercise 1

- Without rotating the neck, slowly lean the head to one side and rest it on the shoulder, whilst breathing out, for about four seconds.

Figure 9.1   Neck exercises

● Again without rotating the neck, slowly lean the head towards the opposite shoulder, resting it whilst breathing out for four seconds.

Repeat this exercise three times.

Exercise 2

● Still without rotating the neck, slowly let the head drop towards the chest and rest it whilst breathing out for four seconds.
● Then lift it back as far as it will go and let it rest whilst breathing out for four seconds.

Repeat this exercise three times.

Arms and shoulders

● With the hands in front of the chest, link the fingers of both hands.
● Lift the arms up above the head, and stretch towards the ceiling.
● Breathe in deeply, holding for four seconds.
● With the arms still raised, bend the elbows to bring the hands down behind the head.
● Breathe out, holding for four seconds.

Figure 9.2   Arm and shoulder exercises

- Straighten the arms and stretch the hands upwards towards the ceiling again, breathing in and holding for four seconds.
- Repeat bending the elbows and placing the clasped hands behind the head, breathing out and holding for four seconds.

Repeat the entire exercise three times.

Lumbar region, legs and feet

Exercise 1

- In a sitting position, place the feet flat on the floor.
- Raise the heels as high as possible.
- Hold this position for four seconds.
- Drop the heels to the floor.
- Raise the front part of the foot and toes off the floor.
- Hold for six seconds.

Repeat the entire exercise five times for each foot alternately.

Exercise 2

- In a sitting position, lift one foot slowly off the floor.

Figure 9.3 Lumbar region exercises

- Spread the toes, hold for four seconds, then point the foot downwards.

Repeat this exercise five times for each foot alternately.

Standing-up exercises

Exercise 1

- Stand on one foot, bend the other leg up behind the thigh and hold the foot with the hand.
- Gently pull the leg upwards and hold for five seconds.

Repeat three times for each leg.

Exercise 2

- Stand upright on one foot and place the other foot on a chair, keeping the leg straight.
- Lean forwards and place both hands on the knee of the outstretched leg.
- Feel the muscle stretching at the back of the thigh and hold for 10 seconds.

Repeat three times for each leg.

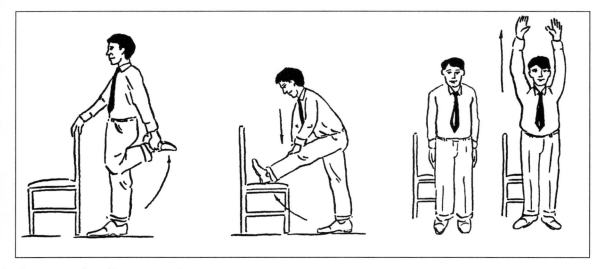

Figure 9.4   Standing-up exercises

Exercise 3

- Hold arms by the sides.
- Then lift both arms above the head, stretching towards the ceiling.
- Hold for five seconds, then relax.

Repeat the exercise five times.

Those who wish to look more closely into the subject of mental and physical relaxation to assist in preparing both the body and the mind for training will find all the exercises above, and many more, in specialist textbooks. They can provide the basis for helping trainees to accept what we, as trainers, are able to inspire in them – such as the attainment of greater knowledge, improved business or sporting techniques – and then, to make use of it to achieve their own personal goals.

Summary

To inspire action from learning trainers must match the five key criteria for enhanced learning:

- **teacher/trainer/coach acceptance**
- **practical and useful ideas**
- **interesting concepts**
- **topic or results acceptance**
- **self-belief**

with the five teaching criteria:

- **bio-rapport**
- **logical presentation**
- **mental stimulation**
- **subliminal influencing**
- **attitudinal development**

to achieve **INSPIRATIONAL TRAINING**.

Afterword

A President of the United States once said, 'It is no coincidence that Fame and Fortune follow those that have the ability to inspire others', and that is the essence of this book.

The techniques described here will undoubtedly improve your ability to inspire students or trainees – young or old, experienced or novice – to take action as a result of your training. It is simple, but not easy. It will take practice, practice and more practice, but without doubt, once perfected, it will bring rewards. The rewards are not just financial, for there is no greater satisfaction to be gained than to see a trainee climb their own ladder of success by increasing their skill level and, more importantly, by increasing their self-belief.

Many readers of this book will already be established trainers seeking ways to improve their existing skills and many will be just starting out. Whether you are experienced or still finding your way, let me share two texts that have helped me.

The first one that many of us already know and is just one of the thousands of such texts that relate the value of persistence. I have chosen to include it because it was the first of its kind that I ever heard. I still remember the time, the place and the circumstances and, indeed, the profound effect it had on my professional career. It was 1972 at the Regency Hyatt Hotel in Chicago, Illinois and I was attending my very first convention. There, I saw, for the first time, people with the ability to command an audience of 2500 individuals from all over the world, to hold them spellbound and, more importantly, to inspire them. It was then that I made my own personal commitment to do the same, and this poem has continually given me the inspiration to continue along that path through all the ups and downs, successes and disappointments.

> When things go wrong, as they sometimes will,
> When the road you are trudging seems all uphill,
> When the funds are low and the debts are high,
> And you want to smile, but you have to sigh,
> When care is pressing you down a bit,
> Rest if you must – but don't you quit.
>
> Life is strange with its twists and turns,
> As every one of us sometimes learns,
> And many a fellow turns about
> When he might have won had he stuck it out.
> Don't give up though the pace seems slow –
> You may succeed with another blow.
>
> Often the goal is nearer than
> It seems to a faint and faltering man;
> Often the struggler has given up
> When he might have captured the visitor's cup;
> And he learned too late, when the night came down,
> How close he was to the golden crown!
>
> Success is failure turned inside out –
> The silver tint of the clouds of doubt,
> And you never can tell how close you are,
> It may be near when it seems afar;
> So stick to the fight when you're hardest hit –
> It's when things seem worse that you must not quit. (Anon)

The second text was given to me in 1994 and it made me understand that, even in failure, there is still victory. That seemed to justify the journey and the sacrifices made along it.

> It is not the critic who counts; not the man who points out how the strong man stumbles, or where the doer of deeds could have done them better. The credit belongs to the man who is actually in the arena, whose face is marred by dust and sweat and blood; who strives valiantly; who errs and comes short again and again, because there is no effort without errors and shortcomings; who knows the great enthusiasms, the great devotions; who spends himself in a worthy cause; who at the best knows in the end the triumph of high achievement and who at the worst, if he fails, at least fails while daring greatly, so that his place shall never be with those cold and timid souls who know neither victory or defeat. (Theodore Roosevelt, Paris, 1910)

Take these two texts, use them or discover your own. Whatever are your dreams, ambitions or aspirations as a trainer, the message is this:

- Focus clearly on what you want to achieve.
- Develop the skills necessary to achieve it, and
- *Just go and do it!*

APPENDICES

Appendix I
Motivational quotations

There are a number of motivational quotations, some of which are reproduced below, which you may wish to give trainees as an aid to self-assessment or to reinforce learning points. These quotations from people who have achieved success in many areas, span several centuries. Those listed below are all designed to provoke and encourage the will to succeed and change. They may be used in the following ways:

- as handouts to reinforce learning points
- to read during training sessions
- as themes for specific training sessions
- as discussion topics for group or even self-analysis
- as future reference for trainees.

There is something much more scarce, something rarer than ability. It is the ability to recognise ability. (Robert Half)

Success is simply a matter of luck. Ask any failure! (Earl)

Progress always involves risk. You can't steal second base and keep your foot on first. (Frederick Wilcox)

Small opportunities are often the start of great enterprises. (Demosthenes)

I do the best I know how, the very best I can, and I mean to keep on doing it to the end. If the end brings me out all right, what is said against me will not amount to anything. If the end brings me out wrong, ten angels swearing I was right would make no difference. (Abraham Lincoln)

One hour of life crowded to the full with glorious action and filled with noble risks, is worth the whole years of those mean observances of paltry decorum, in which men steal through existence, like sluggish waters through a marsh, without either honour or observation. (Sir Walter Scott)

If a man is called a street sweeper, he should sweep streets even as Michelangelo painted, or Beethoven composed music, or Shakespeare wrote poetry. He should sweep streets so well that all the hosts of heaven and earth will pause to say here lived a great street sweeper who did his job well. (Martin Luther King Jr)

Failure is the opportunity to begin again more intelligently. (Henry Ford)

The worst bankrupt in the world is the person who has lost his enthusiasm. (H.W. Arnold)

Do not wish to be anything but what you are and try to be that perfectly. (St Francis de Sales)

Well done is better than well said. (Benjamin Franklin)

Success is a journey, not a destination. (Ben Sweetland)

Adversity reveals genius. Prosperity conceals it. (Horace)

The people who get on in this world are the people who get up and look for the circumstances they want and, if they can't find them, make them. (George Bernard Shaw)

The man who wins may have been counted out, but he didn't hear the referee. (H.E. Jansen)

As I get older, I pay less attention to what men say. I just watch what they do. (Andrew Carnegie)

One man with courage makes a majority. (Andrew Jackson)

The price of greatness is responsibility. (Winston Churchill)

Failures are often divided into two classes – those who thought and never did, and those who did but never thought. (John Charles Salak)

He who believes is strong. He who doubts is weak. Strong convictions precede great actions. (J.F. Clarke)

The secret of happiness is not doing what one likes but in liking what one does. (James M. Barrie)

A great pleasure in life is doing what people say you cannot do. (Walter Bagehot)

Our chief want in life is somebody who will make us do what we can. (Ralph Waldo Emerson)

Yesterday is a cancelled cheque. Tomorrow is a promissory note. Today is the only cash you have – so spend it wisely. (Kay Lyons)

Quality is never an accident. It is always the result of high intention, sincere effort, intelligent direction and skilful execution. It represents the wise choice of many alternatives. (Willa A. Foster)

When you hire people who are smarter than you are you prove you are smarter than they are. (R.H. Grant)

Many receive advice. Only the wise profit from it. (Anon)

Chance favours the prepared mind. (Louis Pasteur)

Don't wait for your ship to come in. Swim out to it. (Anon)

You will become as small as your controlling desire; as great as your dominant aspiration. (James Allen)

Genius is the ability to reduce the complicated to the simple. (C.W. Ceran)

All things are difficult before they are easy. (John Norley)

The only good luck many great men have ever had was being born with the ability and determination to overcome bad luck. (Channing Pollock)

We are continually faced by great opportunities brilliantly disguised as insoluble problems. (Anon)

When two men in a business always agree, one of them is unnecessary. (Anon)

Appendix II
Personal checklists and questionnaires

The following checklists and questionnaires can be used in a variety of formats, such as:

1 self-analysis
2 group analysis
3 self- or group analysis

and used as discussion points or in lecture sessions to encourage and motivate and build confidence. The method will be determined by previously discussed criteria and objectives (see Chapter 5).

The four *learning style checklists* (pp. 162–165) are designed to help trainees identify their own learning style – one of the best methods of helping an individual to learn. Once your trainees have completed these, they should use the assessment sheet (p. 166) to evaluate the results.

The *personality inventory analysis* (p. 167) enables trainees to assess their own personality and that of others and to find out how their own self-image compares with the image others have of them. This is followed by a personal effectiveness grid (p. 168).

These are followed by a self-concept questionnaire and feedback and analysis sheet (pp. 169–171), which can be used to help trainees establish a frame of reference for future growth, and an effective listening questionnaire for trainees to assess their listening skills.

Finally, a suggested format for a personal goal sheet is given (p. 173). This can be kept by trainees as a permanent record of their path to success.

Checklist: Logical learning style

(tick as appropriate)

I work systematically on subjects I don't enjoy as well as on ones I do ❏

I check through everything I write to ensure its flow and accuracy ❏

I pay great attention to detail in all I do ❏

I like to understand how things work and how ideas have been developed ❏

I enjoy solving problems and posing new questions ❏

I like tackling one task and completing it before undertaking another ❏

I am a good critic, asking searching questions and raising doubts ❏

I prefer to work through problems for myself ❏

I like to make lists, work out timetables and have clear action plans ❏

I prefer to listen to ideas rather than talk ❏

I rework any project until I get it right ❏

I adhere to timetables and action plans I have made ❏

I learn best by studying things for myself ❏

I like reading for ideas and coming to my own conclusions ❏

Total ❏

Checklist: Imaginative learning style

(tick as appropriate)

I would not describe my approach to work or learning
as systematic   ❏

I like to spend a lot of time just thinking   ❏

I enjoy making connections between different topics, and
enjoy finding out how ideas link together   ❏

I can spend a long time thinking about work without actually
getting down to it   ❏

I prefer thinking and talking to written assignments   ❏

I like to find new and original ways of completing and
presenting work   ❏

I like to work in bursts of energy   ❏

I like to float ideas with other people   ❏

I am comfortable working without timetables or plans   ❏

I enjoy working out new questions and alternatives   ❏

I would rather work from, and produce, creative diagrams
than straightforward lists   ❏

I don't like detail; I prefer seeing the whole picture   ❏

I enjoy challenging ideas   ❏

I like daydreaming. For me, it's fruitful   ❏

Total ❏

Reproduced from *Inspirational Training* by Ronald Cartey, Gower, Aldershot.

Checklist: Practical learning style

(tick as appropriate)

I like clear purpose and direction ❏

I like planning my work ❏

I like to know exactly what is required or expected before
starting a project ❏

I know what is important to me and what I want to achieve ❏

I like working on my own ❏

I like to get on with a task and not be sidetracked by new
approaches or alternatives ❏

I respect deadlines and am impatient with those who don't ❏

I am usually very well organized ❏

I think in advance about equipment and resources I need
for work ❏

I use lists, charts and graphs that give data rather than attempt
to be works of art ❏

I enjoy getting down to work ❏

I read instructions carefully and work methodically; I like
timetables and agendas ❏

I enjoy finishing a task ❏

Total ❏

Checklist: Enthusiastic learning style

(tick as appropriate)

I get bored easily and enjoy moving on to new things ❏

I enjoy working in groups ❏

I am not interested in detail ❏

I learn by talking through ideas with other people ❏

I like variety and prefer to flit from task to task ❏

When I'm interested I get totally involved; when I'm not
I shy away from topics ❏

I prefer to skip read; trying to absorb everything is a waste
of time ❏

I enjoy writing freely, letting ideas flow rather than thinking
things through first ❏

I don't read through or check my work once it's completed ❏

I like asking lots of questions to find out all I need to know ❏

I like new ideas and approaches ❏

I like to take life as it comes and be spontaneous ❏

Total ❏

Reproduced from *Inspirational Training* by Ronald Cartey, Gower, Aldershot.

Learning style checklist assessment

How did you do?

Enter your scores for each learning style:

Logical   ❑

Imaginative   ❑

Practical   ❑

Enthusiastic   ❑

You are likely to have scores in each category, but your highest score will indicate your predominant learning style. There is no single best style. Each style has its advantages and disadvantages. Knowing these will help you incorporate your strengths in your own learning programme and will provide insight into how to support others with different learning styles in their programmes.

Personality inventory analysis

Tick the **three** characteristics you feel best describe the general type of personality you display most of the time. After doing this, repeat the exercise for each of the other members of your group. Then compare each other's assessment of how they perceive your personality and how you perceive theirs.

Characteristics	Self	Other group members					
		1	2	3	4	5	6
Gentle							
Gracious							
Agreeable							
Understanding							
Considerate							
Calm							
Softly spoken							
Trusting							
Modest							
Sincere							
Warm							
Sweet							
Cheerful							
Carefree							
Confident							
Witty							
Decisive							
Dominant							
Intellectual							
Serious							
Dignified							
Mature							
Animated							
Enthusiastic							
Outgoing							
Radiant							
Vivacious							

Reproduced from *Inspirational Training* by Ronald Cartey, Gower, Aldershot

Personal effectiveness grid

Use this form to assess how effective you think you are. Score each line from 0–100.

	LOW 0 10 20 30	AVERAGE 40 50 60	HIGH 70 80 90 100
Energy			
Knowledge			
Enthusiasm			
Ability to communicate			
Self-understanding			
Ambition			
Concern for others			
Self-motivation			
Problem-solving ability			
Self-confidence			
Self-discipline			
Emotional control			
Self-esteem			
People skills			
Achievement			
Contentment			
Feeling of belonging			
Isolation			
Dominance			
Submissiveness			
Self-acceptance			
Individualism			
Aggression			
Passivity			

Reproduced from *Inspirational Training* by Ronald Cartey, Gower, Aldershot.

Self-concept questionnaire

Score each answer
TRUE = 3   MOSTLY TRUE = 2   SOMEWHAT TRUE = 1   UNTRUE = 0

1   I consider myself an independent minded thinker and decision-maker ❑

2   I often justify, and find reasons for, my mistakes and failures ❑

3   I am seldom envious, jealous or suspicious ❑

4   Losing makes me feel inadequate ❑

5   I normally let others be wrong without showing them up ❑

6   Others' opinions about me mean a lot to me ❑

7   I never feel ashamed, guilty or remorseful ❑

8   I feel threatened by other people's opinions, attitudes and comments ❑

9   I am not prejudiced towards racial, political or religious beliefs ❑

10   I tend to undervalue my own achievements or talents ❑

11   I am willing to accept the consequences of my actions and decisions ❑

12   I sometimes exaggerate a little to protect my image ❑

13   I usually feel warm and friendly towards other people ❑

14   I sometimes feel unable to cope with new or changing situations ❑

15   I express joy, love, hostility and anger without reserve ❑

16   I express criticism without reserve ❑

17   I mix comfortably and feel at ease with new people ❑

18   I put extra effort into pleasing people   ❏

19   I am outspoken about my own opinions and convictions   ❏

20   I need support, recognition and approval from other people   ❏

21   I willingly accept change and look forward to new challenges with confidence   ❏

22   I often draw attention to my successes and myself   ❏

23   I am prepared to take risks to do what I think is right   ❏

24   The actions of my family and associates often makes me feel ashamed   ❏

25   I accept compliments and gifts with grace   ❏

Self-concept questionnaire: feedback and analysis

Find out your score for the self-concept questionnaire by following the steps below. The final score is not important in itself, but all scores are relevant. The questionnaire is designed to provide a frame of reference for growth.

1   Add up the total number of points for all odd-numbered questions ☐

2   Add up the total number of points for all even-numbered questions ☐

3   Subtract the evens total from the odds total ☐

Total ☐

Your score could range from −36 to +36. A perfect self concept would be indicated if you scored 3 on all odd-numbered questions and 0 on even-numbered questions.

Take note of those even-numbered questions where you scored 2 or 3. These are areas in which improvement can be achieved.

Finally, analyse and present findings.

Effective listening guide

Read the questions listed below and rate yourself on each of the listening characteristics, using the following scale:

Always = 4   **Nearly Always = 3**   **Rarely = 2**   **Never = 1**

Do you allow the speaker to express their
complete thoughts without interrupting?   4....   3....   2....   1....

Do you listen between lines, especially
when conversing with people who
frequently use hidden meanings?   4....   3....   2....   1....

Do you actively try to develop ability
to remember important facts?   4....   3....   2....   1....

Do you write down the most important
details of a message?   4....   3....   2....   1....

In recording a message, do you concentrate
on writing the major facts and key phrases? 4....   3....   2....   1....

Do you read essential details back to the
speaker before the conversation ends to
ensure correct understanding?   4....   3....   2....   1....

Do you refrain from shutting the speaker
out because the message is dull or boring,
or because you do not personally know
or like the speaker?   4....   3....   2....   1....

Do you avoid becoming hostile or excited
when the speaker's views differ from your
own?   4....   3....   2....   1....

Do you ignore distractions when listening? 4....   3....   2....   1....

Do you express genuine interest in other
people's subjects and conversations?   4....   3....   2....   1....

Reproduced from *Inspirational Training* by Ronald Cartey, Gower, Aldershot.

Personal goal sheet

Name ....   Date.................

Detailed description	Approx. cost	Date Achieved
Business objectives 1 2 3 4 5 6		
Personal development 1 2 3 4 5 6		
Material wealth/possessions 1 2 3 4 5 6		

Reproduced from *Inspirational Training* by Ronald Cartey, Gower, Aldershot.

Appendix III
Suggested music to aid relaxation

J.S. Bach

Largo from *Concerto in G Minor for Flute and Strings* BWV 1056
Bach and Telemann Flute Concertos: Saar Radio Chamber Orchestra with
Jean-Pierre Rampal (Flute)
Odessy–Columbia Records

Aria to The Goldberg Variations BWV 988
Millicent Silver (Harpsichord)
Saga Records

Largo from Harpsichord Concerto in F Minor BWV 1056
Philharmonia Virtuosi of New York with Judith Norell (Harpsichord)
Greatest Hits of 1720 – Columbia Records

Largo from Solo Harpsichord Concerto in G Minor BWV 975
Janos Sebestyen (Harpsichord)
6 Concerti after Vivaldi. Turnabout, Vox Records

A. Corelli

Sarabanda from Concerto No. 7 in D Minor
Gli Accademici di Milano
Vox Records

Preludio from Concerto No. 8 in A Major
Gli Accademici di Milano
Vox Records

G.F. Handel

Largo from Concerto No. 1 in F (from *Music for the Royal Fireworks*)

Largo from Concerto No. 3

London Symphony Orchestra
Angel Records

Index

Elvis

igloobooks

Published in 2013
by Igloo Books Ltd
Cottage Farm
Sywell
NN6 0BJ
www.igloobooks.com

SHE001 0913
2 4 6 8 10 9 7 5 3 1
ISBN 978-1-78197-916-7

Written by Kim Aitken

Printed and manufactured in China

Elvis

Contents

*Elvis performs
in concert*

Introduction

Born Elvis Presley, dubbed The King of Rock 'n' Roll

Elvis was a fascinating character, a man who came from very humble beginnings in America's South to end up on top of the music world. He died one of the most influential, popular music stars in modern history.

His story began in poverty. Indeed, his psyche was deeply rooted in his upbringing, his world heavily influenced by an overprotective mother and shadowed by the death of his twin brother at birth. His story is not a comfortable, glamorous or straightforward one.

To explore the life of the hip-shaking teen idol means exploring his early childhood, along with his early musical inspiration and his family life. For while his sex appeal and talent came naturally, his look, his sound and his image were developed and nurtured from his teenage youth. The influence of musicians and key musical industry players helped to really define his public persona and to cement his status as The King.

Elvis was famous for his iconic quiff

"Ambition is a dream with a V8 engine."

– Elvis Presley

Elvis' famous hip-shaking moves in Jailhouse Rock

Elvis' career began and ended with music, a sound that represented his soul, his childhood and the mixed racial and social boundaries of his environment, The King created a new musical sound and genre that would sell over one billion records. No recording artist has matched his achievement since.

Arguably, Elvis still holds the largest number of gold, platinum and multiplatinum awards in history. In the United States alone, Elvis has had over 150 different albums and singles that have been certified gold, platinum or multi-platinum by the Recording Industry Association of America (RIAA). He was given 14 Grammy nominations alone. In addition to such accolades, Elvis has had no less than 149 songs appear on Billboard's Hot 100 Pop Chart in America, with over 90 charted albums and ten of them reaching Number One status in the US.

Blessed with movie star looks, he also starred in 33 films and was the first popular music artist to move to the big screen with commercial success.

His romantic life was always complicated. It has been said that from his youth he met and held several girlfriends at the same time. Elvis famously went on to choose a virgin bride and became a husband and a father, although neither of these roles was conventional for Elvis, in any way.

His later years were more difficult for his fans and audiences to digest, and for many the Las Vegas years signalled the decline of Elvis' musical credibility, looks and health. Regardless, his live shows were regular sell-outs and continue to live on today through Elvis impersonators – whose performances also sell-out, over 50 years since his death.

Despite the debate regarding this legacy, Elvis' popularity cannot be challenged. Blending incredible talent, sex appeal, good looks and plenty of personality, Elvis charmed millions and continues to inspire new generations of musicians and stars.

His life, loves and career are legendary.

Elvis performing his later yea

Birthplace sign of Elvis Presley, Tupelo, Mississippi, USA

The King Is Born

Elvis Presley was born and raised in poor Mississippi

The King of Rock 'n' Roll was born just before dawn on January 8th, 1935 in a tiny, two-room house located in a poor neighbourhood of Mississippi, called East Tupelo. A 'shotgun house', the style of which represented poor America, theirs was without electricity and indoor plumbing, built by his father, grandfather and uncle.

Named Elvis Aron (later changed to Aaron) Presley, he was delivered a little over half an hour after his identical twin brother Jesse Garon, who was sadly stillborn. He was to be an only child, raised by young parents, who relied on the help of family and welfare to pay for food and basic provisions – even items like diapers were kindly donated by neighbours.

The fact that Elvis was born in an own-built 'shotgun house', and came from nothing, was symbolic of the birth and growth of his musical career.

His father told an interviewer, Sidney Fields, when Elvis became famous:

"We were poor. When I was sick my wife walked to work many times because she had no carfare. And many times we hardly had any lunch money to give Elvis. But we did eat and had clothes and a roof over our heads. Maybe we got them all on credit, but we had them. We never had much until three years ago, but Elvis never wanted for anything even when we were troubled."

"When I was a child, ladies and gentlemen, I was a dreamer. I read comic books, and I was the hero of the comic book. I saw movies and I was the hero in the movie. So every dream I ever dreamed, has come true a hundred times..."

Elvis, in his acceptance speech for the 1970 Ten Outstanding Young Men of the Nation Award, 16 January 1971

Elvis Presley (1945) standing between his parents outside their home in Tupelo, Mississippi

Elvis' father, Vernon, was only 18 when he was born, and struggled to make ends meet. When Elvis was just three-years-old, Vernon was found guilty of forging a cheque made out to him for the sale of a pig. After Vernon was jailed for eight months, he was unable to make repayments and lost the house, forcing Elvis and his 22-year-old mother Gladys to move in with relatives.

Elvis was devastated by his father's departure, and locals recalled the young boy would sit on the porch crying, wailing for his daddy.

Perhaps because of this misfortune early in life, Elvis and his mother formed an unusually close bond. She was described as over-protective of her only son. Elvis later told an interviewer: "My mama never let me out of her sight. I couldn't go down to the creek with the other kids."

When the interviewer Sidney Fields wrote up his story to accompany the interview in the Daily Mirror, he said of Elvis' parents: "I like these people. They're simple, neighborly, unaffected by the fame and fortune of their son, or the furor he has created."

According to his mother in this same interview after her son's success, she said Elvis was always concerned about his mother and father. When Elvis was only five-years-old, he watched his father help a neighbour put a fire out in their house. He screamed for his daddy. "He was afraid his father wouldn't ever come out," said his mother. "I just told him, 'Daddy will be all right, now. You stop that, hear!' And he did."

Two-year-old Elvis Presley poses for a family portrait with his parents Gladys Presley and Vernon Presley in 1937

Birthplace of Elvis Presley, Tupelo, Mississippi, USA

Equally, his parents worried about him, and said they asked him to stop playing American football after learning that one young boy had died from a blood clot as a result of playing a game. "That scared both of us and we made Elvis quit."

Elvis' unique physical beauty was the result of his mixed ancestry. His seamstress mother was of Scottish, Irish and Native American Cherokee descent, his father from Scottish and German origin. Early childhood photos show Elvis' lop-sided cheeky grin and warm skin tone, with dark eyes and blond hair. He was an unconventionally good-looking boy and would grow up to become a desirable, handsome rock star.

Despite his good looks, Elvis was not a popular child. His first school – East Tupelo Consolidated – recorded average academic results and his peers regarded him as a bit of a loner.

Elvis was raised a Christian, attending church for the First Assembly of God. His mother and father had met at the church, and the family would continue to attend there. While Elvis would later question his faith, his church attendance helped further nurture his belief in music.

Elvis was, as his classmates noticed, shy and a loner. He escaped into the fantasy world of comic books, his favourite being Capt. Marvel Jr. Although he would swap comics with other kids, his social interaction was limited.

It was his love of country music that first got him noticed as a youngster.

Elvis Presley as a child

Elvis Presley with radio DJ and high school classmate George Klein in December, 1970

Elvis Presley's first guitar

In the first term of his first year at school, Elvis' teacher asked her class if any of the students would like to say a prayer. Instead of saying a prayer, Elvis stood up and sang Red Foley's Old Shep. The teacher took Elvis to the school principal who was also impressed by his singing.

Elvis was then asked to sing in a contest at the Mississippi-Alabama Fair and Dairy Show in 1945, which was broadcast on the local radio. Coming a mere fifth, Elvis' talent was yet to be recognised and nurtured.

Elvis' father recalled, "At nine he was picked to sing alone in church. At home we sang as a trio, when Gladys wasn't playin' the harmonica. Elvis always had a natural talent. He can't read a note even now. But you don't have to teach a fish to swim." A year later, at age 10, with frequent home moves around Tupelo, Elvis ended up attending a new school in sixth grade, Milam Junior High, where he was also described as a loner. He was teased for being 'white trash' and the children made fun of him singing hillbilly songs.

Many accounts of Elvis' childhood from sources who knew him, say he was a sweet boy, who never really fitted in. He was also described by other accounts as a lovable rogue or misfit.

His tenth year was also the year he was given his first guitar (accounts differ, with some recalling it was his 12th birthday). Some also report Elvis wanted a bicycle, while others claim he wanted a shotgun. Regardless, the $12.95 guitar was his birthday gift.

I took the guitar, and I watched people, and I learned to play a little bit. But I would never sing in public. I was very shy about it."

– Elvis Presley

Elvis Presley wearing his high school army uniform in 1955

Another home move later, Elvis was living in a largely African-American neighbourhood, nicknamed 'Shake Rag'. He became strongly influenced by a hillbilly singer called Mississippi Slim and gospel music.

Slim held a spot on the Tupelo radio station, WELO. Elvis was obsessed. Slim's younger brother attended school with Elvis and helped him progress his talent by bringing him into the radio station, even tutoring him on guitar and teaching chord techniques.

When Elvis turned 12, Slim scheduled him for two live performances at WELO. The first one was a disaster, with Elvis overcome by nerves; he did not even begin the performance. Fortunately, the second opportunity was fulfilled and Elvis gave his first radio performance at just 12 years of age.

In 1948, when Elvis was in eighth grade, the family moved again. This time, the Presleys moved out of Tupelo, to Memphis, Tennessee. Still a low-income family, they moved into a two-bedroom apartment in a public housing complex.

According to his parents, Elvis skipped the first day of high school out of fear of being disliked. His father said he always wanted to be liked, "And when he isn't, he worries about it."

He continued to be bullied by his classmates, perceived as a 'mama's boy'.

Ironically, Elvis was awarded only a grade C in music at this time. In fact, his teacher told him he had no aptitude for singing.

His shyness for singing publicly continued through his teenage years.

"I never expected to be anybody important."

Elvis Presley

It was during his junior year, however, that he started to receive more and more attention. A self-styled, good looking young man, Elvis greased his hair, grew sideburns and wore dress pants instead of jeans. Fashion conscious from a young age, Elvis tried to emulate his film heroes James Dean and Marlon Brando.

He shopped on Beale Street and frequented the Beale Street gigs, where the blues scene in Memphis was burgeoning.

Elvis' clothes shopping trips were funded by the various jobs he held in his teen years: usher at the local cinema, Loew's, and at Precision Tools.

His mother recalled a teenage Elvis helping out with money, "And even when he was in school he'd go around and pay the grocery bill, $25, $30. We didn't ask him to. He'd just do it himself."

Elvis was also a serious romantic, and having fallen in love at 13 with a girl from church, Magdaline Morgan, he secretly made a marriage licence for them, copied from his parents' certificate. According to reports, even Magdaline herself was not aware of this until after his death.

Family photo from 1954

Walking In Memphis

Elvis' early musical influences and the blues scene in Memphis

Like Elvis' poor upbringing, the musicians who played the blues came from the poor South.

Originating in the early 1900s, the Memphis blues genre was used to describe the mood of musicians playing vaudeville shows along the Mississippi River and Delta. The man credited with establishing the blues was a band man named W.C. Handy, who was inspired to write a song in the genre when he heard a man singing a slow, sad song while playing a guitar by sliding a knife along the strings.

African Americans who had left the Mississippi Delta and other poor, southern areas were moved by this burgeoning Memphis blues scene, which culminated in the Beale Street district, of downtown Memphis. Running from the Mississippi River down to East Street, Beale Street was (and is still today) nearly two miles of blues clubs and restaurants, and is steeped in musical and cultural history.

The street was originally an avenue where trade merchants sold goods, and in the late 1800s travelling musicians would perform along the street. After yellow fever hit the area, the city had to forfeit its charter. The South's first black millionaire, RobertChurch, purchased land around the street, proceeding to renovate and nurture it into a cultural district.

Beale Street became the place to be for African Americans. With a large, mostly affluent black population, Memphis was then the largest city along the Mississippi river. In the period before The Great Depression, records released from Memphis Blues performers regularly sold more than the other blues genres. Different from the Chicago Blues, which featured more electric guitar, the Delta Blues showcased acoustic guitar and wailing harmonicas. In particular, the slide guitar marks the sound of the Delta and Memphis Blues.

The Memphis music scene grew from the blues genre that evolved post-civil war. It represented sadness, hardship, tough living, love and romance. With its moody atmosphere and obsession with music, many have described Memphis as 'home of the blues'.

During the 1930s, amplified guitar pick-ups helped progress the sound of the Memphis Blues. Later, famous blues musicians, including Louis Armstrong, BB King, Muddy Waters and Rufus Thomas performed on Beale Street, further developing the style dubbed the Memphis Blues.

Memphis blues scene where Elvis first discovered his love for the genre

*B.B. King, anoth
musician to heav
influence El*

Beale Street in Memphis is jammed with clubs, bars, restaurants and music shops.

Memphis was certainly home to Elvis' musical beginnings. By the time Elvis was of age to experience Beale Street, some of the nightlife was seedy and boozy, with wailing music heard inside and out of venues.

Even though it was a place where black and white could mix and socialise without judgement or intimidation, Elvis was one of few white people visiting Beale Street. Elvis, along with the thousands of visitors each night, could see blues legends perform, along with street artists while walking home.

That Elvis and Memphis are now well associated together is no surprise.

In Memphis, Elvis had access to not just radio, record stores and church music, he also soaked up music in night clubs on Beale Street and played in a band with other boys from the housing complex in which he lived.

The thriving music scene in the Beale Street haunts, downtown Memphis, were home to black blues and rhythm and blues artists. Elvis was a fan. He would watch acts like Big Memphis Ma Rainey and Rufus Thomas. According to Calvin Newborn, a well-known artist of the time, Elvis also listened to his performances and ended up taking some advice on guitar style and lessons.

Interestingly, BB King recalls knowing the other King from frequenting the music events on Beale Street in Memphis, long before Elvis became a famous singer.

"I remember Elvis as a young man hanging around the Sun studios. Even then, I knew this kid had a tremendous talent.
He was a dynamic young boy. His phraseology, his way of looking at a song, was as unique as Sinatra's. I was a tremendous fan, and had Elvis lived, there would have been no end to his inventiveness."

B.B. King

B. B. King became a big Elvis fan

The romantic, poor Tupelo kid in Elvis must have identified with the music and, in particular, the messages from the blues. Such freedom of expression and emotive, heartfelt music must have made an impression on the teenage Elvis.

It is perhaps no surprise then that the singer Joe Cocker later described Elvis as "the greatest white blues singer in the world".

To listen to singles such as Hound Dog, Reconsider Baby, Stranger in My Own Home Town, That's All Right, Mama,

Mystery Train and Good Rockin' Tonight is to listen to the blues, albeit Elvis' white version of the blues.

These blues influences certainly helped shape his style – later to be described by many as Rockabilly. While he did not necessarily 'invent' Rockabilly, he is widely credited with making it popular by bringing it to the masses, with his own unique twist. In doing so, he also brought social and civil rights to the consciousness of the masses.

While many later complained that Elvis took his experiences from Memphis and became 'the white boy who stole the blues', it is much more likely that he was simply and unconditionally moved and inspired by them.

As the performer Little Richard stated, "He was an integrator. Elvis was a blessing. They wouldn't let black music through, but he opened the door."

To hear Elvis' style is to also hear the influence of Big Mama Thornton, Arthur 'Big Boy' Crudup, The Prisonaires, Lowell Fulson, Chuck Berry, Bo Diddley, Little Richard, and Fats Domino.

Elvis identified with the rhythm and blues genre: he felt the blues.

"Rhythm is something you either have or don't have, but when you have it, you have it all over."

- Elvis Presley

*Elvis was a
big fan of Fats
Domino*

*Elvis was a great supporter of
the civil rights movement*

It seems Elvis took his love of church gospel, country and western music from his early childhood, and added the black rhythm and blues genre he loved from those Memphis teen years. The fusion of these styles, along with the influence of popular music he heard on radio and in the record stores, helped him to create his own unique style.

Self-taught, Elvis' musical ability grew and grew during his teenage years. In addition to his time on Beale Street, he spent the rest of his spare time in record stores, and was a regular at gospel singing nights.

Elvis developed a love for gosp music from his childho

An old wooden church in Mississippi,
the type Elvis would have attended

Memphis was the epicentre of white gospel music in the 50s, and
Elvis adored the four-part harmonies of quartets like those at the
monthly All-Night Singings he attended downtown. They played
a large part in Elvis' musical education, and he would continue to
attend the gospel sings at the Ellis Auditorium with his girlfriend,
long after he attended as a youth with his parents.

But his passion was first cultivated and nurtured in the gospel
choir sounds heard at the First Assembly of God church he had
regularly attended with his parents as a youngster. From the age
of two, Elvis would display a curiosity for music and signing.
His mother recalled, "He would slide down off my lap, run into
the aisle and scramble up to the platform. There he would stand
looking at the choir and trying to sing with them."

Elvis' music is often discussed in the context of gospel, and having won awards and recognition in gospel sound, is widely acknowledged as a key genre in his music.

His country music sound, however, was less publicised and recognised. The country fraternity, however, eagerly recognise Elvis' influence by and for the genre. In more recent years, especially so – he was elected to the Country Music Hall of Fame in 1998.

It is now mostly accepted that he did fuse the Country sound with Rhythm and Blues, In fact, he was successful in the country market first and, interestingly, very quickly. Perhaps because of his appeal with younger listeners, Elvis received great exposure on country radio, played by country disc jockeys (DJs). His notoriety and rising success can be traced back to this country market.

Country Music Hall Of Fame Museum, Nashville, Tennessee

Elvis enjoyed the sounds of the Delta Rhythm boys

Sam Phillips also discovered Johnny Cash

Elvis Rises With The Sun

Discovering his sound with Sun Records and Sam Phillips

While Elvis was busy discovering the sights and sounds of the Memphis Blues scene down on Beale Street, another music lover was determined to bring his passion for the blues to the masses.

Sam Phillips was destined to be the man who invented rock 'n' roll. As the founder of Sun Records, he is credited with helping a young Elvis with discovering his persona as the King of Rock 'n' Roll.

"If you're not doing something different, you're not doing anything."

- Sam Phillips

In the 1940s and 1950s Phillips was a producer, DJ and talent scout who famously discovered talents such as Johnny Cash and Jerry Lee Lewis. He launched Elvis' career in 1954.

To understand Phillips' unique relationship with Elvis requires an understanding of their commonality. Sam Phillips was born in Alabama, the youngest of eight children, and after his father's death while he was in high school, was forced to drop out and support his mother and deaf-mute aunt. Like Elvis, he experienced a poor upbringing and hardship early in his life.

"I was training to be an electrician. I suppose I got wired the wrong way round somewhere along the line."

– Elvis Presley

And like Elvis, Phillips developed a keen interest in music saying, "music moves the soul".

In high school, he played the sousaphone, trombone and drums, and reportedly also led a 72-piece strong marching band.

After Phillips was married and settled with children, he took a job hosting the local radio station Elvis listened to in Memphis. He said he immediately fell in love with Beale Street and the atmosphere there.

Setting up a modest studio, Phillips opened Sun Records and went on to famously sign artists like BB King and Roy Orbison.

Originally, his studio was set up in a small storefront on Union Avenue rented for $150 a month. He also installed recording equipment and called it the Memphis Recording Service, which was designed and marketed for music, weddings, funerals and the like. The business advertised, "We record anything, anywhere, anytime."

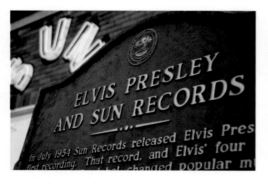

Sun Studio became known as the 'Birthplace of Rock 'n' Roll,'

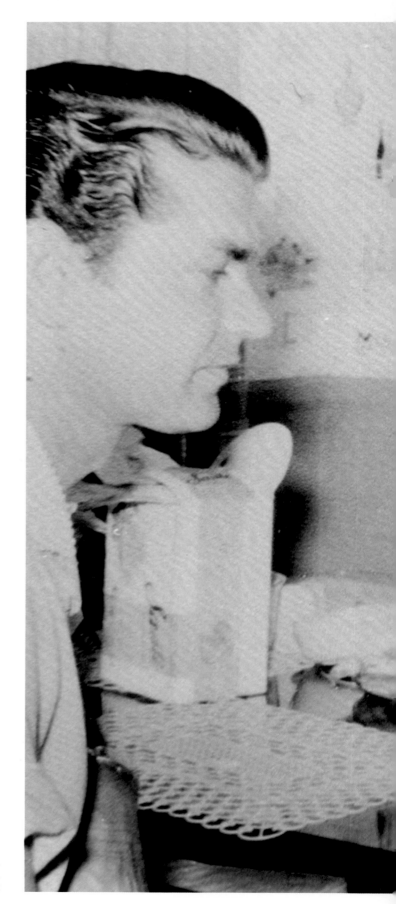

Elvis Presley and Sam Phillips eating ice cream and cake in 1956

Phillips denied reports that he had repeatedly said he could "make a million dollars if he could find a white man who sang black rhythms with a black feel."

Much later, in 1978, Phillips told a reporter with the New York Times, "That quote is an injustice both to the whites and the blacks. I was trying to establish an identity in music, and black and white had nothing to do with it."

With his poor upbringing during the depression, Phillips identified with the performers he had recording in his studios – he could relate to them and bring the best in them. He told the The Dallas Morning News that his aim was to record "the real gutbucket stuff that other labels weren't putting out."

Sun Studios – now an iconic landmark in Tennessee

In the summer of 1953, a young Elvis walked into the Sun Records studio on 706 Union Avenue, in downtown Memphis. He was there to use the DIY record making facility called the Memphis Recording Service. By some accounts, he was there to record some songs for his mother.

Financially, Phillips and Sun Records were struggling. When 18-year-old Elvis came in, it was in perfect time.

Phillips thought that Presley was an introverted man, according to reports. Nonetheless, Phillips said:

"After listening to his voice, seeing his demeanour… and what I thought was a very different style…I was highly impressed with what I thought he could do as an artist."

Sam Phillips, in a recorded interview on Elvis 7 April, 1992

The self-recording service advertised at Sun Studios

Left-right; Elvis Presley, Bill Black, Scotty Moore, Sam Phillips in the Sun Records studio

"When Elvis came in and he performed those first two songs, I was blown away by this guy's talent. By that I don't mean that I heard the finished thing, but I just heard some instinctive things about this person's intonations and stuff.

"Of course, we didn't talk about 'intonations' and all of that jazz, but that's what I was hearing and feeling! You know, that's how you communicate, and so it didn't take a genius to recognise that this person Elvis had real potential.

"My honest opinion was that he might be that white guy who could get the overtones and the sexual feel in there without anything being vulgar; just that actual thing that gets hold of somebody and says, 'Hey, listen to me!'"

- Sam Phillips, For Elvis Fans Only, August 2, 2004

Although Phillips noticed The King's voice and charisma, as he recorded versions of My Happiness and That's When Your Heartaches Begin for a $4 fee, it would be another year before they would begin to work together.

Elvis cashing one of his first checks in 1956

Elvis recording and playing at RCA

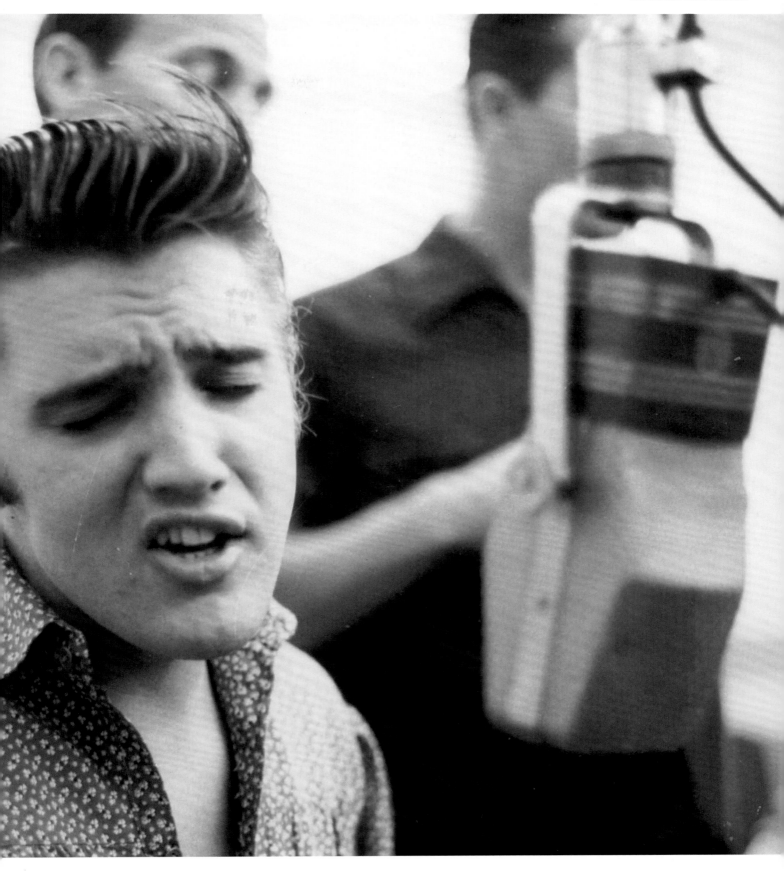

Bill Black, bass player.

It was reported that Phillips had so many other artists consuming his time and attention that he struggled to focus on Elvis straight away. Some other accounts suggest that Phillips was not actually in the studio at the time, and only heard his second recording in the new year of 1954. At this time, Elvis was working as a driver for Crown Electric Company and studying at night school to be an electrician.

During the summer of 1954, at the suggestion of his studio assistant, Marion Keisker, Phillips invited Elvis in to the studio. Keisker recalled asking Elvis what his singing was like and he replied, "I sing all kinds." And "I don't sound like nobody." Her notes on his session read: "Good ballad singer. Hold."

There was no real method to their approach; it was about trying out different arrangements until they discovered the right sound. At first, Phillips was not impressed with how Elvis delivered the songs he requested. After asking him to sing some pop songs of the time in his own way, Phillips decided was something about Elvis, but with bassist Bill Black and guitarist Scotty Moore, who were in a country and western outfit called Starlight Wranglers, working on

material and experimenting with sounds. Some sources recall the three rehearsed for months before recording in the studio.

Elvis did not actually have a band at the time – it was Phillips who introduced Black and Moore, and decided to shape Elvis' voice and rhythm guitar sound. With his guidance, Elvis learned production qualities and the "feel" that Phillips described when they happened on a perfect cut.

Phillips' ear was good. He could recognise a unique sound that would sell – and finally they came up with That's All Right (Mama).

It happened just at the last minute.

Phillips recalled they had started packing down the instruments to close a long, tedious session one evening, July 5, to the point where the door to the studio was open and everyone was ready to leave. Elvis started on his rhythm guitar singing from Arthur Crudup's 1946 blues hit: "That's All Right, Mama…" and Phillips froze.

*Scotty Moore on the set
of Jailhouse Rock*

*Elvis' first single,
That's All Right
(Mama)*

"There was no question in my mind. That was the sound, the feel, even the tempo."

- Sam Phillips, For Elvis Fans Only, August 2, 2004

With a fast rhythm and no drums, the bass going fast to keep time with his vocals, guitar wailing in and out, Phillips asked what they were doing. They apparently said they didn't know.

"Well, back it up, try to find a place to start, and do it again," Phillips said.

A maximum of four takes later, and the single was ready. Just days later, the Memphis DJ Dewey Phillips played the song on his radio show and listeners phoned in to ask who it was singing. He ended up playing the record over and over that same show. Some reports indicate Elvis was invited in for an interview that night too. Rock 'n' Roll was born.

Phillips was innovative for his time, using new techniques like pulling back on the volume of the vocals, to blend with the instruments of the band, and introducing an echo on the vocals, achieved by running the tape through a second recorder head.

Phillips knew Elvis before the fame, the hip-swivelling controversy and the Vegas years. He helped shaped the future King of Rock 'n' Roll, by encouraging him to be raw and very unlike the man Elvis wanted to sing like – Dean Martin.

Steering Elvis away from a crooner style and towards the rockabilly, bluesy and raw Elvis that was recorded on the single That's All Right (Mama) Phillips launched the career of the newest sounding singer – with a genre all of his own.

"Elvis had sex written all over him from the day he walked in the door. I don't mean anything about him being good-looking, because he really wasn't as good-looking as he would develop a little later on, but he had sex written all over him, and the right kind," said Phillips.

"When this man opened his mouth it had sex, when you saw him on stage you couldn't take your eyes off him, and that was even as a male. I don't want to use the word 'charisma', but this guy - and I'm talking about him in a total, total personal way, in addition to fantastic talent as far as his singing was concerned - had a certain ability for contact, and to a measured degree he could give you that sexual feel, or whatever feel was needed, if a song indicated that it had that potential."

Elvis wanted to sing like Dean Martin

Elvis Presley joins his guitar player Scotty Moore (left) and bass player Bill Black on a weekly broadcast of 'Louisiana Hayride' at the Shreveport Auditorium.

Phillips later said there was something in Elvis' soul and his spirit, to survive the entertainment business and all the years of commentary, at such a phenomenal, global level. And he certainly was granted a background at Sun Records that gave him the "inertia" to feel confidence in himself and his ability.

Despite popularity and notoriety, the Sun label was not performing well financially. A practical businessman, Phillips ended up selling Elvis' contract to RCA Records for a whopping $35,000, which was at the time, unheard of.

Sam Phillips may not have made the biggest or best investment in Elvis, who would go on to become worth $4million annually at the height of his fame, however he is largely recognised as being the legend who discovered Elvis. He used the money from selling the contract to develop other musicians and hits, including Perkins' hit Blue Suede Shoes.

In Last Train to Memphis: The Rise of Elvis Presley, author Peter Guralnick said Phillips's accomplishment was recognising "the unlimited possibilities, and untapped potential, in the popular appetite for African-American culture."

He was inducted into the Rock 'n' Roll Hall of Fame in 1986. The Sun Records studio is now a tourist attraction and was named a National Historic Landmark.

Elvis records the soundtrack for his film 'Love Me Tender'

Recording at RCA again in 1956

The King Takes The Throne

Elvis' meteoric rise to success

Following the great chemistry Elvis had with Black and Moore at the 1954 recording, The King happened on his first local hit song. Moore became his manager and local shows soon followed.

Come later that same year, happening country radio show The Louisiana Hayride invited Elvis to appear. He also made it onto local television some six months after, and a few more of his recorded singles Good Rockin' Tonight and I Don't Care if the Sun Don't Shine grew his popularity in Memphis. During this period, Presley hired a new manager in the local DJ Bob Neal. Neal encouraged Elvis to audition for a talent show in New York, although he did not win the hearts of judges.

The judges must have later questioned their scouting abilities, considering it was only a few months later that an Elvis gig in Florida started a riot.

Still only a local country act, Elvis received his first Number One record, with his adaptation of Junior Parker's Mystery Train, in September of 1954. His ascent to fame and stardom was quick, taking a little under a year from his first recording to his first Number One.

It was around this time that Elvis was getting more attention from music promoter Colonel Tom Parker, who had met him through Neal. Parker started to get more involved in Elvis' career and by the time Sun Records had sold his contract to RCA, Parker was getting his connections in the music publishing arena also involved.

When the contract went through, Elvis used his $5000 advance to buy his mother a pink Cadillac, as he'd promised her as a young boy.

In 1956, Parker signed Elvis to a manager's contract, which allowed him 25 per cent of the star's earnings. The contract held firm right up to Elvis' death and to royalties and estate earnings long after his passing.

Elvis on the Louisiana Hayride tour

Elvis with manager,
Colonel Tom Parker

49

Elvis Presley performing on the Milton Berle Show
in Burbank, California on June 4, 1956

Despite this outrageously generous cut (the standard was 10 per cent), Parker was good for Elvis' rise to rock stardom. Parker managed him through his first record for RCA and his national television appearance on Stage Show, a popular programme hosted by the Dorsey Brothers, Tommy and Jimmy, who were big band members. Elvis then followed with another six appearances on the same show.

Under Parker's wing, Elvis went on to perform on the Ed Sullivan, Milton Berle and Steve Allen shows, all popular in their own right.

Parker set up the first recording with RCA in Nashville, in January, with the usual Black and Moore support. He also added the pianist Floyd Cramer and guitarist Chet Atkins, plus three backing singers, for fuller sound. What followed was Heartbreak Hotel, the single that gave Parker leverage to secure Elvis on national TV with channel CBS. Heartbreak Hotel became his first Number One pop song.

Following filming at CBS in New York, Elvis recorded a further eight tracks in the RCA studios of the Big Apple. This recording included Blue Suede Shoes, a famous and extremely popular song of The King's.

In March, RCA released Elvis' self-titled debut album. It included five songs from unreleased material at Sun Studios. They completed the mixed menu of the album, as there were two country songs and one pop song to complement the rock 'n' roll feel of the other tracks. It was not only the first rock 'n' roll album to get to Number One on Billboard's chart, but stayed at the top for ten weeks.

Elvis Presley holding framed
gold record of Heartbreak Hotel

Come April, national TV station NBC had Elvis on its Milton Berle Show. It was well received. Just a short time later, Elvis had a scare.

Taking a flight back to Nashville, Elvis and his bandmates were left extremely unsettled after the engine failed and the plane nearly went down. Just as Elvis seemed to have many lives, so he had many hits to come. And while many assume that Elvis' Las Vegas career began much later, in fact he had tested the waters with performances in Vegas at this early point in his career. Parker had Elvis on The Strip for two weeks, performing to a lackluster audience of middle-aged folk. They were not his target audience.

Following this, he started a tour of the American Mid-West, with 15 cities in 15 days. It was on this tour that Elvis began featuring a cover of Big Mama Thorton's Hound Dog as part of his closing act.

His popularity was reaching fever pitch.

Alongside his television appearances, in the middle of the year Elvis was contracted to shoot his first film, Love Me Tender. Costing $1million to make, and released a short three months after filming began, it only took three days to break even. Elvis was so watchable, be it singing or acting, audiences could not get enough of him. He signed with Paramount Pictures for a seven-year movie contract.

After all of the success and attention that followed the Milton Berle Show, and of course the excellent TV ratings, it should have come as no surprise that Steve Allen and Ed Sullivan were to follow. National television channel giant NBC booked Elvis to appear on Steve Allen, filmed in New York that July.

Elvis later described the show as the most ridiculous of his career. In truth, it was a ridiculous performance. Set up by the Allen team, he was to appear wearing a bow tie, top hat and tails singing Hound Dog to a basset hound on air.

Allen later wrote of Elvis that he found him "strange, gangly" and that he found his "charming eccentricity intriguing" – he was hardly enamoured of the singer's style and abilities and fit Elvis into his show format for light entertainment and laughs. Steve Allen's direct competition was Ed Sullivan. The competition between the two show hosts was well known, and Elvis benefited from their intense rivalry.

Elvis agreed to a series of three appearances on the CBS network's Ed Sullivan Show for a record-breaking $50,000. Sullivan put in the offer after Allen's episode that featured Elvis outdid his in the ratings.

And more record-breaking was to follow: the first appearance took 82.6 per cent of the whole television audience, a figure of almost 60million viewers. The irony was that show was not hosted by Sullivan himself, as he was recovering from a car accident. The actor Charles Laughton instead interviewed and hosted.

*Movie art for the film
'Love Me Tender', 1956*

Singing 'Hound Dog' on the Steve Allen show

Elvis' moves and provocation were to cause intense debate and gain Sullivan even more attention. For the first two Ed Sullivan shows, Elvis was filmed from top to toe. The camera angles and filming was fairly conservative when he danced and gyrated, and yet the reaction from the audience was the same – intense screaming and near hysteria.

Elvis must have realised the impact of the show: this first appearance in September would garner him

celebrity status on a never-seen-before level, millions of fans, and another record-breaking one million advance orders on his newly recorded Love Me Tender.

But he also appeared to consider the hosts and restrictive formats of the shows with some disdain. At a concert in Memphis, he declared to the audience, "You know, those people in New York are not gonna change me none. I'm gonna show you what the real Elvis is like tonight."

In October, his second appearance aired. Come November, the film Love Me Tender was released, to box office success and a panning from critics. The film was originally titled The Reno Brothers, but Paramount cleverly changed the title to match his chart topping single. And four musical edits were added to the acting film, taking it from a regular acted movie to the first of Elvis' famous musical films.

Following more controversy and conservative pressure, the last of Elvis' Ed Sullivan Show appearances, aired in January of 1957, was famously filmed only from the waist up.

Many speculated that Parker had masterfully engineered this waist-high filming to generate even more publicity, although this remains unfounded. Regardless, Elvis still made an impact with his performance. As his hair fell seductively in his face, he provocatively mouthed the words.

In the first year of his national TV debut, Elvis made ten top singles, four of which were Number One hits. He had millions of fans and outraged just as many with his suggestive moves and raw sex appeal.

The controversy, all the talk and the sheer number of fans meant Elvis had hit the big time. He had made it. After one year going from local star to national, in the short year that followed he had surpassed not only his own expectations, but critics' too.

Female fans push on police barricades under Studio 50 awning as they wait for Elvis to appear on The Ed Sullivan Show

Elvis performs on The Ed Sullivan show again, 1957

Elvis' parents remembered a young Elvis had promised them, "'When I'm grown up I'll buy you a big home and two cars. One for you and Daddy and one for me.' All his life he'd say out loud what he was going to do for us, and he'd say it in front of other people. And you know, I believed him.

"And when he got to 19 and started making money, he told us: 'You've taken care of me for 19 years. Now it's my turn.'"

It was following the Ed Sullivan Show airing in January that Elvis received notice from Memphis that it was likely he would be drafted to serve in the military later that year.

From early 1957, Elvis was already established as America's most popular act and was an international star. The singles Too Much, Teddy Bear and All Shook Up would hit Number One on the charts. Even where his music was not officially released, Elvis was a star.

And just as Elvis had purchased a pink Cadillac car for his mother with his first advance, his first home would also be bought for his parents, as well as himself at 1034 Audubon Drive in Memphis.

Later, he moved into a 23-room Memphis mansion, Graceland, an old church that was the dream home for his family.

It was also at this time in his career that Elvis began working with songwriters Jerry Leiber and Mike Stoller. Penning Loving You, the soundtrack to his next film, the pair helped Elvis secure his third straight Number One album.

What followed with Leiber and Stoller was a winning combination, whom Elvis considered his "good luck charm". The team went on to write the majority of the tracks for Jailhouse Rock, of which the title track also went straight to the top of the charts as a Number One single.

Elvis Presley with songwriters Leiber and Stoller (1957)

Elvis Presley strolls the grounds of his Graceland estate in circa 1957

The Elvis' Christmas album was also written by Leiber and Stoller and became the best selling Christmas album of all time.

On December 20, Elvis' military draft notice came through. He requested a 60-day deferrment to finish the film King Creole (a dramatic film based on the novel A Stone for Danny Fisher) and, during filming, the single Don't (also a Leiber and Stoller special) was released, which gave Elvis his tenth Number One.

The year of 1957 closed with Elvis landing more top 100 songs than any other artist (according to Billboard). Elvis was responsible for more than half of the RCA singles sales and merchandise brought more than $22million in addition to the earnings made from his films and music.

It was time for Elvis to serve in the Army.

With his parents, family members and some friends, Elvis reported to the Memphis Draft Board on March 24, 1958, where he and other recruits were transported to the Kennedy Veterans Memorial Hospital. Elvis' army serial number was 53 310 761. After swearing in, he was bused to Arkansas where he and the other recruits were given the G.I. haircut. Stationed in Texas, Elvis was then assigned to the Second Armored Division's "Hell on Wheels" unit.

"Hair today, gone tomorrow."

- Elvis coins the phrase, in a quote to the media following his drafting

Elvis whilst stationed in Germany in 1958

Elvis Presley stands in line with other enlisted men and officers on a military base, Germany

Elvis in Fort Chaffee, AZ, at the beginning of his military service, 1958

Elvis' reporting for duty was, now like the rest of his life, as far from ordinary as you could get. It was like a media 'circus', with hundreds of reporters and photographers circling him as he arrived. Some photographers even accompanied him to the base, where he was sworn in.

In opposition to the amusing comment on his hair, Elvis also appeared to have a desire to be taken seriously and declared, "The Army can do anything it wants with me." He did not wish to be treated specially or any differently from other soldiers.

However, Presley was different. And even while he was stationed in Texas for training, he had a visit from a businessman called Eddie Fadal, who he had met on tour. According to Fadal, he was so concerned with keeping his career alive during his army service that during a two-week leave in early June, Elvis cut five sides in Nashville.

While Elvis was in training, his mother was diagnosed with hepatitis and Elvis was approved emergency leave to visit her on August 12. Sadly, just two days later she passed away, aged 46, of heart failure.

He would later name her death the greatest tragedy of his life. At her funeral, Elvis said, "You know how much I lived my whole life just for you," which showed the impact his mother had on his life and how intensely close they were. Some say he never recovered from her passing.

Following his training in Texas, Elvis was assigned to the 3rd Armoured Division and was stationed in West Germany.

The Army also had a big impact on his life, some of which would be very positive and some of which was less so. He made friends in the Army and took it seriously, which was reinforced by soldiers' accounts who said he was generous and determined to be considered a good solider, just like a normal man. He donated his Army pay to charities and bought televisions for the base. He studied and practiced karate from his training.

Whether the timing of his mother's death prompted or influenced some of his choices during this period is unknown, but seems likely. Elvis was introduced to amphetamines while on duty, by a sergeant. The affect the drugs had on his energy, strength and weight loss impressed him, and he encouraged others to try them too. Unfortunately, this introduction would have grave consequences on his health and lifestyle later in his life.

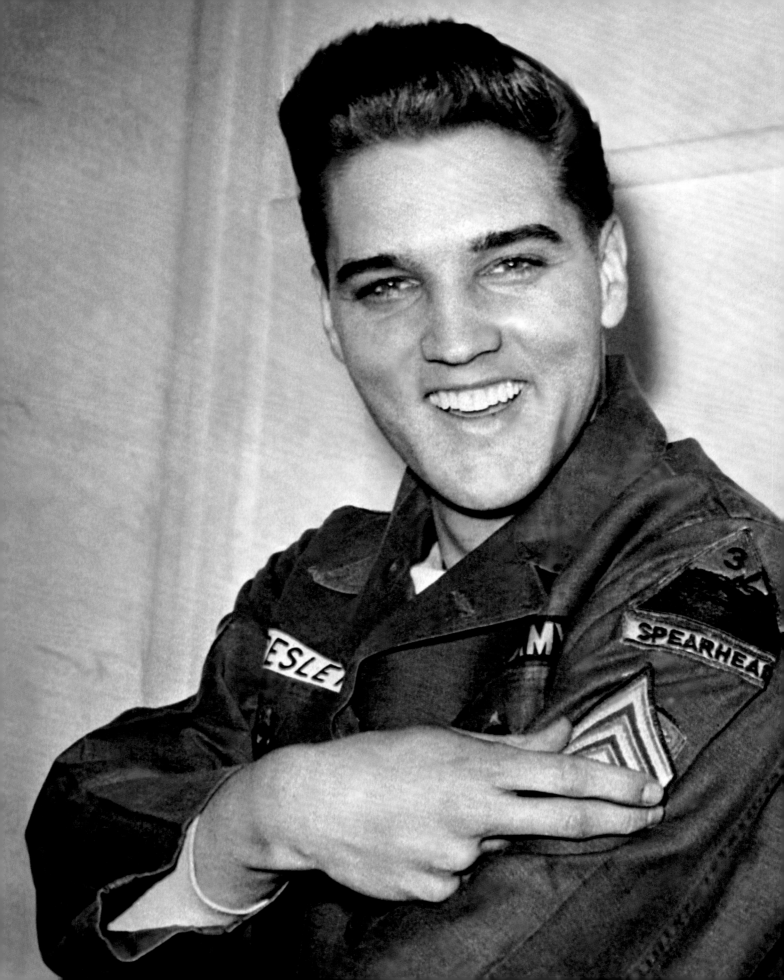

Around six months later, Elvis was promoted to sergeant. He was discharged that March.

While Elvis had concerns for his career during his army tenure, he was well protected by Parker's plans and management while he was on duty. Some reported that Parker even encouraged Elvis to serve to gain respect, and that this would also be best as a soldier rather than in serving the Special Services. It was rumoured Elvis was offered the Air Force, where he would have been able to perform and keep in touch with the general public. Parker was clever, though, he continued to release singles while Elvis was away, even securing a total number of ten hits in his absence. They included two Number One singles:

- **Wear My Ring Around Your Neck (Number Two, 1958)**

- **Don'tcha Think It's Time (Number 15, 1958)**

- **Hard Headed Woman (Number One, 1958)**

- **Don't Ask Me Why (Number 25, 1958)**

- **One Night (Number Four, 1958)**

- **I Got Stung (Number Eight, 1958)**

- **(Now and Then There's) A Fool Such as I (Number Two, 1959)**

- **I Need Your Love Tonight (Number Four, 1959)**

- **A Big Hunk o' Love (Number One, 1959)**

- **My Wish Came True (Number 12, 1959)**

Incredibly, especially for the time, while serving in the Army, in just one year – 1958 - Presley earned $2 million.

In addition to the support and clever planning of Parker, RCA producer Steve Sholes also prepared for his Army absence by releasing a steady stream of new, unheard materials. They also compiled four albums over the two-year period and packaged it Elvis' Golden Records, climbing to Number Three on the LP chart.

Left to right; Colonel Tom Parker, Eddy Arnold and Steve Sholes at the RCA Recording studios for his last recording session for two years, on March 10, 1958

Elvis Presley shows his sergeant insignia on February 14, 1960 in Friedberg, Germany

Private Presley

Elvis as lover and friend, husband and father – from accounts of his only wife Priscilla, the women he romanced, close friends and family

Much has been said of Elvis Presley's love life. The media and public fascination with his sex appeal and attractiveness made it inevitable. Much of it, however, is yet to be substantiated.

While Elvis was on the road to becoming a star, he had a relationship with June Juanico, and it was said of her that she was the only woman Elvis' mother really approved of. Whether or not this is true is unknown. Juanico wrote a book about Elvis, titled Elvis in the Twilight of Memory and in it she claimed they did not consummate their relationship, mainly because she was scared of falling pregnant. She also claimed that his manager Parker encouraged Elvis to date and be seen with beautiful women, for publicity.

Of the women who dated Elvis, some have said he enjoyed an active love life, while others claim he would not pursue sex with them. Anne Helm, an actress Elvis dated, said he "really liked sex. And it was special."

This differs from his relationships with actress June Wilkinson, who he met on the set of King Creole, saying, "He invited me to dinner at the Beverly Wilshire Hotel... Then Elvis gave me a tour of his suite, sat me on the bed in his bedroom and sang to me for two hours. That was it. The next day... we had dinner again. He was very sweet, and he was friendly. He had more than sex on his mind. He got me to the airport on time, and our paths never crossed again."

It was during Elvis' military service that he met Priscilla Beaulieu, a pretty 14-year-old brunette.

After a seven-and-a-half-year courtship, they married in Las Vegas May 1, 1967.

Fifteen-year-old Priscilla stands amid a group of fans as she says goodbye to her boyfriend, Elvis Presley

Elvis dating a young woman in 1956, before he met Priscilla

Priscilla Beaulieu was born Priscilla Ann Wagner in Brooklyn, New York in 1945. After her father, a pilot, was killed in a plane crash when she was a child, her mother and Paul Beaulieu raised Pricilla. Captain Beaulieu was a United States Air Force Officer, who married her mother and raised Priscilla as his own.

The Beaulieus were stationed in West Germany at the same time as Elvis in his army duty. While in Germany as a regular 14-year-old, Priscilla would "hang out" at the Eagles Club, listening to the jukebox, just like any other teenager. One day, a man named Currie Grant who claimed to be friends with Elvis approached her. He offered her the chance to meet him.

In a television interview with Larry King many years after Elvis' death, at Graceland, Priscilla said of meeting Elvis:

"I met him when I was 14. I was in Germany and he was stationed in Germany. And I was invited to go visit with him. I was actually, I was at the Eagles Club, which was a place that military families had gone to, you know, eat lunch, you know, have entertainment. And I was writing home letters to all my friends, missing them very much. And there was a guy and his wife that were there. And he introduced himself and asked me, you know, what I was doing there, how long I had been there.

"I had just -- oh, my goodness, it was only three weeks that I -- I had just gotten there. He asked me if I wanted to visit Elvis and did I like him. And I said yes. And I'm saying this very quickly to get it over with. I said I have to, you know, ask my parents, never, ever thinking that, you know, I would meet him."

Elvis and Priscilla in the early 1960s

In September of 1959, she joined Grant and his wife at Elvis' house.

In Priscilla Presley's interview with Sandra Shevey of Ladies Home Journal in August 1973, not long after their divorce, Priscilla Presley talked about her romance, marriage, and divorce with Elvis.

She said of their first meeting, "It was a very casual evening - a family atmosphere. Elvis was sitting in a chair when I arrived and he got up and shook my hand. Then reality hit me, and I thought, 'What am I doing here?' Priscilla recalls that her parents were waiting up when she got home. 'They asked me how it was, and I told them exactly what had happened: that Elvis was very nice and warm and cordial, but that I never thought I'd see him again. Then he called."

"At first, my parents said that I shouldn't date Elvis, that I was too young, which was true. My mother felt that it was an once-in-a-lifetime opportunity; and besides, it was not harming me. Finally she prevailed upon Dad to consent. But he set up a 12 o'clock curfew'. 'Each date with Elvis was the same. Usually he'd have his father pick me up in a car. Elvis' mother [Gladys Presley] had died in 1958. In Germany, Vernon was dating a pretty blonde named Devanda 'Dee' Elliot. Sometimes they would join us and some friends for a movie or something'.

"I was never impressed with dating Elvis. Perhaps I thought that it was all a dream. Or maybe it was because Elvis was very down to earth. He made me comfortable."

Priscilla wore a navy sailor dress with patent shoes. She said of her behaviour at this time, "I was so nervous, I really didn't know what to say. I was quite shy".

Apparently Elvis said of her "Oh! A baby! You're just a kid" which was understandable considering he was ten years older at 24 years of age.

Priscilla, now sixteen, waits with others to greet Elvis at the end of his army tour of duty

Elvis Presley is greeted with a gift from Nancy Sinatra upon his arrival from Europe

In unauthorised biographies, some authors claimed Elvis preferred much younger women as a way of keeping young himself.

By her account, he seemed to be trying to impress her by playing her songs. Even though she was hugely excited about meeting him, she did not tell any of her classmates at school for fear they'd think she was making it up.

Though conscious of her age, Elvis wanted to see her again. They spent the following six months seeing each other. Priscilla described Elvis as gentle, fun, vulnerable and insecure. She also said "He was a father to me. He was my mentor."

Only a couple of months before her 15th birthday, Elvis was discharged from the army and moved back to the US. It was rumoured that he was dating Nancy Sinatra within days of his return.

Three weeks later, Elvis telephoned and told her she was the only one. From her autobiography Elvis and Me, over the following two years Priscilla would become used to rumours and his denying them. Hurtfully to Priscilla, he made little of their relationship at a press conference back in the States, and he began dating Anita Wood along with other actresses.

From Priscilla's account, Elvis would discuss everything with her, including his relationship with Anita Wood. Patiently waiting on the sidelines for her King for two years, she frequently questioned her role in his life but never complained.

Out of the blue, in March 1962, Elvis called Priscilla and asked her to visit in Los Angeles. Aware that her father would object, she gave Elvis the responsibility of convincing him. Elvis ended up agreeing to a list of her father's rules, including waiting until she was on summer vacation, that he buy her a first-class round trip airfare, to send a detailed itinerary of her activities in LA and that she be chaperoned, write to her parents daily and stay with his friends, the couple George and Shirley Barris.

Cleverly, and somewhat sneakily, Priscillla wrote the daily letters in advance of her trip and had Elvis' butler post them on her behalf.

Further deception took place when they shared a suite at the Sahara Hotel and Casino. Elvis took Priscilla shopping, and advised her what to wear, how to do her make up and even how to style her hair. Priscilla claimed he was very instructional on her appearance, telling her that he liked women with heavy make up.

"I was definitely under a spell of what I thought was love," Priscilla said of his controlling her appearance.

She also recalled that prescription drugs were a part of his everyday life, something she saw the first time she visited him in LA. Innocently, she did not think anything of them as they were prescribed and, even later in his life, did not think he had a problem or an addiction.

He would take sleeping pills in increasing doses over the years, and then would require prescription drugs such as Dexedrine to wake up.

She returned to visit Elvis at Graceland for Christmas, and again needed to persuade her parents to allow her to travel to him. At the end of that trip, Elvis attempted to persuade her father to allow Priscilla to finish school in Memphis. He offered the finest Catholic school and his promise she would graduate. He also promised she would be chaperoned, and would live with his father, Vernon and his new wife and not at Graceland.

Elvis Presley and his father
Vernon Presley, 1958

According to Anita Wood, Elvis was seeing both Priscilla and her at the same time. She claimed that in early 1962:

"I was coming down the backstairs into the kitchen, I heard Elvis say, 'I'm having the hardest time making up my mind between the two' ... I knew exactly what he was talking about. And I had a lot of pride ... so I just marched my little self right down the stairs ... And Elvis took me into the dining room and his dad was sitting at the table. And we sat down at the table and I said, 'I'm gonna make that decision for you, I heard what you said and I'm leaving.' And I remember that I started crying, it was a very difficult decision to make. I must say that was probably the most difficult decision that I've ever made in my life. I have to say that. After having dated someone like Elvis for five years, and as close as we were for this to end. And when I left, I knew there would be no going back ... I said, 'I'm leaving', and I called Andy, my brother, to come pick me up and we sat there and talked a little bit longer, but nobody could eat."

In October of 1962, Elvis got his way. While he was filming Fun in Acapulco in Hollywood, he hosted the Beaulieus and
charmed them with his hospitality. Captain Beaulieu and Vernon Presley had Priscilla enrolled in the all-girl Immaculate Conception Cathedral High School. Before long, Priscilla was living at Graceland, with Vernon driving her to school. She had pocket money and was soon driving herself when she got her driver's licence.

Graceland circa 1970

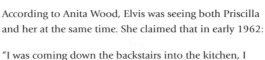

*Elvis Presley on the set
of 'Fun in Acapulco'*

Priscilla also said Elvis treated her with great care and respect, and did not take advantage of her saying, "We cannot compare it to today. We still had morals, high standards. There was a lot of care." She went on to claim, "Any sexual temptations were against everything he was striving for, and he did not wish to betray me, the girl waiting for him at home who was preparing to be his wife." In her autobiography, she explains they would kiss and "make out" but it never went further.

According to her account, Elvis told her that they had to wait until they were married before having intercourse. He said, "I'm not saying we can't do other things. It's just the actual encounter. I want to save it."

Some biographers have dismissed Priscilla's claims, suggesting they had a sexual relationship. But, according to Priscilla, while the couple slept in the same bed together over the six years they lived

together, he would not make love with her before marriage, "somewhere, he, along in his past, said that he wanted a virgin."

Priscilla said, "Fearful of not pleasing him—of destroying my image as his little girl—I resigned myself to the long wait. Instead of consummating our love in the usual way, he began teaching me other means of pleasing him. We had a strong connection, much of it sexual. The two of us created some exciting and wild times."

She even confessed in her autobiography that they took Polaroids of their fantasies and that they were quite playful with their sexual expression, although she stressed in an interview: "Nothing was harmful; nothing was done with bad intent. Nothing was done, you know that I don't think is unusual. They were just games."

Elvis Presley and Joan O'Brien play nurse and patient in 'It Happened At The World's Fair'

*Ann Margaret starred in
many films with Elvis*

*With Ursula Andress
in a still from the film,
'Fun in Acapulco'*

In addition to Elvis' parents confirming he had a temper, so too Priscilla described his jealousy and bad temper. In her book, she claimed he threatened to dismiss an employee who was too friendly to Priscilla. According to Priscilla, Elvis would throw a chair at her if she was not fond of something he sang; that he would shoot the television using his gun if the programme was not to his liking. She said, "He'd just blow them off the air; that simple. And the television would be replaced like that."

Yet, Elvis' own promiscuity conflicts with this value and expectation of her monogamy and faithfulness.

Priscilla discovered a packet of love letters from Wood in the attic at Graceland. Elvis apparently said he did not make love to Wood the whole four years he was with her. "Just to a point," he said, "then I stopped. It was difficult for her too, but that's just how I feel."

Priscilla also understood that Elvis had affairs with co-stars of his films, even while he was in love with Wood.

Even though Priscilla had the company of Elvis' family, the maids and secretaries, she reported being lonely when he was away.

While Elvis filmed Viva Las Vegas reports came in that Elvis and the female star, actress Ann Margret had started a relationship. Priscilla heard the rumours, which continued long after the movie production was finished. The chemistry between the two stars was obvious, both on and off-screen. During filming, she would try to telephone Elvis, and every time he would delay the call.

Priscilla was devastated. Because of the publicity surrounding the affair, Priscilla went to join Elvis in the following weeks while he filmed for his next movie. What followed was surprising – a jealous Ann-Margret announced to the press that she and Elvis were engaged. Unsurprisingly, the story went national.

Elvis ended up asking Priscilla to return to Memphis until the press coverage died down. Losing her temper at this, Priscilla threw a vase at the wall and Elvis starting packing her bags telling his father to book a plane back to Germany.

In the end, on his return to Graceland, he confessed to the affair and promised it was over.

Ann-Margret was the only co-star of Elvis' to attend his funeral. After his death, she wrote her memoirs and referred to Elvis as her soulmate.

Just before Christmas in 1966, Elvis went down on bended knee and proposed to Priscilla, with a three-and-a-half carat diamond ring, circled by 20 smaller detachable diamonds.

Elvis' manager, Parker, made the wedding arrangements while Elvis was off filming Clambake. A Supreme Court Justice presided over the nuptials, at the Aladdin Hotel in Las Vegas, in a small suite on the second floor.

Priscilla wore a white organza gown trimmed in pearls with lace sleeves and a full train. On her head, she wore a crown made of rhinestones and a three-quarter-length tulle veil. Elvis wore a black brocade suit. Fourteen guests attended the wedding, including Dee and Vernon and Priscilla's parents, the Beaulieus.

Ever the opportunist, Parker had booked a press conference immediately after the ceremony, and some of the press was even invited to the breakfast reception for 100 guests that followed.

With their honeymoon a mere few days long – in their Palm Springs, California home – Elvis carried his new bride across the threshold singing The Hawaiian Wedding Song, then carried her straight to the bedroom. The newlyweds then returned to Memphis to host a reception in Graceland for family, friends and staff. Apparently even a few lucky fans were in attendance.

Priscilla and Elvis went to their ranch near Horn Lake, Mississippi for another few days of privacy. Just as fast as the wedding itself, it was only two months later that Elvis announced on set at his latest film Speedway that Priscilla was pregnant.

Elvis Presley And Priscilla Beaulieu
At Their Wedding, 1967

73

Not having been married long before her falling pregnant, Priscilla said she considered an abortion. Not because they did not want children, but because of the timing and her fear that he may find her unattractive. In her book, she said Elvis had remarked on "women using pregnancy as an excuse to let themselves go."

Priscilla controlled her weight while pregnant, dieting to the extent that she weighed less at full term than prior to the pregnancy. She reported the couple had an active love life during her pregnancy. And then the rumours came about Elvis and his co-star of the film Speedway, Nancy Sinatra.

Elvis reassured her that the rumours were untrue, saying she must have been sensitive because of her pregnancy. While six months pregnant, Priscilla received a telephone call out of the blue from Nancy Sinatra, who was Frank Sinatra's daughter, offering to throw her a baby shower. Elvis convinced her to accept, even thought Priscilla found it peculiar coming from a woman she hardly knew. However, she and Sinatra got along well.

Shortly after the baby shower, Elvis asked Priscilla for a separation, saying he was confused. Days later, he changed his mind.

On February 1, 1968, their only child, Lisa Marie, was born.

In an interview with Sidney Fields, Elvis' parents talked about his nature, how he'd been brought up and his values.

"He's never sassed us, and he's never been uppity. Big people are still the same as little people to him, and he's considerate of both the same way. We're country folk. He's a country boy, and always will be. How can any boy brought up like mine be indecent or vulgar? Especially when he's so good to us and his friends. Why, he always wants to do what's right," said his mother.

Elvis and Priscilla proudly show their newborn baby, 4 day old Lisa Marie

His father continued, "He never touch a drop of liquor in his life, and he wouldn't know dope if he saw it.

"He's a sympathetic boy, and tender-hearted. It hurts him when someone thinks bad of him. Maybe this will tell you what he's like. He was usherin' at the movies this time, and on his night off he was downtown with his friends and he sees this Salvation Army lady takin' up the Christmas collection. But the box was empty. Elvis put his last $5 bill in it, and started drummin' up a noise to get that box filled. It was filled."

His own values and upbringing would have an impact on how he wanted to behave as a husband and father. By Priscilla's, and indeed, all accounts, Elvis was a doting father to his only daughter.

Priscilla said of his parenting, "He adored having a child. He adored Lisa. He just loved watching her grow up. He was a very caring father."

Elvis was generous to fault with his daughter, he rarely disciplined her and allowed her almost anything she wanted.

Priscilla, on talking with Larry King about jewellery she bought Elvis, said of his generosity:

"The pendant is a gift that I gave him, actually, in 1967, I believe. It was from our favourite jeweller at the time, Harry Levitch. It's a calendar in the back marking his birthday with a ruby and diamonds on the side. You know, Elvis did like a lot of flash.
He loved jewellery and he liked getting jewelry. He was more of a giver, though. He loved giving gifts more than he did receiving gifts."

Despite these extravagances, Elvis also liked regular things, such as watching old movies. His favourites included It's a Wonderful Life and Wuthering Heights.

The family at home

Elvis doted on Lisa Marie

The year of Lisa Marie's birth was also the year of Elvis' return to the limelight. From 1967 to mid-1968, his singles climbed no further up the charts than number 28. To a rock star accustomed to regular Number One hits, this was devastating. To overcome this, his manager Parker began to focus again on Elvis' television appearances to raise his profile and popularity, organising a Christmas special that aired in December of 1968.

It became known as the '68 Comeback Special and viewers tuned in to watch in record numbers. He had found renewed fame and success, which was positive for the marriage, but also meant regular touring and time away from his young family.

After the success of his Comeback, Elvis again filmed away from his family, for an MGM production titled Elvis on Tour. It went on to win a Golden Globe for Best Documentary Film. While his success returned, and with it his career fulfillment and happiness, Elvis' family life was becoming just the opposite.

In 1971, Elvis had an affair with Joyce Bova, who had become pregnant and aborted the baby. He was unaware of this at the time, but it signalled his lack of discretion and care for his immediate family and reputation. In addition to the absences from home, Priscilla thought Elvis was no longer interested in her sexually, that he could not see her the same way after she became a mother.

She grew lonelier. Elvis was taking pills to fall asleep and Priscilla found more letters from girls in their Palm Springs home. After Elvis asked her not join him on tour as much, her paranoia and sadness about his promiscuity worsened. She also had two affairs of her own, and just four years later their marriage was over. Priscilla claimed that after her confession to an affair with Mike Stone, her karate instructor, Elvis forced himself on her and said, "This is how a real man makes love to a woman."

Tom Jones poses with Elvis Presley and his wife Priscilla, Las Vegas, Nevada, 1st July 1971

Priscilla Presley poses for a portrait holding her little poodle circa 1965

Elvis Presley and his wife Priscilla leave the courthouse hand in hand following a short divorce hearing on October 9, 1973

They separated. In just five months time, Elvis had moved his new girlfriend, songwriter and ex-beauty queen Linda Thompson, into Graceland. Thompson was reportedly a virgin and she said their did not consummate their relationship until they had dated for a few months. Thompson was a fan of gospel music and shared Elvis' curiosity for spiritual and religious enlightenment.

It was claimed that their earlier passionate relationship eventually became depressing and dispassionate. Thompson said of Elvis, "There were times when he was very, very, difficult. There was a lot of heartache and he exhibited a lot of self-destructive behaviour, which was very difficult for me, you know, watching someone I loved so much destroy himself."

Elvis and Priscilla filed for divorce in August of that same year. When the couple divorced, Priscilla recalled "The judge couldn't believe it." They remained very close even after their divorce.

According to Elvis' friends, however, he was not happy about the divorce and worried about his age and his career. According to many, Elvis never got over the failed marriage.

Sadly, before his death, Priscilla joked with Elvis that maybe it might be their time again, together. Elvis joked, "I'm seventy and you're sixty. We'll both be so old, we'll look really silly, racing around in golf carts."

"Elvis epitomised charm, charisma. But I think his laughter. Elvis had the most contagious laughter. He just -- once he started laughing, that was it. Everyone would start laughing. And sometimes it was uncontrollable. He couldn't stop. And he laughed over the silliest things, you know? He just -- he just had a great sense of humour. He loved to have fun. He loved to play games."

- Priscilla Presley, on what she missed most about Elvis after he died

The King Is Back

On return from military service, Elvis was keen to regain his career status as The King

When Elvis returned to television after his Army service, it was only a short two months later and it would be for an unheard-of amount of money. Parker had booked Elvis for just eight minutes of singing time, for $125,000. Titled the Welcome Home Elvis episode for a television programme hosted by Frank Sinatra, who must have overcome his disdain for rock 'n' roll.

Elvis was also desperate to regain his status at the top of the charts. The pressure to deliver was massive and

he was already being asked what his immediate plans were now he was a regular citizen again. It was two years since he had been in a recording studio and at the press conference on his return, he seemed not to know what the process would be, "As far as when I'll record, I really don't know," he said. "Probably this week or next week. And what I'll record, I don't know yet. I've got quite a few songs to choose from, I've collected over two years. I don't know exactly what type or what instruments I'll use… I really don't know yet."

"Well, the first thing I have to do is to cut some records."

– Elvis at Press Conference at Graceland, March 7, 1960

*Elvis at a press conference following his
return from the army*

But Parker and RCA knew exactly what was planned for the session in two weeks time. One session in Nashville, then a break while Elvis filmed the Sinatra television special, then back in the studio to records new material.

Parker allegedly brought Are You Lonesome Tonight? Into the studio to be recorded, at the request of his wife for Elvis to record it, being one of her favourites.

RCA had organised an A-list group of musicians to record with Elvis for his return, including Hank Garland on guitar, Bob Moore on bass, Buddy Harman on drums, Floyd Cramer on piano, Boots Randolph on saxophone, and the Jordanaires on vocals. Elvis insisted his old band members Scotty Moore and D.J. also be included. Using new technology, as Ernest Jorgensen explained in his book on Presley's recording sessions, "This would be the first time Elvis was recorded on a three-track machine, giving more space to each player (as well as a separate track for Elvis's voice) and making real stereo records possible. For a group of sophisticated players like this, three-track was a distinct advantage: The music they made could be reproduced in finer detail."

The first session was an 11-hour recording, the second one almost 12-hours long. According to engineer Bill Porter, there was serious tension in the control booth where the RCA management team watched on. They needn't have been concerned.

As the biographer Peter Guralnick declared, "There was nothing on the session that could not be said to be of a very high standard." Some declare it his best artistic and commercial work in his career. There were 18 songs in total, being:

• **Make Me Know It**

• **Soldier Boy**

• **Stuck on You**

• **Fame and Fortune**

• **A Mess of Blues**

• **It Feels So Right**

• **Fever**

• **Like a Baby**

• **It's Now or Never**

• **The Girl of My Best Friend**

• **Dirty, Dirty Feeling**

• **Thrill of Your Love**

• **I Gotta Know**

• **Such a Night**

• **Are You Lonesome Tonight?**

• **The Girl Next Door Went A'Walking**

• **I Will Be Home Again**

• **Reconsider Baby**

Jorgensen said, "Elvis had never been heard like this before… There was new depth to his voice; his interpretations were increasingly sophisticated; the group was probably the best studio band in the business; the song selection was imaginative and varied, the technical quality excellent…

Floyd Cramer was drafted in on keys

Boots Randolph, a new recruit to Elvis' band

Elvis gets back into the studio

Elvis and Frank Sinatra pose with a fan

"Most surprisingly of all, the new album pointed in no one musical direction... It was as if Elvis had invented his own brand of music, broken down the barriers of genre and prejudice to express everything he heard in all the kinds of music he loved.

"As a document of Elvis's first comeback, Elvis Is Back was irresistible."

Stuck on You had four weeks at Number One on Billboard's "Hot 100" pop chart. Then It's Now or Never spent five weeks at Number One, and Are You Lonesome Tonight? followed with six more weeks at Number One. The album itself was his first to be released in true stereo, and it reached Number Two on the charts. The RIAA labelled it a Gold Album in 1999.

The RCA executives and Parker were pleased. Elvis' fans were still buying his records and when the previously critical (of rock 'n' roll) Frank Sinatra said, "Presley has no training at all. He has a natural, animalistic talent. When he goes into something serious, a bigger kind of singing, we'll find out if he is a singer," Elvis looked set to prove he was.

Inspired by Elvis' admiration for Tony Martin's There's No Tomorrow, the single It's Now or Never was quite different to Elvis' sound before. The same could be said of Are You Lonesome Tonight. The diversity of singles featured on the album, along with the diversity of his vocals, would cause some critics to rethink their prior judgements of Elvis.

For example, It Feels So Right was rock 'n' roll rebellion, and The Thrill of Your Love was gospel-inspired. The album also covered blues, and had Elvis on rhythm guitar throughout the tracks.

With superb warmth and depth, this stereo album sounded great and looked great. It featured full colour photographs of Elvis, taken just before he was discharged from the Army.

More critically acclaimed than any of his other albums recorded across his career, it continues to be praised and was awarded four-and-a-half stars by Rolling Stone Magazine in 2011, saying "Elvis is Back! Might be the

King's greatest non-compilation LP: wildly varied material, revelatory singing, impeccable stereo sound'.

Many have commented on his return and surmised that while he was on duty with the Army, Elvis must have worked hard on his voice range and quality, building its strength and power for his return. Of the tape cut and left off the released album, it was said the rejected recordings were not too removed from the quality of those included. With a high quality band and Elvis' more mature, rich vocals, these unreleased edits could easily have been used.

Elvis Presley plays drums in a moment off camera while filming the movie 'Flaming Star', 1960

Elvis was self-critical and apparently apologised before taping Fever, saying, "If I hit a few bad notes here because I can't my bearings right, you know, but uh, we got plenty of tape."

Both the artist and the band were keen to reach near perfection. In some takes, there would be adjustments to musical arrangement or tempo in order to reach the pinnacle of musical excellence. With a full, long day in the studio for both recordings, there was no doubt Elvis and his band worked exceptionally hard to deliver the commercial success and critically acclaimed quality of Elvis is Back.

Following his success with the album release and his television debut, there was last medium Elvis needed to conquer on his return from service: cinema.

Slated by the critics, his first film on return from the Army, GI Blues was fluffy and unimaginative, like many of his movies. However, Elvis' soundtrack to his first film on his return from service, GI Blues, went to Number One in October and the film itself did well at the box office. Elvis' movie career was a disappointment to him in many ways, despite the commercial success.

Elvis in costume for G.I. Blues

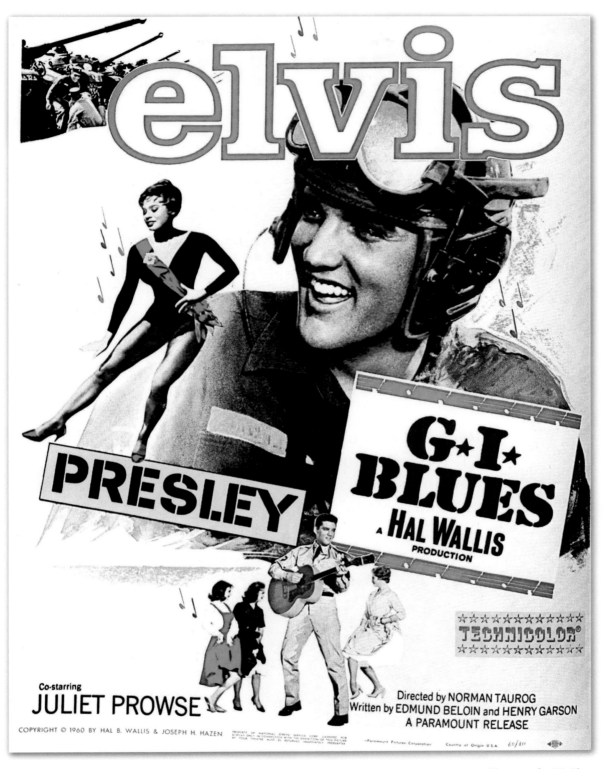

Film poster for G.I. Blues

The Music & The Moves

Famous for his lopsided grin, sideburns, greased hair and husky voice, Elvis added to his appeal with some seriously outrageous moves for his time.

"Some people tap their feet, some people snap their fingers, and some people sway back and forth. I just sorta do 'em all together, I guess."

-Elvis Presley in 1956

His moves began to find their exaggerated form around the time he hit the big time in 1957, and became a key part of his act through the 60s. And the mere presence of The King, let alone his famous pelvic moves, sent the audiences into a tizz. Elvis' long-time support band member Moore remembered the live performances around this time:

"He'd start out, 'You ain't nothin' but a Hound Dog,' and they'd just go to pieces. They'd always react the same way. There'd be a riot every time."

"Rock and roll music – if you like it, if you feel it, you can't help but move to it. That's what happens to me. I can't help it."

– Elvis Presley

Signing autographs for adoring fans

In fact, even at this early point in his national popularity, there were security concerns surrounding his performances. fifty national guardsmen were stationed at the concerts he performed for at the Mississippi-Alabama Fair and Dairy Show. What followed was chaos. A performance in Wisconsin prompted the local Catholic diocese to write to the director of the FBI, J Edgar Hoover, advising him,

"Presley is a definite danger to the security of the United States... [His] actions and motions were such as to rouse the sexual passions of teenaged youth... After the show, more than 1,000 teenagers tried to gang into Presley's room at the auditorium... Indications of the harm Presley did just in La Crosse were the two high school girls... whose abdomen and thigh had Presley's autograph."

His television performances seemed to worsen the visibility and controversy of his moves. It was Milton Berle who first encouraged Elvis to go on without his guitar and Elvis obliged with a raunchy, slow version of Hound Dog and matched it with raunchy, slow grinding movements of his hips.

The audience rush the stage at the Mississippi Dairy Show

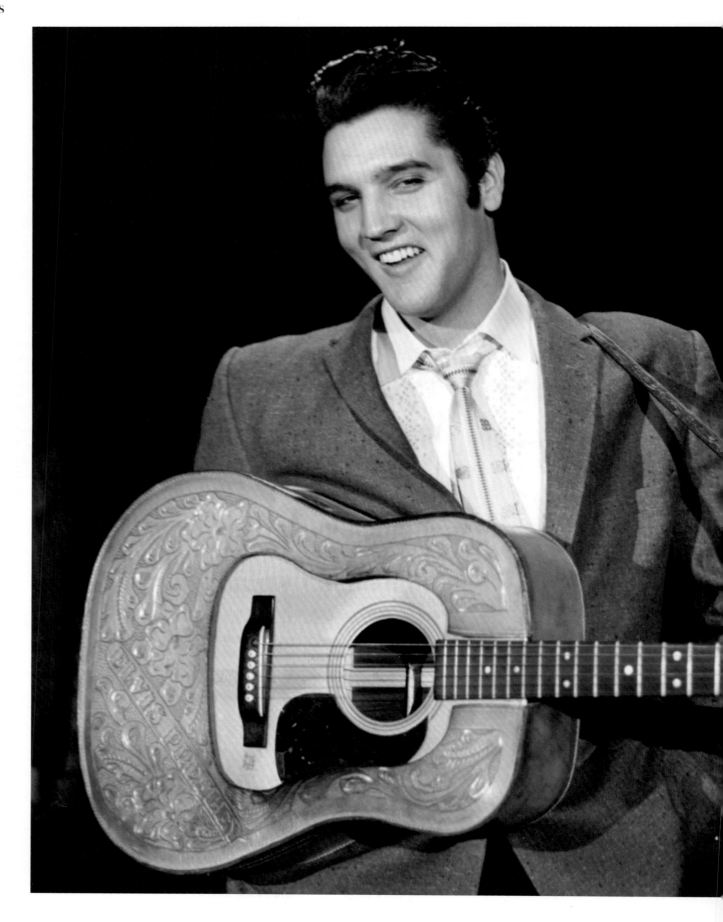

Critics berated him with dismissive comments regarding his voice and focused on his hip swivelling, with reviews such as Ben Gross' of the New York Daily News "... Elvis, who rotates his pelvis... gave an exhibition that was suggestive and vulgar, tinged with the kind of animalism that should be confined to dives and bordellos".

Even Ed Sullivan, prior to inviting him to this show with that record-breaking amount, apparently informed his producers, on reviewing the Berle show tapes, that Elvis' moves were inappropriate for Sunday viewing for families.

But Elvis' least favourite was the term "Elvis the Pelvis", spurring him on to say that it was a childish comment to come from a grown man.

The controversy surrounding his moves and his live act continued. In August of 1957, Elvis was ordered by a judge from Jacksonville, Florida to tame his movements.

From accounts of the performance that followed, Elvis kept his body still, and teased both the audience and the order by wiggling his little finger suggestively.

"The first time that I appeared on stage, it scared me to death. I really didn't know what all the yelling was about. I didn't realize that my body was moving. It's a natural thing to me. So to the manager backstage I said, 'What'd I do? What'd I do?' And he said "Whatever it is, go back and do it again."

-From a 1972 taped interview used in MGM's documentary Elvis on Tour

Elvis grabs the microphone during a performance, 1955

"I'm not trying to be sexy. It's just my way of expressing myself when I move around."

– Elvis Presley

Elvis' second appearance on The Ed Sullivan Show

Elvis continued to tour during the year of '57, to riots, crazed fans, fainting and crying girls.

In Vancouver, the crowd destroyed the stage at the end of the act and a riot broke out. In Philadelphia, he was pelted with eggs. In Detroit, the local newspaper warned "the trouble with going to see Elvis Presley is that you're liable to get killed."

Later, in the words of his obituary for Elvis, Lester Bangs credited him as "the man who brought overt blatant vulgar sexual frenzy to the popular arts in America."

His physical and sexual appeal was undeniable. That his moves promoted this is also undeniable. But his now grown-into, handsome, dark good looks were on their own striking. Even the male critics of his time were expressive of the fact. Mark Feeney said, "He was once beautiful, astonishingly beautiful".

Television director Steve Binder, said, "I'm straight as an arrow and I got to tell you, you stop, whether you're male or female, to look at him. He was that good looking. And if you never knew he was a superstar, it wouldn't make any difference; if he'd walked in the room, you'd know somebody special was in your presence."

Backstage at the Milton Berle show

*Elvis Presley (left) and Liberace exchange
personal trademarks while standing together.*

Possessed with this natural sex appeal and blatantly
employing raunchy pelvic movements on his live
performances, Elvis captured the eye and the imagination
of women and men, teenagers and critics across the
world. But his sound, voice and musical genre were just
as appealing and intriguing.

For many music fans, even today, Elvis Presley introduced
them to rhythm and blues. The link from his blues roots
to his pioneering rock 'n' roll is obvious when listening
to many of his songs. Starting with his first recording of
That's All Right, Elvis' sound was the white man singing
the blues. Elvis often altered the song lyrics of rhythm
and blues numbers he covered, to make room for his fast
tempo'd Rockabilly style.

Elvis' musical roots in country, gospel and rhythm
and blues were obvious. but he always returned to
gospel, inspired by its uplifting and moving style.
His attendances at the All Night Singings at the Ellis
Auditorium in Memphis would give him style influence
for his sound – as well as his moves.

*Another seductive pose to
promote his upcoming films*

Acts like the Statesmen Quartet featured highly emotional vocals. Ironically, it was at church and at these gospel nights that Elvis first witnessed the power of the jiggle, where the leader of the Quartet employed a sprinkling of leg jiggling.

His musical influences continued to be wide-ranging, and like any music fan, he had a comprehensive knowledge of his favourite genres. Leiber and Stoller reported how impressed they were by his understanding of the blues. And equally, his knowledge of gospel was impressive. Even Elvis himself announced to the press: "I know practically every religious song that's ever been written."

In late 1957, Elvis dropped by Sun Records studios. Phillips was no longer Elvis' sponsor or manager. That day he captured a recording of an impromptu session. Elvis was jamming with Carl Perkins and Jerry Lee Lewis, which resulted in the Million Dollar Quartet (although the fourth member of the recording, Johnny Cash, was only there briefly and reports were he did not record with the other three).

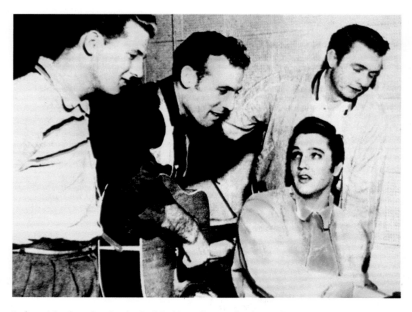

Left to right; Jerry Lee Lewis, Carl Perkins, Elvis Presley (sitting), Johnny Cash - The Million Dollar Quartet

Elvis Presley and Johnny Cash pose for a portrait in December of 1957

Elvis' sound grew from his love of gospel, fused with country and blues, into his own distinct sound heightened with a raw, emotive, rhythmic twist. Once he'd moved from Sun to RCA, he continued to grow his sound and his moves – blending electric guitar to further the rockabilly style with a tougher edge.

Interestingly, on his return from military service, Elvis pushed his sound into another realm, with what was then described as a more mild rock beat. This lighter sound flowed into the soundtracks of his post-Army filmography.

Considering his meteoric rise to success, it must have been important to Elvis to return to civilian life with musical and film success. Not even before a month out of his Army fatigues, Elvis went back to the recording studio to work on his first stereo album Stuck on You and had met up with Frank Sinatra to tape the television programme The Frank Sinatra-Timex Special. This was interesting, considering Sinatra had previously been highly vocal and critical of the rock 'n' roll genre.

Some accounts of Sinatra's criticism claim it was directly about Elvis, the following presented quite regularly in stories: "His kind of music is deplorable, a rancid smelling aphrodisiac. It fosters almost totally negative and destructive reactions in young people."

Elvis Presley plays a double-necked electric guitar, 1962

Whether this was actually said by Sinatra, of Elvis, is yet to be proved and it seems questionable.

The following, however, is a direct quote from an article in the Los Angeles Mirror News (October 28, 1957):

"My only deep sorrow is the unrelenting insistence of recording and motion picture companies upon purveying the most brutal, ugly, degenerate, vicious form of expression it has been my displeasure to hear—naturally I refer to the bulk of rock 'n' roll.

"It fosters almost totally negative and destructive reactions in young people. It smells phony and false. It is sung, played and written for the most part by cretinous goons and by means of its almost imbecilic reiterations and sly, lewd—in plain fact, dirty—lyrics, and as I said before, it manages to be the martial music of every sideburned delinquent on the face of the earth … this rancid-smelling aphrodisiac I deplore. But, in spite of it, the contribution of American music to the world could be said to have one of the healthiest effects of all our contributions."

Sinatra was not a fan of rock 'n' roll

That same day, Elvis was apparently asked his reaction to Sinatra's comments about rock 'n' roll. From reports in several LA newspapers the following day, there were various versions of his response presented. The one most attributed is from the Herald-Express, by Gerry McCarthy, who quoted Elvis as saying:

"He has a right to his opinion, but I can't see him knocking it for no good reason. I admire him as a performer and an actor but I think he's badly mistaken about this. If I remember correctly, he was also part of a trend. I don't see how he can call the youth of today immoral and delinquent. It's the greatest music ever and it will continue to be so. I like it, and I'm sure many other persons feel the same way."

This conversation is a fascinating insight into the debate that raged at the height of Elvis' success. Right from a young age, Elvis divided opinions: his peers, his teachers and talent scouts. Some found his looks, his style and his voice too different, too unusual. The majority, however, ended up determining him a cultural and musical icon, a revolutionary.

*Elvis and Frank Sinatra
joke together in 1965*

*Elvis recording with
the Jordanaires*

Ballads such as Are You Lonesome Tonight? also went to
Number One. It seemed that whatever musical journey
Elvis took his fans on, they loved. His later career also
went through various permutations, from the strong,
almost aggressive rock sound of his 1968 Comeback
Special, to his later soul and funk infused recordings of
the tracks on Suspicious Minds.

Elvis' last recordings in the 70s had a country sound and
were often played on local country radio stations, taking
him back to where he came from, musically and as a star.

In addition to Elvis' much-talked about musical style, his
voice has had a variety of reviews, commentary and has
been declared both a baritone and a tenor. His range was
brilliant, with some describing it as two octaves and a
third, others stating it was two and a quarter octaves. His
vocal capacity for high Gs and As is similar to those an
operatic baritone would possess.

Much has been written of his vocal style, in an emotional sense (surely steeped in his gospel musical upbringing). Lindsay Waters, music scholar, states: "His voice had an emotional range from tender whispers to sighs down to shouts, grunts, grumbles and sheer gruffness that could move the listener from calmness and surrender, to fear. His voice can not be measured in octaves, but in decibels; even that misses the problem of how to measure delicate whispers that are hardly audible at all."

In this way, it is difficult to compare Elvis' style, voice and vocal ability or range to anyone else.

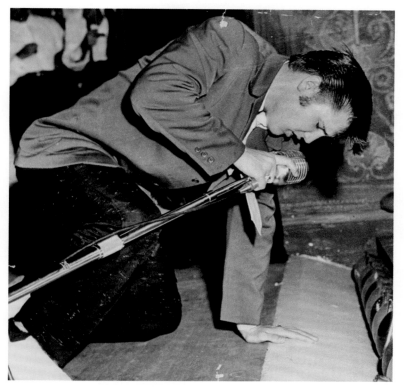

Elvis' distinctive vocal sound combined whispers, grunts and sighs

"A live concert to me is exciting because of all the electricity that is generated in the crowd and on stage. It's my favorite part of the business - live concerts."

– Elvis at a press conference prior to his 1973 television special, "Elvis - Aloha from Hawaii, via Satellite"

Hollywood & The Movies

Elvis was keen to be considered a genuine and talented actor. He looked up to James Dean and Marlon Brando and dreamed of being a movie star. Despite Elvis' natural success with music, he knew he would have to learn a lot and work hard to become an actor.

Starting out in film, Elvis said in an interview with the press, "I've talked to veteran actors. I've talked to a lot of producers and directors in Hollywood, and they all give you advice … they told me that I had good possibilities."

"I think I'm gonna enjoy it. I really do"

Elvis' phenomenal roll call of films is 33-long.

While many fans are aware of his work with Hollywood producer Hal Wallis, from Paramount Pictures, he actually only appeared in nine films out of 33 in total for Wallis. The majority of his films were for for Metro-Goldwyn-Mayer.

Beginning with 1957's Jailhouse Rock the last 1969 film, The Trouble with Girls in 1969, Elvis starred in 12 films for MGM. The studio also produced Presley's documentary films in the 1970s.

His first few films are generally viewed to be the better ones of his career, perhaps because he was involved in choosing the options.

Elvis' very first film was a nerve-wracking experience for the team of filmmakers and, presumably, for Elvis himself. Indeed, the transference of singer and rock star to movie actor was and continues to be challenging. It was set for release in 1956 and those behind it were undecided as to whether Elvis would prove a success on the big screen. He had participated in three days of screen tests in March for Wallis at Paramount in Hollywood and it took a week for Wallis to offer a contract. The contract was signed in April, for one film and an option for six more.

Elvis relaxing on set circa 1960

"I have never read a line. I never studied acting, never been in any plays or anything—I just got out there."

– Elvis on acting, in an interview in 1956

Elvis alongside Judy Tyler in 'Jailhouse Rock'

Originally titled The Reno Brothers, at the time of signing, Elvis was still a rising star and had not received national attention – that all changed when he appeared on The Milton Berle and Steve Allen Shows that summer. With all the fuss and fan worship that soon followed, they included four songs and adapted it from a straight acting film into a musical re-titled Love Me Tender.

Interestingly, it has been reported that the final scene in the movie had two possible outcomes – for the main character played by Elvis to live or to come to a violent death as described in the original script. After much debate, including a vote between the 20th Century Fox board of directors, they reached a compromise with Elvis' character dying to save the life of his screen brother, followed by a shot of him walking up to Heaven singing the theme song.

Even more interestingly, the film house gave theatres the choice of two endings: the final edits being one version with his character appearing in a shadowed form as his family walk away from the grave and the second version ending on his death. The surveys that came back showed most theatres went for the softer version so as not to incite upset in filmgoers and fans of Elvis.

While much talk and reservation came with Elvis' launching a film career, he actually won over the film crew and his fellow cast. His co-star Richard Egan praised Elvis to the press, saying, "This guy is genuine. There's nothing phony about him and he works hard. He's not conceited. He IS self-assured, but that's fine with me. I'm all for him and all of us associated with him in the picture are rooting for him." (from an interview with Charles Gruenberg of The New York Post)

A publicity handout for 'Love Me Tender'

He went on to say to Sheilah Graham's Hollywood Today review, "Elvis is a surprising type of actor. He's the male Monroe. He's completely without guile. You give him lines and he says them the way he would in real life. And that's the best kind of acting—when you're not."

The film was launched and screened on Broadway at the Paramount Theater in New York on November 15, 1956.

Unsurprisingly, considering Parker's tendency to maximise Elvis' appearances when there was an offering to promote, he had booked the singer for a series of public appearances coinciding with the opening of the film.

The film opened at the Paramount in Toledo just a day before his stage show played the city's Sports Arena on Thanksgiving Day. As it turned out, both his show and the film did very well in ticket sales. Parker would later choose to starve audiences of Elvis in person whenever one of his films was released. It was in fact, why audiences continued to watch his films: to see The King on screen.

Following the key learnings from Elvis' film debut, Wallis understood that a Broadway premiere was not necessary – as long as the films were released where teenage fans lived, there would be great ticket sales.

He also knew the fans were there to see Elvis and to see him sing, not necessarily to watch him act. As long as Elvis was the star, on the promotional posters and in the full feature length of the film, the sales would continue to come in.

Presley dances in front of his band in a movie still from 1956

This formula was employed for Elvis' next movie, Loving You, where Elvis sang almost first thing in the film, only six minutes into the movie. Generally considered his best, the next three Elvis movies were more serious. According to reports, he had pushed for more serious roles in the early 60s, including Flaming Star and Wild in the Country. They did not do as well at the box office.

Playing a bad boy rock 'n' roll rebel in Jailhouse Rock, Elvis received positive critical feedback on his acting. It premiered in Memphis on October 17, 1957, and was released nationwide on November 8.

It continues to be a much loved film of his, and in 2004 the US National Film Registry selected it for preservation for being "culturally, historically, or aesthetically significant."

King Creole proved to be a rare example of how a serious acting role could be combined with Elvis singing on screen. However, even when it was obvious that such a combination wouldn't work in every film, Parker continued to pressure the studios to include music. In his fourth movie, Elvis gave the best performance of his film career, portraying an angry and confused young man.

"As the lad himself might say, cut my legs off and call me Shorty! Elvis Presley can act. It's a pleasure to find him up to a little more than Bourbon Street shoutin' and wigglin'. Acting is his assignment in this shrewdly upholstered showcase, and he does it, so help us over a picket fence."

- *Howard Thompson of the New York Times*

On return from military service, Parker had Elvis booked on a tight film schedule. The films were mostly predictable, small budget musicals. Each turned a profit.

Hope Lange And Elvis Presley In 'Wild In The Country'

Elvis Presley stands shirtless in a scene from the film 'Flaming Star', 1960

A Hollywood movie producer once said: "A Presley picture is the only sure thing in Hollywood." Another sure thing was high sales of the soundtracks. There was a formula for these too. Leiber said it was "three ballads, one medium-tempo [number], one up-tempo, and one break blues boogie". But with Elvis averaging three films a year, the timing was tight not only on filming, but on song writing and production.

The Jordanaires' Gordon Stoker said of the soundtracks, "The material was so bad that he felt like he couldn't sing it."

Again, regardless of critics' attacks on the music material, from 1960 to 1964, three of his soundtrack albums reached Number One.

Under the management of Parker, however, and certainly while Elvis was away on duty for the Army, he had less and less of a say in which roles were his. This meant the serious, more credible roles went by the wayside. Nevertheless, the films were always a success in ticket sales, if not in critic's reviews.

Parker had the ultimate control while Elvis served in the Army. He worked with the Hollywood studios to set up an approach, and 'Elvis formula' that would generate high ticket sales and repeat success.

Parker was a fantastic negotiator. He strategically bumped Elvis' salary up by playing the studios off one another and demand higher salaries for each new contract. A good example of this was the first movie Elvis was to star in after returning to civilian life. In place of the $25,000 Wallis paid for Elvis' 1956 contract, Parker negotiated an incredible increase of $150,00 on top for GI Blues. Plus, he negotiated a cut of the movie's profits.

Parker did not interfere, however, with the script, production or indeed any aspect of the film making process. He encouraged Elvis to do the same and accept orders.

Talking with a Fox executive for Elvis' first film, Parker said, "There's no sense in sending me the script. The only thing I'm interested in is how much you're gonna pay me."

"We don't have approval on scripts—only money. Anyway what's Elvis need? A couple of songs, a little story and some nice people with him. We start telling people what to do and they blame us if the picture doesn't go. As it is, we both take bows and if it doesn't hit maybe they get more blame than us. Anyway, what do I know about production?—nothing."

- Colonel Parker in an interview with Variety magazine

The only element Parker pushed for in Elvis' films was the music. He knew that the fans wanted to see Elvis sing and that would mean commercial success. One report of the 1960 film Flaming Star came back with the story of the director David Weisbart having stated, "I cannot see how it is possible for Elvis to break into song without destroying a very good script."

Allegedly, Parker responded "We want all the best possible results for this picture, including the hundreds of thousands of dollars worth of exploitation represented by a good record release by Elvis."

After testing with audiences, however, on this occasion the director won, with only the title tune and one other song appearing in Flaming Star.

"This isn't a very popular view, but Colonel's formula was correct. The serious stuff—the movies that didn't have many songs in them—flopped. That's a pretty good argument. On the other hand, by the time Elvis figured out he was being screwed around, it was too late. He signed too many contracts. If the Colonel handed him a contract, he'd sign it and never look at it … And when you've already been paid for the pictures, and you've already spent half the money, you've got to do them. All those pictures were presigned. So Elvis had no choice."

Lamar Fike, Elvis' friend and confidant

Elvis Presley In 'Flaming Star, 1960

The Colonel continued to release films whilst Elvis served in the Army

A musical comedy, his first after his return from the Army, GI Blues was slated by critics. It was, however, to become the template of Elvis' future movie formulas.

Made in 1960, it was lightweight and only finished 14th on Variety's list of the year's top grossing films. Just one month later, they released Flaming Star, a western drama largely considered his best acting of the three westerns he starred in. Star came in much lower in box office sales, a point attributed to the fact that the movie does not feature any Elvis songs. The audiences told the movie producers through these sales what they wanted to see: Elvis singing.

Elvis admitted as much in an interview with Parade magazine in 1962:

"I'm smart enough to realise that you can't bite off more than you can chew in this racket. You can't go beyond your limitations … A certain type of audience likes me. I entertain them with what I'm doing. I'd be a fool to tamper with that kind of success. It's ridiculous to take it on my own and say I'm going to appeal to a different type of audience, because I might not. Then if I goof, I'm all washed up, because they don't give you many chances in this business."

Elvis' seventh film was titled Wild in the Country, in which both his acting and script was criticised for being "sheer nonsense" by the New York Times reviewer Bosley Crowther.

Blue Hawaii, released with 14 songs and filmed with beautiful South Seas scenery, made up for the previous poor reception to Wild in the Country. The music and the comedic script gave it the winning formula to make it Elvis' most successful film of his career.

Elvis' last day serving in the Army

The soundtrack album to Blue Hawaii became the most successful LP of Elvis Presley's career. It went straight to the top of Billboard's album chart and stayed at the Number One position for an incredible 20 weeks.

The film led to sales of the soundtrack LP, and the album led to repeat ticket-buyers for the film. In the plot, Elvis plays a very likeable, energetic adult tour guide to a group of teenage girls. Famously, Angela Lansbury plays the funny girl role as Elvis' mother.

More light story lines followed with his films Follow That Dream, Kid Galahad, Girls! Girls! Girls!, It Happened at the World's Fair and Fun in Acapulco. The roles Elvis played in these films varied from prizefighter, fisherman and playboy pilot.

In Fun in Acapulco, Elvis sings 11 songs, and as his character is a lifeguard who travels to Mexico, he sang some Mexican songs. His serious rock 'n' roll days were left behind to make way for light, scenic musical numbers. Released in 1963, the film came out at a time when Elvis was beginning to feel unhappy with his career.

In 1964, MGM's Kissing Cousins began to negatively impact Elvis' perception – as the director Don Siegel said, Elvis was "kind of a joke in the industry as an actor". In this film he sings nine songs.

Parker being heavily involved in the money making aspect of Elvis' film career, was beginning to insist on tighter budgets and even tighter shooting schedules. Viva Las Vegas pulled in $4.67 million to finish at number 11, while Kissin' Cousins suffered a number 26 spot with $2.8 million.

For, despite Viva Las Vegas being one of 1964's top box office films, production costs ate up the predicted high profits of its release. Viva is one of the most exciting Elvis films to watch, mainly because of the chemistry between Elvis and Ann-Margret. It also featured great music and lots of it.

Stella Stevens and Elvis Presley on board and holding hands in a scene from the film 'Girls! Girls! Girls!'

The second half of the decade did not perform quite as well. Still, the gospel single Crying in the Chapel was a top ten hit and the gospel album How Great Thou Art was to win Elvis his very first Grammy Award for Best Sacred Performance.

After Elvis married, his career of films and accompanying soundtracks written and produced to the formula that sold tickets continued until the release of Clambake resulted in low sales. Audiences appeared to have had enough of the now tired Elvis formula.

His filmography that followed included Roustabout, Girl Happy, Tickle Me, Harum Scarum, Frankie and Johnny, Paradise Hawaiian Style, Spinout, Easy Come Easy Go, and Double Trouble.

Tickle Me was Elvis' first non-musical comedic role. In the majority of his other films, he chases girls, while playing a singing lead role, some more heroic than others.

Again, critics despised it, with The New York Times warning, "Elvis Presley had better watch his step after 'Tickle Me,' his latest color musical film. This is the silliest, feeblest and dullest vehicle for the Memphis Wonder in a long time. And both Elvis and his sponsors, this time Allied Artists, should know better.

"In such trim packages as 'Viva Las Vegas' and 'Fun in Acapulco,' the Presley formula—colorful settings, tunes and pretty girls aplenty—took on real, tasty sparkle. But yesterday's flapdoodle, even weaker than the preceding 'Girl Happy,' should strain the indulgence of the most ardent Presley fans. See for yourself, girls. It looks made up as it goes along."

Elvis Presley In 'Roustabout'

Clambake followed, with Elvis playing a wealthy young man pretending to be a normal ski instructor. It was his first film as a single man, following his divorce. His acting was the last thing on his mind, and many have said this was his worst performance of his movie career. He had put on weight and his audiences were starting to show disinterest in his appearances on the big screen in the same way he was.

His last six films were unremarkable. Stay Away Jose, Speedway, Live a Little Love a Little, Charro!, The Trouble with Girls, and Change of Habit saw gradual declines in ticket sales.

The next three films to feature Elvis were documentaries and would prove much more successful with audiences. Following his '68 Comeback Special, Elvis fascination had peaked again and the live and behind the scenes footage of The King doing what he did best, performing, would help strengthen his status as The King of Rock 'n' Roll once again. In 1970, Elvis' performance at the International Hotel in Las Vegas was scintillatingly captured in Elvis: That's the Way It Is and the 15-city concert tour of Elvis' in 1972 recorded in the hugely popular Elvis On Tour.

For many, That's the Way It Is was a revelation, and a revolution in documentary filmmaking. Indeed, if fans did not get to see him in Vegas, they could take it all in with this film. MGM kept the focus on Elvis, with the editing featuring slices of fan commentary appearing throughout. Aside from the fan edits, the film featured a simple three-part format, in chronological order.

Elvis Presley in the movie 'Speedway'

"The first 20 minutes of the film are devoted to studio rehearsals, cross cut with fast excerpts from personal interviews with fans. The rehearsal horseplay comes off very well. Then onto Vegas for about 26 minutes of pre-opening preparation by both Presley and the hotel staff. Finally, most of the remaining hour-plus comprises actual show numbers culled from several live performances."

- Variety magazine

The director, Denis Sanders, captured the essence of Elvis live, and punctuated the film with snippets featuring fans to highlight the phenomenon that was Elvis fever. This is also evident with the inclusion of a feature on an Elvis fan convention. Elvis, who was 35-years-old in this documentary, appears in good shape and powerful on stage.

This time, the New York Times review was kinder:

"The callow youth who gyrated to fame and wealth as a kind of national joke is now a handsome man, a bit jowlier, true. But the face has character. The personality is a bit more suave but stronger. The powerhouse drive that used to flail about wildly is shrewdly disciplined and siphoned until it explodes into his extraordinary sense of rhythm. Tired? Elvis? He's ferocious. Most impressively of all, he comes over as a genial, reasonably balanced guy… Years later, the Presley act has an actor and a good one."

The only criticism leveled at the documentary was the lack of behind the scenes Elvis, to show what kind of person he was. There are a handful of moments where the viewer catches a glimpse – when he is nervous about to go on stage for example. But there is no footage of Elvis' family, his wife and daughter, or his manager. It was a glimpse of Elvis' live persona more than the man off-stage.

Elvis backstage during his USA tour, 1970

The follow-up documentary Elvis on Tour was a more entertaining view of Elvis live, with the producers and directors Pierre Adidge and Robert Abel taking the viewer on a journey using panels, where footage was spliced on screen. It's in this documentary that the viewer can see Elvis in jumpsuits, and it signals the beginning of his final years.

"Bill Belew's wardrobe for Presley's on-stage concert appearances make the star resemble Captain Marvel, which isn't far off the mark considering what Presley has accomplished in an 18-year period of worldwide fame. The musicianship is updated of course, but the adroit insertion of some old Ed Sullivan guesting footage places the early days in complementing, not contrasting context."

- *Variety magazine*

This documentary was less successful with audiences, taking just $500,000 in 105 cities over the first weekend. The New York Times was even less supportive of the film, with reviewer Canby opining that the film was nowhere near an intimate portrayal of the star, "The camera never catches him in a truly candid moment. Close-ups do not reveal anything but, rather, they enshrine an ideal… while getting on and off airplanes, on and off buses, and in and out of limousines. Strip away the storybook myth and—lo—there is a storybook myth underneath; a nice, clean-cut, multi-millionaire pop idol who is, offstage, hard-working and friendly and something less than a riveting personality. The essential blandness of the offstage Elvis has the effect of diminishing the impact of what we see of the onstage performances."

Five years later, Elvis would be dead.

Elvis performs on stage in 1972 in a studded jumpsuit

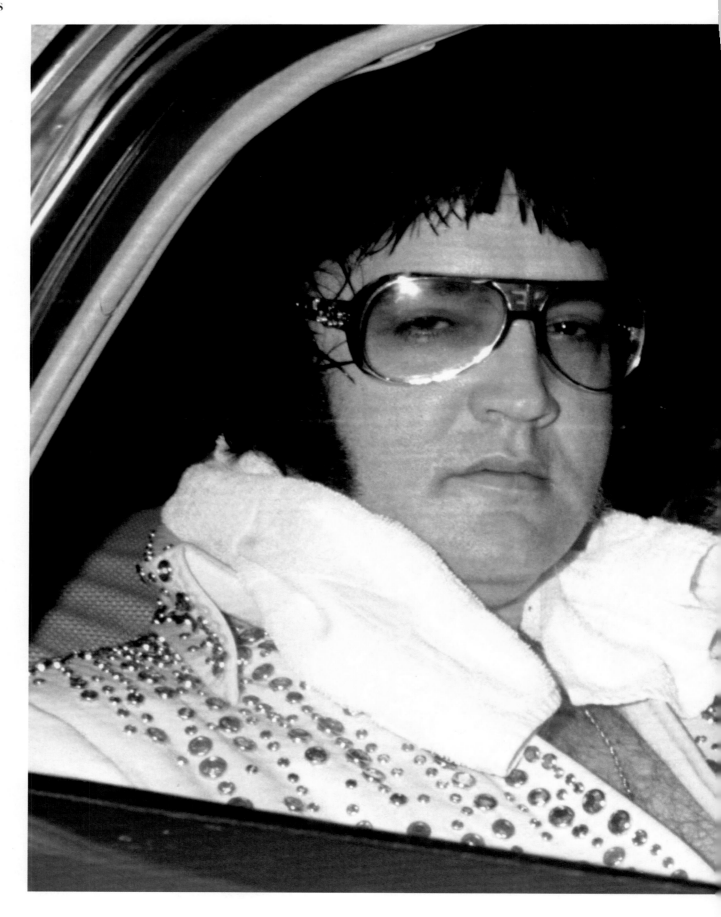

The final film to be made and released in 1981, posthumously, was considered by many fans as the best of the three documentary films, simply titled This is Elvis.

Named "The definitive film biography of The King" by Dave Marsh of Rolling Stone magazine, This is Elvis is a fascinating journey.

The documentary makers had full access to Elvis' estate and included for the first time some home movie sequences. The first version of this film featured staged versions of events, with voice stand-ins, the remastered version released a couple of years later begins with Elvis arriving at Graceland the last night of his life.

While the film is not in chronological order, it covers the majority of Elvis' career highlights. Only the first three of his movies are covered though. There is more focus on the wedding of Elvis and Priscilla, Lisa Marie and it shows clips of his appearances across various media, including television.

The viewer also sees some less complimentary footage, hearing Elvis' friend talk in some detail about Elvis' drug use and his peculiar behaviour later in his life. The film shows Elvis in his later years, overweight and forgetful of lyrics on stage in Vegas. It is considered to be a well-put-together documentary of Elvis' life, featuring the good, the bad and the ugly.

"So maybe we never win an Oscar—but we're going to win a few box office awards. Check the list of the 10 top box office stars—Elvis is right there. And here's a guy who carries his pictures by himself—the rest of the guys on the list have three or four stars to back them up."

- *Colonel Parker*

Elvis and Linda Thompson arrive at the International Hotel, Las Vegas

Elvis, Father of Lisa Marie

His only child, daughter Lisa Marie, was nine years old when he died

On learning of her pregnancy, Priscilla was devastated. Sharing her family story with British newspaper The Guardian in 2012, she wrote "I thought, "Oh my gosh, here I am married and now I'm pregnant and I'm not going to look attractive any more." It was certainly a rocky time. It was hard for Elvis too because he was a sex symbol – the most wanted sexual specimen in the world. And he was apprehensive about what his fans would think about him being a dad and how that would affect his status as a sex symbol."

According to Elvis, he said his biggest accomplishment in life was his daughter. He liked that his name would carry on after his death, and considered it incredible he had helped create Lisa Marie. It was said that she was the light of his life.

He adored Lisa Marie. He spoiled her.

The recipient of regular gifts, jewelry and toys, Lisa Marie had the life of a young princess, befitting of the daughter of The King. One story tells of his overindulgence, flying her by private jet so she could see and play in the snow. For her first birthday, he rented out the whole amusement park, called Libertyland, for Lisa Marie and her friends.

Family at home 1968

Elvis and Priscilla Presley with their daughter, Lisa Marie, 1968

Elvis and Lisa Marie at Graceland

According to Jim Curtin, in Elvis, Unknown Stories Behind the Legend when Lisa Marie's first baby tooth came out, Elvis left a $5 bill under her pillow. Priscilla had to tell Elvis off, because it was such a high amount at the time, with most kids only receiving 50 cents.

Elvis was so extravagant with gifts for his daughter he even bought her a golf cart, and a pony. While he showered Lisa Marie with love and material affection, Priscilla wrote, "Elvis wasn't a hands-on dad. And living at Graceland was difficult but I knew when I got married that he was going to have his guys around all the time. I could not domesticate Elvis, and I accepted that. He didn't really have that much to do with the practical stuff but I took naturally to becoming a mother. I thought, "My God, this is a product of Elvis and me and I'm going to be there for her." The moment you have the child, everything changes. It is terrifying and it is beautiful and it changed my life and it brought Elvis and me closer together."

"I was the disciplinarian and there were times when Lisa didn't like it but you can't live life without boundaries. I was very subtle and very calm, and she knows this now. Lisa was four when Elvis and I divorced and we were very civil and we really wanted him to stay in her life and they spent plenty of time together. Elvis and I didn't suddenly not like each other."

Elvis had been reported to say proudly that Lisa Marie was a true Presley.

She loved performing in front of the mirror, singing into a hairbrush and soaked up the attention and fuss from fans of Elvis. The young Lisa Marie also enjoyed posing for family pictures.

Elvis was very proud to be the father of his only child, Lisa Marie. He even named his private jet after her.

When Lisa Marie talked to television host Diane Sawyer, about her memories of Elvis as her father, she remembered him singing her lullabies, even waking her at odd hours, "Oh yeah, he'd always wake me up to sing in the middle of the night, get on the table and sing. I remember him as my dad, but he was a very exciting dad."

Elvis' private jet 'Lisa Marie'

Both father and daughter had a passion for singing, and when Lisa Marie was old enough to learn lyrics to songs, she would try to impress her father with her renditions. Sometimes she learned his songs, and later would famously film and sing digitally-managed duets with her father after his death, to mark anniversaries of his passing.

Lisa Marie was not baptised, although Priscilla was raised a Catholic and Elvis a Baptist Christian, they had agreed she should decide herself.

She talked with Sawyer of what it was like to see Graceland, the rooms enshrined to Elvis and how it was when he died, "It's hard. It's also really comforting,' she said. 'I don't know if anyone has, you know, the place that they were raised, you know, held in a capsule like this. It's not often that you have that."

Lisa Marie described her awareness of his unhappiness, saying, "I think that he was in trouble. He was not happy. He was, you know, obviously crying out for help.

"If I was watching TV in my room, he'd come to my room and sort of stumble to my doorway and start to fall, and I had to go catch him. You know, things like that. And he'd try to pull himself out of it if he saw me, things like that."

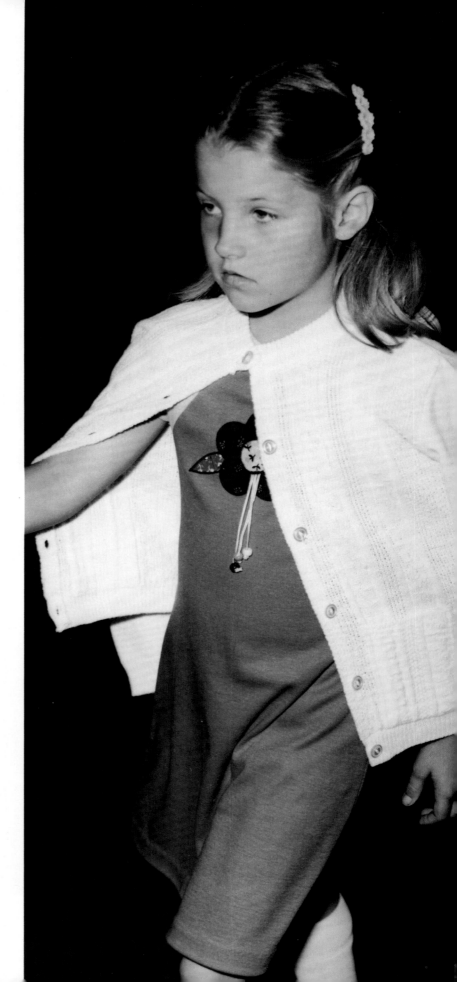

Lisa Marie aged nine in 1977

Back to back performances began to tire Elvis

Sadly, she told Sawyer she would say to him, "Don't die. Are you going to die?"

When Elvis collapsed, Lisa Marie saw the paramedics take his body away. Describing the event, she said she "couldn't really process what was happening" but did vividly recall the day of the public viewing of Elvis' body.

"I did a lot of strange things that day, because it didn't really settle in. I rode my golf cart. I ran around and smoked cigarettes at nine, in the guard shack somewhere. I was crazy. I don't know, I did, like, wacky things."

Lisa Marie inherited his father's looks, her remarkable resemblance due to her eyes and lips. The following excerpts from her interview with Playboy magazine are a fascinating insight into how Lisa Marie perceived Elvis as a father.

When asked how her parents' divorce affected her, when she was just five-years-old Lisa Marie replied, "When they divorced, I would go out on the road more and miss more school, which I liked. People say I didn't get to see him very much, but I was with him quite a bit. All of a sudden, a car would show up at school, and he was calling for me to go out on the road. "

Following the divorce, Lisa Marie would spend time with him often at Graceland, she said of those times, "[Seeing her father was] Nocturnal: Go to bed at four or five a.m. and get up at two or three the next afternoon. It was always a lot of fun. There is not one bad memory. There was always a lot of energy and life in the house. He was very mischievous.

"The only two rooms upstairs in Graceland are mine and his. When he slept, he was a bear in hibernation."

And when asked further about her father's addiction to prescribed pills, she said, "I was aware of his demise. [Softly] His temper was getting worse, he was gaining weight, he was not happy. I saw him taking different pills, like a potpourri of capsules, but I didn't know what they were. He was obviously not in good shape. But he didn't want me to see that. So he would try to mask it for me.

"I was there when he died. I was there for most of the summer. I'm actually not going to go into his death, the day of, the whole thing. Just so you know."

Elvis Presley's funeral procession, 1977

Elvis meets President Nixon in 1970

In the Ladies Home Journal interview, not long after her
divorce from Elvis, Priscilla said of having Lisa Marie,
"Elvis and I were ecstatic over the birth of our daughter.
If the baby had been a boy, we were going to name him
John Barron. I liked the name Barron. It has a very strong
feeling to it. But when it was a girl, we decided on Lisa
Marie - for no special reason, only because it is a very
feminine name."

"When the baby got a little older - she's five now - I
started going out more with other women whose
husbands were in Elvis' group; we'd go to the park,
go shopping, or go out for lunch. If Elvis got time off,
we'd take a trip, but we were seldom by ourselves. For
instance, our stay in Hawaii was supposed to be a cozy
family vacation. Elvis had finished filming Blue Hawaii,
and he wanted to show me the islands. So we rented a
bungalow with a private beach. But with an entourage of
twelve people (each guy and his wife), how intimate can
you become? I accepted it, but occasionally if I became
resentful, Elvis would tease me out of it."

Regarding how Lisa Marie understood the divorce of her
parents, Priscilla said,

"She thinks daddy is on a business trip so it works out.
And Elvis is no absentee father. When he's on tour, he
often calls her, and when he's in town, he sees her a
lot. She spent last weekend with him, and I took her to
watch him perform in Las Vegas for her birthday."

On her 25th birthday, Lisa Marie inherited the Graceland
estate, estimated at that time to be worth $100 million.

*Priscilla Presley & Elvis Presley
in Hawaii, 1968*

Lisa-Marie inherited Graceland

The King Is Back Again

As if he had many lives, Elvis had a third return to musical success – his 1968 Comeback Special

Pictured during his performance at NBC studios, 1968

After a lacklustre few years filming a series of formulaic movies and experiencing a lack of creativity with his music, Elvis was keen to be born yet again. What followed was a powerful moment in Elvis' time as The King of Rock 'n' Roll.

The '68 Comeback Special was originally to be a Christmas show, but Elvis defied Parker's instructions and went with the director Steve Binder's suggestion that it be just like old times. Binders, who was also co-producing the show, had to convince Elvis the audience would respond to a rock 'n' roll, old school Elvis.

Ultimately very different from the proposed format Parker had arranged, it aired in December 1968, titled Elvis. The show featured a support band with a small audience and Elvis in tight black leather. It was the NBC's highest rating show that season, with figures harking back to his first year of success, a total of 42percent of the viewing audience.

Journalist Jon Landau of Eye magazine declared, "There is something magical about watching a man who has lost himself find his way back home. He sang with the kind of power people no longer expect of rock 'n' roll singers. He moved his body with a lack of pretension and effort that must have made Jim Morrison green with envy."

The single released to coincide with the TV special If I Can Dream hit the charts, climbing to number 12. The album, the soundtrack to Elvis, hit the top ten.

Elvis during his '68
Comeback Special
on NBC

A series of recording sessions followed this positive reception. The sessions led to the much-loved From Elvis in Memphis, the first album unattached to an Elvis film in eight years. The album featured In the Ghetto, which hit Number Three on the charts. Other hit singles that followed included Suspicious Minds, Don't Cry Daddy and Kentucky Rain.

In addition to the successful recording, Elvis was receiving offers for live performances from around the world. Come May, Vegas' International Hotel announced Elvis was scheduled to perform nearly 60 shows over a four-week period.

With a new band, led by guitarist James Burton, Elvis and Parker organised for the inclusion of two gospel groups, The Imperials and Sweet Inspirations. With his early history of lackluster performances in Vegas, Elvis was concerned. But Parker managed a massive PR programme around his appearances and even had music journalists flown in for the opening night.

The first gig held an audience of 2,200, many of whom were celebrities. When Elvis walked on stage without introduction, he was greeted with a standing ovation. Two more standing ovations followed. He was modest in his receipt of the praise that also followed. Elvis pointed to Fats Domino when a journalist addressed Elvis as The King. Elvis said: "That's the real King of Rock 'n' Roll."

Parker cemented Elvis' musical re-birth with a five-year contract with the International Hotel, for an annual earning of $1million. He was to play every February and August. A short while later, Elvis released the double album From Memphis to Vegas/From Vegas to Memphis, including live performances from the hotel and the sound sessions. Suspicious Minds became his first American Number One in more than seven years. It was sadly to be his last.

Elvis during another performance at NBC, 1968

In early 1970, Elvis was performing two shows a night, over a long two-month period at the International Hotel. Another live album was issued from these appearances, called On Stage.

By late February, he had performed six recording-breaking shows, with the highest attendance recorded at the Houston Astrodome. MGM continued to film documentary footage at the International, titling that release Elvis: That's the Way It Is. His jumpsuit-wearing appearances marked another shift in his metamorphosis as a performer.

It was at this time that Elvis was named one of the US Junior Chamber of Commerce's Ten Most Outstanding Young Men of the Nation in 1971. He was also the first rock star to be awarded the Lifetime Achievement Award (then known as the Bing Crosby Award) by the National Academy of Recording Arts and Sciences, the Grammy Award organisation.

By this point, Elvis was touring the country, selling out venues and frequently breaking box-office records. Over his lifetime, he performed a total of nearly 1,100 concerts. Having performed two benefit concerts for a television special, Aloha From Hawaii, Elvis was continuing to find form. Airing in January of 1973 to high ratings, the soundtrack reached Number Eight.

It was the first global concert satellite broadcast. Elvis was now reaching millions of viewers live across the globe.

From this show, Elvis's attire became iconic and instantly recognisable. American writer Bobbie Ann Mason said: "At the end of the show, when he spreads out his American Eagle cape, with the full stretched wings of the eagle studded on the back, he becomes a god figure."

Elvis Presley arrives in Hawaii
for his televised concert

The Vegas Years

The costumes, the sell-out performances, the relentless show schedule of Elvis' Vegas years

Following his '68 Comeback Special, Elvis wrapped up his movie contracts and returned to the stage in 1969. His last live show being the benefit concerts in Pearl Harbour and Honolulu, Hawaii in 1961, it would be eight years before he returned to live shows and to Vegas.

His arrival in Vegas did wonders for the city, and initially, for him too. He attracted a new audience to Vegas, with much younger city folk travelling to The Strip to see Elvis perform. After almost a decade locked into dull movie deals he was bored with, Presley found his live shows in Vegas reinvigorated him. He was also feeling like he needed a reinvention.

Telling a journalist, "I've been away from people - real people - too long. Working for Hollywood was fine, and I've got no complaints about the way I was treated, but they put me on a production line. I was making films back-to-back, sometimes three a year, and although there was plenty of music in them, I had no say in what I sang or how I sang it.

"Whenever I tried to make a point, or change something, some guy in a suit would come over, surrounded by lawyers and accountants, and they'd tell me that I signed my name to a contract and I gotta do what they tell me. Well, I was a good boy and I didn't argue, because my mama always told me to mind my manners."

"We do two shows a night for five weeks. A lotta times we'll go upstairs and sing until daylight - gospel songs. We grew up with it...it more or less puts your mind at ease. It does mine."

– Elvis during Vegas live shows, taken from a 1972 taped interview used in MGM's documentary Elvis on Tour

Wearing black leather for his Comeback Special

The International Hotel advertises
performances by Elvis Presley

"But I was bored with movies, bored with the people, and bored with my life. I felt I'd sold my soul to the Devil. I look on today as the day I get back to doing the work that God put me on Earth to do. My big problem, though, is that maybe Vegas won't want to know me."

American songwriter, Mike Stoller later told a BBC documentary team that, "There was a coolness factor, a hip factor. He brought something to Vegas that it needed."

Tom Jones told the same documentary, "Elvis wanted to prove a point after the movies. I was one of the few solo artists around who was still successful, so in 1968 he'd come to Vegas to watch me perform and see my body movements, which he had always been known for, too.

"He wanted to see and hear me firsthand to know whether audiences still wanted that sort of thing.

"He loved being Elvis Presley. There was no doubt about that. He loved it when he was great and who could blame him? But then I think he started to dislike himself. He lost his desire to be Elvis Presley."

Parker's wife, Loanne, said of Elvis, "He was the first entertainer to make a profit in the show room. Before that, the casinos used to subsidise the entertainment because they knew they'd get their money back at the tables. But Elvis changed all that and drew the big players in. The women were thrilled because they went to see the shows at night while their men were in the casino. Everyone was happy. When Elvis was in town, everything lit up."

From 1969 to 1976, Elvis performed to a very heavy concert schedule. Inevitably for Elvis, they were always sell-out shows. His fans and supporters must have been keen – selling out 2,200 seats two times a day over a month. In what would now be considered too gruelling a concert schedule for any performer, he was performing two concerts daily, usually one in the afternoon and the following as late as midnight. What followed was to seriously impact his physical and mental health and wellbeing.

Opening in the summer of '69, his four-week gig featured 57 shows, which broke attendance records. Incredibly, Newsweek reported not just positive press reviews, but a record-breaking Las Vegas show attendance of 101,509 and another Vegas record of gross sales at $1,522,635. Rumour has it Elvis celebrated the news by giving a diamond-studded Rolex watch to each of his 30 members of his entourage and bought 14 Cadillacs, one for each of his close friends.

Elvis was paid $100,000 a week, which was unheard of at the time (it is the equivalent to a couple of million by today's standards).

Elvis' live show then went on the road in the 70s where he continued to break box office records. At Madison Square Garden, Elvis performed four sold-out shows in. Between 1969 and 1977, Elvis clocked up almost 1,100 live performances.

Understanding how popular and successful his shows were, it is surprising to learn of how nervous and full of self-doubt Elvis would be about performing. From observers at the International Hotel show on July 31st, 1969, he paced back and forth nervously.

As the audience's rumble simmered down to a quiet hush, and the orchestra played, Elvis ruled the stage and performed an incredible show.

Elvis Presley on stage during his 1972 Madison Square Garden Concert

It was during these Vegas years that Elvis began wearing elaborate costumes. Perhaps to disguise his growing insecurities and odd behaviour, the costumes would be a distraction. Whatever his motivation for wearing them, they were fitting of the Vegas setting. With broad shoulders, he had costumes designed with capes and V-cuts from his neck to his waist. He wore gold chains and medallions and was generally keen on what Priscilla called "flashy" jewellery.

Elvis' home-town friend, Jerry Schilling, said of the outfits, "Elvis and all of us became Vegas-ised. Nothing he did, was in moderation. If a few sequins looked good on his jumpsuit in the lights, then at the next show there had to be more. If a high collar worked for him, the collars kept getting higher. The belt buckles kept getting bigger.

"As the years went on in Vegas, so did the wardrobe. Elvis was fanatical about his clothes."

As his health declined with his increase of prescription drugs, Elvis began to put on more and more weight. His now trademark jumpsuits had to be re-made each time Elvis arrived to Vegas. But, his costume maker Gene Doucette recalls, "His body made a perfect 'V'. He went from wide shoulders down to perfect hips and you can't ask for more than that when you are trying to design a sexy outfit for a stage presentation.

"His clothes became as integral a part of Elvis as his music, his lighting and his whole show. With all the stones on them, the clothes were really heavy, perhaps adding 25-30lbs extra for him to carry. And all the time the costumes were becoming ever more flamboyant."

Observers could see that as Elvis' behaviour worsened, he became more and more preoccupied with the clothes he wore on stage. He asked for bigger collars, more rhinestones.

His behaviour worsened on stage too. Guests noticed he slurred his words, would ramble and rant to the audience, and forget the lyrics to his songs, those he had sung over and over many times before.

Performing in his signature white, studded suit

Apparently, Elvis had five different doctors prescribing drugs to him, and because of patient-doctor confidentiality, none of them knew what each other were prescribing or had any contact with each other to understand the impact the various pills were having together.

Several people recall Elvis having an icy wake-up call from Parker to rouse him from a pill-induced slumber before one of his shows. Come the early seventies, Elvis was taking painkillers, amphetamines, barbiturates and medication for a sinus problem. This prescription cocktail must have had grave affects on his health.

After a while, Elvis became less interested in hiding the pills and covering up his addiction.

Linda Thompson, his girlfriend after his divorce from Priscilla recalled "One night I saw all these prescription bottles on his bedside table. I said, "Elvis, are you sick?" He said, "No, no, honey, I had a little sore throat."

"He needed a lot of care, physically and emotionally. There were times he was my baby, other times my brother, my lover, or just my friend. He would shower gifts - cars, diamonds, even houses - on friends and strangers alike. He was so incredibly generous and we would call him either crazy or a fallen angel."

In a 1974 concert at the Hilton, Elvis was surreptitiously recorded ranting on stage to his fans about various rumours and people in his life. Later released by a Las Vegas news team and reported by George Knapp, a journalist with Eyewitness News I-TEAM, who are a television investigative unit in southern Nevada, the recording has been variously interpreted as sad and shocking.

Elvis is parodied in a sketch show in 1976

It was reported that Elvis appeared disoriented and started talking about the rumours regarding his drug use. The following quotes are excerpts from the recording, reported by Knapp, and his news team:

"I hear rumors flying around--I got sick in the hospital. In this day and time you can't even get sick. You are strung out. By god I'll tell you something, I have never been strung out in my life, except on music. I got sick that one night, I had a hundred and two temperature, and they wouldn't let me perform, from 3 different sources I heard I was strung out on heroin. I swear to God, hotel employees, jack, bellboys, freaks who carry that luggage up to your room, people, you know maids. And I was sick. But all across town, strung out."

According to Knapp and his team, Priscilla was in the audience during this particular show, and the following excerpt from the recording is about her: "...my ex-wife Priscilla. She's right here. Honey, stand up...turn around, let them see you...boy she's a beautiful chick, you know, (…). Now my little daughter Lisa Marie, she's six years old, look at her jump up. Pull your dress down Lisa, pull your dress down before you jump up like that. And at the same booth is my girlfriend Sheila. Stand up Sheila, turn completely around...."

"No the thing I'm tryin to get across, we're the best of friends, always has been. Our divorce came about not because of another man or another woman but because of circumstances involving my career. I was traveling too much . . .after the settlement, it came out about two million dollars . . . after that I got her a mink coat. She got me, listen to this, tonight, a $42,000 Rolls Royce. That's the type of relationship we have...."

Performing live in 1976

Then Elvis referred to Priscilla's new boyfriend Mike Stone.

Elvis continued, "She likes this Stutz that I have. It's not a car it's a Stutz, no it's called a stud. A Stutz, and she likes the stud...Mike Stone ain't no stud, so forget it..."

In another Vegas show, it was reported that four men attempted to attack Elvis. As security men rushed the stage, Elvis employed his karate skills and managed to remove one of the attackers himself.

There were also rumours he believed that this attack was organised by Priscilla's boyfriend Stone and that Elvis was paranoid about Stone. There were even stories that Elvis had asked his bodyguards to check out the possibility of a contract killing of Stone, before Elvis changed his mind. These stories were not substantiated, but it was widely agreed Elvis was affected by and under the influence of drugs during his Vegas years.

Ironically, he was previously reported to have been very anti-drugs and alcohol, presumably because he had known family members to be alcohol dependent. His awareness of the dangers of prescription drugs was not as strong.

Indeed, to some it seemed that Elvis' upbringing meant he had very strong ideas of right and wrong, but little worldliness that would help him choose right and wrong for himself.

His purist views were obvious when the hotel casino offered Elvis thousands of dollars worth of gambling chips every day, and he refused them because of his religious beliefs.

In 1976, Elvis finished his 837th and final show in Vegas, going home to Graceland.

"He definitely believed he had been blessed by God. It wasn't just an accident - he had been picked out. He used to question it, though. "Why me?" he would say."

– *Tom Jones on Elvis Presley*

1976 was a busy year for live performances

Memphis Mafia

The tight friendship circle Elvis kept from his late teens to his death

In his childhood and adolescence, Elvis was unpopular with his peers, both male and female. He struggled to get the attention of girls and boys considered him awkward, a loner and too much of a 'mama's boy'. So when he found fame and fortune in his late teens and early twenties, Elvis' popularity must have come as a shock.

He felt safe with people of his own kind, with similar backgrounds and upbringing to him. He was not used to associating with the rich and famous in the music industry and Hollywood.

For the first time, Elvis headed up a large group of friends, who wanted to be with him. According to biographers, the group of friends who would later be dubbed The Memphis Mafia began with Elvis' first cousins Junior and Gene Smith. Along with a high school friend, Red West, they went everywhere with Elvis.

The Memphis Mafia would later grow in numbers, although the inner circle only ever included one woman. Judy Spreckels became Elvis' confidante and said that she "was with him and the guys all the time."

"There wasn't a crowd then, just a few guys… [being his friend] had nothing to do with being a yes man for him and obviously he trusted me."

It was during the early 1960s that Elvis' close circle of friends, who he kept right up till his death, were named the 'Memphis Mafia'. The name came from a journalist who observed their dark suits and sunglasses, whih were apparently requested by Elvis in order that they all look respectable. Apparently, the friends thought it an amusing title and, along with Elvis, did not object to it.

As the story was told, it happened when the friends arrived at a hotel by black limousine, and someone in the crowd yelled, "Who are they, the Mafia?"

Who were the Memphis Mafia?

Elvis Presley arriving with bodyguard Red West

Marty Lacker, was one of the original circle. He met Elvis as a teenager, as he went to the same high school as Elvis, in his final year. He was one of two best men at Elvis' wedding and was considered Elvis' right hand man. He said of the group, "Most of the guys had responsibilities and they were far from leeches, hangers on or whatever else they were called. They all had jobs to do so that Elvis could do his and as far as being there for the money, that's laughable because there really wasn't much in that area to be there for. Most of us were not there for the money, we were there because we all cared about Elvis and each other like brothers."

In late 1971, Lacker arranged for the Memphis City Council to rename Highway 51, which runs in front of Graceland, as Elvis Presley Boulevard. He was also responsible, along with Parker, for arranging the Elvis recording at American Studios in 1969 that basically brought Elvis back to the top of the charts. He was close to Elvis from 1957 until he died in 1977.

Gene Smith was Elvis' cousin, and as part belonging to a close family, they had a close friendship growing up together. Elvis considered Smith to be a very important person in his life, and would often travel with him. Many have said Smith went everywhere with Elvis. It was reported that the cousins suffered a disagreement in the early sixties, but would later come together and spend time at Graceland with each other.

Junior Smith was another cousin, who sadly became disabled during the Korean War. When Elvis got a call that Junior had died, he took the news badly.

Elvis posing in a police uniform, Presley kept friends in the police force, particularly the narcotics department

Billy Smith, a third cousin of Elvis' who made in into his close knit circle, was the youngest of the group and reportedly Elvis' favourite. A loyal friend and constant companion, Billy Smith was good to Elvis right to the end of Elvis' life.

George Klein was another fellow graduate of Humes High School in 1953. When George started working in radio, he blossomed into one of Memphis' most popular DJs. Elvis said of Klein, 'George will be my friend forever.'

Lamar Fike began working for Elvis in 1957. Fike had a good sense of humour and while working for Elvis became a good friend, often travelling with him on tour and working as his lighting director.

Larry Geller joined Elvis' inner circle when he became his hairdresser in 1964. He was different to Elvis' other friends, being a spiritual person who encouraged Elvis to read about religion, spirituality and mysticism. He peaked Elvis' curiosity, which was no surprise considering his religious start to life and the unique experiences he had in life, "I mean there has to be a purpose...there's got to be a reason...why I was chosen to be Elvis Presley. ... I swear to God, no one knows how lonely I get. And how empty I really feel."

Joe Esposito, who acted as Elvis' road manager and personal aide for nearly 17 years, handled money and cross-referenced the extensive travel arrangements. He said, "it was a party like you wouldn't believe. Go to a different show every night, then pick up a bunch of women afterwards, go party the next night. Go to the lounges, see Fats Domino, Della Reese, Jackie Wilson, The Four Aces, the Dominoes - all the old acts. We'd stay there and never sleep, we were all taking pills just so we could keep up with each other." Esposito was the other best man at Elvis' wedding.

Elvis Presley and Joe Esposito (right) leaving JFK

Joe Esposito, Elvis Presley and Diane Goodin leaving a hotel

Over the years, many people would become involved with the Memphis Mafia, but the most prominent members in Elvis' later years are widely acknowledged to be (in no particular order) Red West, Sonny West, Marty Lacker, Billy Smith, Gene Smith, Joe Esposito, Nick Adams, Lamar Fike, Alan Fortas, , Richard Davis, Dave Hebler, Al Strada, stepbrothers David and Billy Stanley, Larry Geller, Charlie Hodge and Jerry Schilling.

Samuel Roy says that "Elvis' bodyguards, Red and Sonny West and Dave Hebler, apparently loved Elvis—especially Red; these bodyguards showed loyalty to Elvis and demonstrated it in the ultimate test. When bullets were apparently fired at Elvis in Las Vegas, the bodyguards threw themselves in front of Elvis, forming a shield to protect him." The author adds that the people who surrounded Presley "lived, for the most part, in isolation from the rest of the world, losing touch with every reality except that of his 'cult' and his power."

According to Presley expert Elaine Dundy, "Of all Elvis' new friends, Nick Adams, by background and temperament the most insecure, was also his closest." Guralnick says that the singer "was hanging out more and more with Nick and his friends" and that Elvis was glad Parker "liked Nick." June Wilkinson also confirms that the singer "had an entourage who spoke with Southern accents. The only one I remember was Nick Adams, the actor."

For many of his friends from Memphis, they worked with Elvis and were employed by his estate. For some of them, it may have been the only way out of the poverty they grew up in. By many accounts, most of the friends were fiercely loyal to Elvis, although this was challenged by many in later years as various Memphis Mafia members revealed stories about Elvis for well paid tell-all books that went on to be published.

*Elvis arrives at the Hilton Inn
with his bodyguards in 1976*

By writer Patrick Humphries' account, they "acted as Elvis' bodyguards, babysitters, drug procurers, girl-getters, mates and car buyers."

"…various members of the Memphis Mafia had … played vital roles in keeping Elvis' numerous dirty secrets out of the public eye. A couple of them had been arrested with false prescriptions attempting to collect drugs for Elvis, quite a few had taken physical hits in the service of protecting Elvis and none were paid more than $500 a week. For that they were often shouted at, abused and belittled by the King when he felt like it."

By other accounts, writers like Jerry Eden claim they were only it in for the money, saying it made him "sick to see Elvis' two-faced cousins, members of the so-called Memphis Mafia, who hung around him for the money, clothes, cars, and leftover girls."

"[They] were mostly his second and third cousins from Mississippi. With the exception of a couple of the guys, like Charlie Hodge and Red West, most of his friends were simply ignorant hillbillies out to get everything they could from him… They had a real sweet thing going that's for sure. They called themselves bodyguards, but in reality they were only flunkies falling over each other to kiss El's ass."

Author Jerry Eden claims there was no love lost between Priscilla and the group of men, "When Priscilla came on the scene, she made them move out of Graceland, keeping just a couple of them in the house to act as bodyguards."

Many reported the negative influence this circle of friends had on Elvis, including Elvis' pianist Ton Brown. Brown saw Elvis regularly during the last two years of his life and said of his declining health and wellbeing, "But we all knew it was hopeless because Elvis was surrounded by that little circle of people … all those so-called friends."

Elvis leaves the Hilton Hotel with his bodyguards in June 1972

According to biographer Peter Guralnick, "Hollywood was just an open invitation to party all night long. Sometimes they would hang out with Sammy Davis, Jr., or check out Bobby Darin at the Cloister. Nick Adams and his gang came by the suite all the time, not to mention the eccentric actor Billy Murphy..."

When Buzz Cason, a backing singer for Elvis, asked Lamar Fike how Elvis managed to party every night, Fike replied, "A little somethin' to get down and a little something to get up." Sadly, Elvis' addiction was obvious to his friends and either they did not, would not or could not help him with it.

The group of friends famously also used the acronym TCB, which stood for Taking Care of Business. The circle of friends was given gold necklaces with TCB

and Elvis had his private jet painted with the initials. Elvis, who bought them new Cadillacs and houses for wedding gifts, often gifted the friends generously.

The group, who would remain loyal to Elvis, was often criticised and doubted by journalists in particular. Journalist John Harris said, "it was no wonder that as he slid into addiction and torpor, no-one raised the alarm: to them, Elvis was the bank, and it had to remain open."

Whether or not the group was lecherous and after Elvis' money, they certainly had some fun and mischievous times together. There are stories abound regarding what the Memphis Mafia got up to. Again, without evidence, there were stories about the Mafia playing key roles in finding girls for Elvis, and for themselves.

Elvis Presley and singer Sammy Davis, Jr. backstage in Elvis' dressing room, opening night at the Showroom International Hotel on August 10, 1970

One of Parker's assistants, Byron Raphael, claimed he also had this role to fulfill. According to Raphael, the actress Natalie Wood felt rejected by Elvis, who would not have sexual intercourse with her. She then said to the Memphis Mafia that she "was not the only one to think Elvis and the guys might be homosexual, especially since Elvis often wore pancake makeup and mascara offstage to accentuate his brooding intensity, à la Tony Curtis and Rudolph Valentino, his favorite movie actors."

The loyalty of some of the members of the Memphis Mafia was questionable later in Elvis' life. In 1977, the West cousins joined with Dave Hebler to write an expose on Elvis, which was dubbed 'The Bodyguard Book'. It is generally thought they cared no longer for their loyalty to Elvis after Vernon, Elvis' father, fired the trio following what he considered to be rough handling in their roles as bodyguards.

It was said that Vernon Presley gave the reasons for their dismissal and delivered the news, saying that they had received complaints about how the bodyguards had reacted to fans as part of their role in protecting Elvis, and that Elvis' expenses were mounting.

The Wests were given a few weeks pay as severance and after they requested to speak with Elvis, he refused. It was reported they were upset about this, especially as they had worked for and been a part of Elvis' inner circle for 20 years. Elvis was said to be angry and hurt that the book was coming out. Titled Elvis: What Happened? it revealed Elvis' drug abuse and private stories about The King of Rock 'n' Roll.

Elvis and his father pictured after his first Las Vegas performance in 1969

Parker attempted to settle with the trio for a large monetary amount, but could not reach agreement. It was later said that they also tried to offer the publishers a settlement amount, which also did not work out.

When the trio held press conferences about the book launch, they claimed they wrote it to help Elvis understand the effect his medication addiction was having, to help him to seek help and get clean from the addiction.

Elvis's youngest stepbrother recalled Elvis "was devastated by the book. Here were his close friends who had written serious stuff that would affect his life. He felt betrayed. Red was honest with Elvis about his medication problems and I think this was one of the reasons he was fired. For the guys they were fired, but not by Elvis. That must have hurt."

To many, it was unfortunate that several members of Elvis' inner circle would later pen a book, Revelations from the Memphis Mafia, where many unsavoury stories about Elvis and the members of the Memphis Mafia would surface, who were sometimes rumored to be gay themselves, more than once insisted that the "gay rumors" that "got going when Elvis started hanging out with Nick Adams" were false, suggesting that it was not uncommon for gay men to be attracted to Presley, but that he was "prejudiced about homosexuals."

Much later, in 2007, Sonny West wrote and published Elvis: Still Takin' Care of Business, which was described as a gentler, kinder portrayal of life and friendship with the King.

In an interview with The Elvis Info Net website, Billy Smith talked of the inner circle known as the Memphis Mafia, of Elvis and their time together.

"I do remember him singing a lot for the family and different ones. He always had a love for music even at very young age. Very early on I remember once when Elvis pulled me out of a garbage can! I fell in head first. I was little, and I was trying to get some bananas out that the man from the fruit stand had thrown away. Elvis saw me as he passed and pulled me out!

Elvis Presley with girlfriend Linda Thompson arrive at the hotel after a concert - March 21, 1976

"Elvis was always my hero. And we were always close, even with the eight year age difference. He always looked after me, and I always wanted to be with him.

"I was always close to Elvis even as a young child. He always seemed to want me around him and was very protective of me. I always loved Elvis very much and would do just about anything to please him and be with him. We could talk about anything, and we did! He felt comfortable with me and trusted me. At least, he always told me did.

"When he was sick, I usually stayed with him. I usually went to the hospital and stayed with him there. I had so much respect for him. He did a lot for me and my family in the early years and for my family in the later years. He always told me that he loved me. Maybe it's because I was where he was before it all happened, and that was the link. . . we were family. He was my hero."

On Larry Geller's version of events with Elvis, Smith said,

"Larry Geller was okay. I don't agree with some of the tales he tells, but Larry was there for a while. He seems to remember his importance more than some of the other guys remember it. But, why bust his bubble. As I said, everyone had a job to do. Larry was his hair dresser.

"I was with him on many of the recording sessions. "The Memphis Mafia" was with Elvis almost 24 hours a day, at least one or two of them. And, in the early days, they lived with him."

Elvis Info Net also secured an interview with Lamar Fike, who revealed the following in response to various questions about their time together as part of the Memphis Mafia.

"The fun times outweigh the sad. Looking back just about every situation had its funny moments. We lived life to the fullest and the fun flowed from this.

"You've got to understand, Elvis was only human even if many want to sanctify him to a higher level. On an emotional level he was no different to you or I...he had feelings, strong feelings, and he was searching for what eludes so many of us, inner fulfilment and inner peace."

*Elvis with his bodyguards
after a concert in 1974*

The Later Years

The years most Elvis fans would prefer to forget, Elvis' health and wellbeing declines while he continues his demanding tours

It could be said of Elvis that he was fortunate enough to have experienced two or even three careers. After a very quick ride to success as the King of Rock 'n' Roll, he returned from two years at Army duty, which at the time was a very long period between albums. Then after finding critical acclaim again with Elvis is Back! he suffered from a slow, grinding progression of films that bored his fans towards the end, just as it did him. He uniquely had another famous comeback in 1968, and was to become more popular than he was before.

His fan base was huge, with Elvis fellowship becoming almost cult-like. And, yet, Elvis seemed to doubt himself more and more. Like most people, Elvis was full of contradictions. He was self-confident and enjoyed being liked and popular, but at the same time he was riddled with self-doubt and insecurity, with a deep need to be liked.

While outwardly charming and accepting of his fame, even describing autograph requests as something he had grown used to, his behavior became increasingly paranoid and private. He was reported to have become mistrustful of the general public, and was known to rent out cinemas in order to watch a film peacefully, as well as amusement parks at night time.

It seemed everything Elvis did was in excess. When he was a young boy, he was unpopular with the girls. So when he became famous and had attained sex symbol status, he had a number of women at any one time. He had affairs while he had girlfriends; he had affairs while he was married.

Elvis performs in one of his last concerts in 1977

Likewise, his relationships with men were in excess. When he was viewed as a 'mama's boy' and was unpopular at school, Elvis did not have many friends. As his success increased and he rose to fame and fortune, Elvis kept as many friends close as he could, even inviting them to live with him at Graceland and going on tour with him. The Memphis Mafia was a much larger, more involved version of Sinatra's famous Rat Pack.

It seems that following his introduction to amphetamines while in the Army, Elvis became increasingly dependent on them in his later years, and certainly while performing in Las Vegas. While not confirmed, he was rumoured to be abusing pharmaceutical drugs, barbiturates, tranquilisers, and amphetamines. It was also said that he had tried prescription pills as young as in his teens, and yet he was outwardly and outspokenly adverse to recreational drugs and alcohol.

Indeed, he would state that he rejected drugs and alcohol, and it would appear that he never drank, or

used so-called recreational drugs. However, he was obviously unaware of the dependency linked to over the counter drugs and amphetamines.

Because of his outspoken values on recreational drugs, and having been known to denounce them to fellow celebrities, President Nixon at the White House ironically awarded him an honorary Drug Enforcement Administration Agent's Badge.

Sadly, the recording released of him ranting on stage in Vegas and the witnessed performances of him rambling between songs showed his deterioration.

And just as with drugs, Elvis relationship with food and his weight went from one extreme to another. At the height of his fame, when he was filming an average of two movies a year, he had to keep a close eye on his weight, his food consumption and exercise, in order to keep slim for the camera.

Not long after his contract for the movies ended, and Elvis found freedom in his career again, he began to overeat – he loved sweets and puddings. His weight soon ballooned with the bloating, a side effect from the prescription drugs. He was also growing obese and his health declined quite rapidly.

His work schedule was another extreme. Elvis went from cultivating a two-way artistic music relationship with Sam Phillips at Sun Records, to what could be interpreted by outsiders as a one-way, commercial business relationship with his manager Colonel Parker. Parker continued to push schedules, demands and financial gain from Elvis, locking him into long contracts with first his movies, and then ironically, again with the Vegas years.

The frantic tour schedules did not help. And the overly generous deal signed with Parker meant Elvis was tied into his commitment to Parker's arrangements. It was said that Parker suffered a gambling addiction and had also managed a very complex deal with RCA, which meant Elvis did not receive royalties.

Additional financial pressure came from Elvis' father, who was managing his finances, and not particularly well, by accounts. The financial outlook for Elvis, with his expensive homes and extremely generous way with gifts for friends and family, was not positive. It was likely this had an impact on Elvis' state of mind and happiness.

He came from nothing, a poor Tupelo kid who lived his later years in extravagance, wealth and privilege. And yet, not one of these areas of his life of excess – fame, fortune, career, women, friendship, and health – brought him happiness or fulfillment.

What was life like for Elvis in his later years?

Rolex given to Elvis Presley by Colonel Tom Parker is shown at Christie's on November 23, 2012 in London, England. Estimated at £6000 - £8000

Elvis Presley confers with Colonel Tom Parker on the set of one of his films.

Again, Elvis lived his life with contradiction and so his later years were paradoxical. Finding fame as the rebel rock 'n' roller, The King would end up closing his career and his life on the well-established entertainment circuit of Las Vegas.

The rebellious man dubbed the King of Rock 'n' Roll was raised with an earnest, polite, religious, upbringing. He would talk as a Southern gentleman, calling a lady 'ma'am'. And then lose his temper and call guests unseemly names.

He was a night owl, who was terrified of not being able to sleep and would end up taking prescription pills just to do that. And consume more to wake up again.

In later 1974, things began unravelling for Elvis. Even though Elvis did not like the idea of his father remarrying after his mother's death, he was upset that Vernon and his stepmother Dee separated. At the same time, Elvis' own relationship with Linda Thompson had also come to a close. As two sensitive, close and spiritual people, it was difficult for Elvis to let go of Thompson.

In addition, Elvis' long-term pianist, David Briggs, had enough and wanted to return back to Nashville, to the studios.

Perhaps compensating for his losses at this time, Elvis' weight had ballooned. When his regular band members saw him around this time, after a while apart, they noticed the dramatic increase and how it changed Elvis' appearance remarkably.

Tony Brown, his new pianist, recalls the moment Elvis arrived, "He fell out of the limousine to his knees. People jumped to help and he pushed them away, like, 'Don't help me!' He always did that when he fell. He walked onstage and held on to the mike for the first thirty minutes like it was a post. Everybody was scared."

Elvis Presley with girlfriend Linda Thompson, 1976

Elvis' guitarist in the band, John Wilkinson, watched on too,
"The lights went down and Elvis came up the stairs. He was all gut. He was slurring. He was so f*****d up. It was obvious he was drugged, that there was something terribly wrong with his body. It was so bad, the words to the songs were barely intelligible. He could barely get through the introductions. We were in a state of shock. I remember crying. He cut the show short, yet it seemed like it went on forever."

Things got mildly better for the next three nights of the tour, where he showed more enthusiasm and seemed to be more with it. However, it wasn't long before it worsened again, and when they were in Detroit for another show, Wilkinson recalled "I watched him in his dressing room, just draped over a chair, unable to move. So often I thought, 'Boss, why don't you just cancel this tour and take a year off?' I mentioned something once in a guarded moment. He patted me on the back and said, 'It'll be alright. Don't worry about it.'"

His tour continued, relentlessly, and Elvis went through the motions, performing one city a day. In 1975, things did not get better for Elvis. While he should have celebrated turning 40 on January 8th, instead he lamented he was getting old, worrying about his age.

By now, Elvis' doctor, whose name Elvis shortened from Dr George Nichopoulos to simply Dr Nick, would have concerns over Elvis' health.

Just 20 days after his birthday, he was admitted to hospital for an enlarged colon and a detoxification. Nichopoulos kept Elvis in for what was to be several days, but they found more problems on his arrival. In addition to the enlarged colon and detox, Elvis had a biopsy on his liver, which showed he had quite severe damage. According to the attending physicians, it was due to drug abuse.

A rare, untroubled, smile
from Elvis in 1975

Nichopoulos had said the colon problem was caused by bad diet, mainly The King's love of fried food and sugar. In order to overcome the damage to both, he needed to change his diet and stop taking the pills.

Normally, Elvis took the winter holidays off and started work after his birthday each year. But in 1975, he had agreed to a New Year's Eve performance, to 80,000 people in Michigan. According to reports, his financial woes were worsening, and despite all the extravagances and the record earnings of his Vegas and concert years, Elvis had borrowed against Graceland and needed the money.

To everyone involved in the performance, it was not his finest.

It seemed the different arrangements and layout of the band and staging was not communicated and so

Elvis was not best prepared. It was freezing. Wilkinson said, "The trumpet players' lips were so cold they could barely blow their horns. It was so cold our strings kept changing key. Oh, we were glad to get out of there."

Elvis' famous bad temper got the better of him. He apparently shouted at everyone on the way back home, and was furious at how it unravelled.

Parker, however, had managed to secure $800,000, understood to be another record for the takings of one artist at the time, for one night's performance. At this time, Parker had also made another lucrative deal Elvis could not refuse. For $6million, he sold off the rights to RCA for all material recorded by Elvis up to 1972, amounting to over 350 tracks and 50 albums.

By 1976, things were getting out of control.

Elvis and his road manager, Joe Esposito depart for another concert

Under pressure from RCA to record more material, which had previously managed three albums annually, Elvis refused to go back to the studios in Nashville. RCA asked for Hollywood or Memphis. He refused.

Unbelievably, RCA were so desperate for Elvis to record new songs that they sent a reported $200,000 worth of recording equipment to Elvis, at Graceland. They even flew his band from Los Angeles and studio executives from Nashville to join him at Graceland. The band and the team waited for Elvis to join them in the den at Graceland. It hit midnight, and still there was no Elvis. Then word came that Elvis was sick and a doctor was seeing to him.

There was a different version of events of this particular night, as told by Elvis' close companions and bodyguards, Red and Sonny West, and Dave Hebler. They told their story in a book called Elvis: What Happened?, a tell-all book that was published just weeks before his death.

Much has been said of this book, and others that followed from the supposed loyal friends of the Memphis Mafia, in particular whether the authors were merely disgruntled ex-employees or were sharing the truth. According to the Wests and Hebler, Elvis was upstairs in his room, surrounded by automatic weapons, pistols, rifles and rockets. Many have recalled Elvis' obsession with guns and weaponry, and that he had a collection later in life.

Red West claimed Elvis handed him a list of names and photographs of people that had been shared by the Memphis police, and that "Elvis had it all planned. He wanted myself and Dave Hebler and Dick Grob, the former cop [who had gone to work for Elvis some years earlier], to go out and lure them, and he said he was going to kill them."

Elvis Performing in Concert at the Philadelphia Spectrum in 1976

In early 1977, despite the hero worship of Elvis in the cities he toured, Elvis was barely delivering an average performance. Some shows were good, some were average and some were awful. Some were even more critical of him at this time, with the journalist Tony Scherman writing, "Elvis Presley had become a grotesque caricature of his sleek, energetic former self. Hugely overweight, his mind dulled by the pharmacopoeia he daily ingested, he was barely able to pull himself through his abbreviated concerts."

For a show in Louisiana, March 31st, Elvis was a no-show. After calling his hotel room and waiting, the show was cancelled; the audience was told Elvis was sick.

Checked in again at the Baptist Hospital under the care of Nichopoulos, Elvis was in fact sick. The press was informed he was being treated for exhaustion. In fact, he had been abusing uppers, continued a bad diet, refused to exercise and was not sleeping.

There was cause for concern. He had been using prescription pills every day over the past two years and now he was taking them in random doses that were putting him at risk of overdose. Linda Thompson recalls him being unconscious a number of times.

Nichopoulos was by now Elvis' only physician, apparently organised so that the doctor could keep a close eye on his patient and know exactly what was prescribed and how much. It seemed a better solution than prescriptions coming from variety of doctors, with no way of knowing how much and what drugs he was ingesting.

While Elvis was in some degree of denial, considering his pills as medicine, he also was aware they made him feel good.

Elvis' ex-girlfriend, Linda Thompson's
Birthday Party At Gatsby's - March 23, 1977

Elvis Presley performs in concert at the
Milwaukee Arena on April 27, l977

While Nichopoulos' argument that he could start to wean Elvis off the prescription drugs was a good one, it was brought into question when it was discovered after Elvis' death that he had prescribed his patient an average of 25 pills a day, totaling 5300 in a short seven month period.

Elvis checked himself out of hospital after five days. Elvis' last week was unremarkable. He saw friends, spoke to them on the telephone and played racquetball. He watched gospel shows on television.

He spent time with Ginger Alden, his last girlfriend. He read the Bible, ate cheeseburgers and took his pills.

On August 15th, 1977 Elvis woke at 4pm, ate breakfast and played with Lisa Marie on the lawn, watching and laughing as she racew around in her electric cart.

Elvis' requested an appointment with his dentist at 10.30pm that same night. His dentist, Dr Lester Hofman, saw Elvis and met Alden for the first time. He x-rayed her teeth and gave Elvis two fillings.

Back home at Graceland, Elvis apparently called his doctor to ask for more painkillers, because of the fillings. Elvis talked about his concert play list with one of his security men who said he told him "We'll make this tour the best ever."

Elvis then changed to go and play racquetball again in the early hours of the morning, this time with his cousin Billy Smith and his wife, Jo. As was customary at this time, Elvis and Alden went to bed at around 4 am. Around half an hour later, Elvis sat at a piano and played some gospel numbers.

At 9am the same morning, August 16th, Alden woke to find Elvis still reading.

Telling her he was going into the bathroom to read, as he could not sleep, she warned him "Okay, just don't fall asleep."

Dancing erratically with his guitar on stage in 1977

Elvis Presley in Hawaii with Ginger Alden, March 1977

Death & Legacy

In the early hours of August 16, 1977 Elvis Presley was strung out, unable to sleep. He told his girlfriend Ginger Alden he was going into the bathroom to try to sleep; she later said she knew he was going in to the bathroom to take more pills.

At this point, it was likely to be the third round of pills he had taken in six hours. According to the medical examiner later, as many as ten different types of prescription pills were found in his system, including Codeine, Ethinamate, Methaqualone, barbiturates, Placidyl, Valium, Demerol, Meperidine, Morphine, Chloropheniramine, and antihistamines.

At 1.30pm Alden woke and knocked on the bathroom door. Hearing no reply, she went in and found his body slumped on the floor in front of the toilet.

Alden screamed for help and Al Strada and Joe Esposito rushed to her aide and called the fire department. With an ambulance racing to the scene, Elvis' daughter Lisa Marie and his father Vernon came in to see what was wrong.

Lisa Marie was rushed out of the bathroom, but not before she apparently cried out "What's wrong with my daddy? Something's wrong with my daddy, and I'm going to find out."

A few hours later, at 4pm Elvis' father Vernon greeted reporters on the steps of Graceland and told them, "My son is dead."

The King of Rock 'n' Roll was dead.

It was hard to believe that only a couple of months before, on June 25, he had delivered his last live show.

Those around him at the time recalled he was mortified that his previously loyal, close family and friends, three of his bodyguards who were sacked by Vernon, would release the gossipy, tell-all book Elvis: What Happened? He had apparently attempted to stop its release by offering money to the publishers of the book.

The book was released in the United States just four days before he died.

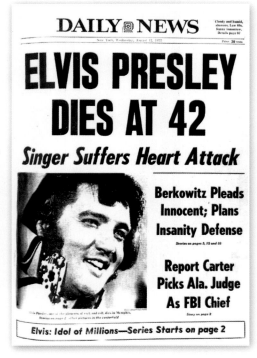

Front page of the Daily News dated Aug. 17, 1977

While the family decided to keep the autopsy report private, it was later revealed that Elvis had died of heart failure, and had an enlarged liver and advanced arteriosclerosis.

The autopsy report has been challenged many times, and was re-opened again in 1994, where the Coroner Dr. Joseph Davis determined, "There is nothing in any of the data that supports a death from drugs. In fact, everything points to a sudden, violent heart attack.

"Whether or not combined drug intoxication was in fact the cause, there is little doubt that polypharmacy contributed significantly to Presley's premature death."

Award-winning Elvis biographer Guralnick, however, states of Elvis' death, "Drug use was heavily implicated. No one ruled out the possibility of anaphylactic shock brought on by the codeine pills... to which he was known to have had a mild allergy."

More reports and speculation followed, and as historian and pathologist Michael Baden states, "Elvis had had an enlarged heart for a long time. That, together with his drug habit, caused his death. But he was difficult to diagnose; it was a judgment call."

After medical examiners discovered the volume of prescriptions given to Elvis, the Tennessee Board of Medical Examiners charged Nichopoulos with being criminally liable for his death and indiscriminate, although he was later acquitted of the charges. His license was suspended for three months and was later permanently revoked after the same Tennessee Medical Board brought new charges of over-prescription.

Thousands of fans and press had gathered at Graceland, mourning the loss of their rock 'n' roll King.

Two days after his passing, on August 18th, Elvis Presley's funeral was held at Graceland with an open casket. With near hysteria building amongst fans who had gathered at the gates, on the day of his funeral, two women were killed, and a third seriously injured, after a car drove into a group of fans.

A young man in an 'Elvis RIP' t-shirt attends a memorial service for Elvis Presley, August 1977

After the funeral, a long procession to the cemetery went past 80,000 people.

He was buried in a mausoleum, at the Forest Hill Cemetery in Memphis.

Then President of the United States, Jimmy Carter, issued a statement,

"Elvis Presley's death deprives our country of a part of itself. He was unique, irreplaceable. More than twenty years ago, he burst upon the scene with an impact that was unprecedented and will probably never be equaled. His music and his personality, fusing the styles of white country and black rhythm and blues, permanently changed the face of American popular culture. His following was immense. And he was a symbol to people the world over of the vitality, rebelliousness and good humor of this country."

Later, one of Elvis' cousins, Billy Mann, provided the National Enquirer with a photograph of the open casket, after accepting $18,000 for it. It was reportedly the Enquirer's biggest selling issue ever.

Even Elvis' girlfriend Ginger Alden succumbed to the lure of a $105,000 deal with the Enquirer in return for telling her story. However, she apparently settled for less on breaking the exclusivity arrangement she had signed with the Enquirer.

Elvis continued to top the charts, even after his death. Way Down reached the top of the country charts only a few days after his funeral and burial.

As crazed fans attempted to break into the mausoleum, in October Vernon agreed to move his body. Elvis and his mother were exhumed and buried again, this time in the Meditation Garden at Graceland.

With a so many people involved in Elvis' life, his Last Will and Testament brought a lot of attention. Originally, Lisa Marie, Vernon and Elvis' grandmother Minnie Mae were to inherit Elvis' estate. Interestingly, neither Priscilla, nor any of his romantic loves were included and did not stand to inherit anything from Elvis' estate.

View of the front page of the Commercial Appeal newspaper the day after the death of Elvis Presley

View of the front page of the Memphis Press-Scimitar newspaper the day after the death of Elvis Presley

Police officers on motorcycles escort a white hearse containing the body of American rock and roll singer Elvis Presley

Lisa Marie Presley inherited her father's estate

Along with witnesses Charles F. Hodge and Ann Dewey Smith, Ginger Alden was a third witness and signatory on his Will.

(b) After payment of all expenses, taxes and costs incurred in the management of the expenses, taxes and costs incurred in the management of the trust estate, the Trustee is authorizes to accumulate the net income or to pay or apply so much of the net income and such portion of the principal at any time and from time to time to time for health, education, support, comfortable maintenance and welfare of: (1) My daughter, Lisa Marie Presley, and any other lawful issue I might have, (2) my grandmother, Minnie Mae Presley, (3) my father, Vernon E. Presley, and (4) such other relatives of mine living at the time of my death who in the absolute discretion of my Trustees are in need of emergency assistance for any of the above mentioned purposes and the Trustee is able to make such distribution without affecting the ability of the trust to meet the present needs of the first three numbered categories of beneficiaries herein mentioned or to meet the reasonably expected future needs of the first three classes of beneficiaries herein mentioned. Any decision of the Trustee as to whether or not distribution, to any of the persons described hereunder shall be final and conclusive and not subject to question by any legatee or beneficiary hereunder.

(c) Upon the death of my Father, Vernon E. Presley, the Trustee is instructed to make no further distributions to the fourth category of beneficiaries and such beneficiaries shall cease to have any interest whatsoever in this trust.

(d) Upon the death of both my said father and my said grandmother, the Trustee is directed to divide the Residuary Trust into separate and equal trusts, creating one such equal trust for each of my lawful children then surviving and one such equal trust for the living issue collectively, if any, of any deceased child of mine. The share, if any, for the issue of any such deceased child, shall immediately vest in such issue in equal shares but shall be subject to the provisions of Item V herein. Separate books and records shall be kept for each trust, but it shall not be necessary that a physical division of the assets be made as to each trust.

An excerpt from The Last Will and Testament of Elvis A. Presley

His father, Vernon, was provided for in his will

'We Love You Tender Book Launch', 1980

The Graceland home is close to, although not exactly, as Elvis left it. And the second floor, where his bedroom is located, is not available to tour and remains closed off.

Graceland was added to the National Register of Historic Places in 1991 and a National Historic Landmark in 2006. In 1993, Graceland purchased the shopping centre plaza that was built across the street in the 60s. The shops and attractions there are now known as Graceland Plaza.

The Graceland property is still owned by Lisa Marie, along with her father's personal effects. She sold 85 per cent of the business of Elvis' estate in 2005, to an entertainment company, of which her mother Priscilla retains a seat on the board of directors. She owns the remaining 15 per cent.

In addition to managing the estate, Priscilla also pushed for state law to guarantee the rights over deceased celebrity images. As such, Elvis Presley Enterprises Inc (EPE) now owns the rights to the name Elvis Presley and any merchandise created and sold in the US must pay royalties to EPE in advance.

From 1979, the EPE business has brought hundreds of lawsuits on people or businesses distributing or using the King's images without their permission.

The interest in Elvis Presley lives on. In addition to websites and online blogs written about The King of Rock 'n' Roll, hundreds of books have been published and the Graceland mansion is the second most visited home in America by tourists, after the White House.

Elvis' albums and songs have been reissued, remastered and repackaged countless times, and will continue to sell. His legacy is enormous, and wide reaching.

From 1977 until 1981, six singles of Elvis' were released and went on to become top ten hits on the country charts.

Elvis has been inducted into four musical halls of fame, including the Rock and Roll Hall of Fame in 1986, the country Music Hall of Fame in 1998, the Gospel Music Hall of Fame in 2001, and the Rockabilly Hall of Fame in 2007. He was awarded the Blues Foundation's WC Handy Award in 1984, the Academy of country Music's first Golden Hat Award, and the American Music Award's 1987 Award of Merit.

His music is still relevant today and will no doubt continue to be in future. For 2002's World Cup soccer advertising campaign, Nike used a remix of Elvis' A Little Less Conversation, by Junkie XL (titled Elvis Vs XL), and it went on to top the charts in over 20 countries. In 2003, a remix of Rubberneckin' (from 1969) topped the US chart. The following year the Elvis 50th Anniversary release of That's All Right also topped the US chart.

In 2005, three singles of Elvis', Jailhouse Rock, One Night and It's Now or Never went to Number One in the United Kingdom. Of the 17 singles issued that year, each hit the UK's top five.

In the early and second half of the 2000-2010, Elvis ranked in the highest income earners. The year of his 75th birthday, 2010, Viva Elvis: The Album was released, with his vocals added to new instrumental recordings of his songs. He ranked second on Forbes list that year, with an income of $60 million. By 2011, there were 15,000 licensed Elvis products.

The star of Elvis Presley on the Hollywood Walk of Fame

Incredibly, Elvis continues to hold the record for the most songs ever charted on Billboard's Top 40 and Top 100. Joel Whitburn, chart statistician, announced that Elvis' total was 104 and 151 songs on those charts, respectively. Other biographers and historians have recorded slightly different amounts, but all declare he had over 100 songs on both charts.

Elvis also holds the record for having 80 cumulative weeks at Number One. He also still holds the records for the most Number One hits and Top Ten hits in the UK, with 21 and 76 respectively.

Elvis had achieved what many would have declared impossible. He made a return from two years out of the limelight while serving for the Army, breaking new records. He returned from soft, fluffy movies and the critic's dismissal of him to make a comeback that broke new records again.

He filled Madison Square Garden for four consecutive shows, breaking every attendance and box office record. He broke ground by reaching a billion people live (and on delay) with his 1971 Aloha From Hawaii satellite show. He even won a Golden Globe for Elvis on Tour and a Gospel Award Grammy for He Touched Me.

Elvis continues to have fans worldwide, and some are fanatical about Elvis's death, believing it was a hoax – that it was faked so he may retire in peace.

Still today, there are reported sightings of Elvis that hit the newsstands and media. The theory surrounding this 'fake death' is based on discrepancies on his death certificate and accounts from those claiming he was planning it to avoid continued attention.

For many other fans, Elvis lives on in the nightly shows audiences can take in along The Strip in Las Vegas. For some, being an Elvis impersonator means making a good living.

There are estimated to be over 80,000 Elvis impersonators globally, although it is difficult to substantiate this number. The Elvis impersonator is such a well developed category now that it is considered there are three main types of impersonator, including the look-a-likes, who focus on Elvis' fashions and look, the sound-alikes, who focus on their vocal impressions of Elvis singing and talking, and the impersonators who are a combination of the two. Elvis impersonators provide a source of fascination on their own, and movies such as Elvis and 3000 Miles to Graceland have been produced on the topic.

Elvis Presley receives a platinum record from a man commemorating his live album 'As Recorded at Madison Square Garden' selling 1 million copies

Above; Elvis Presley during a live performance of 'Aloha from Hawaii'

Opposite page: Elvis Presley on stage singing in performance at Madison Square Garden, 1972

Index

Singles

Picture Credits

All images featured in this book are courtesy of Getty Images © Getty Images.

Page 140 - Waring Abbott/Michael Ochs Archives/Getty Images

Pages 144-145 - Ron Galella/WireImage/Getty Images